THE WAY OF
CHINESE PAINTING

MAI-MAI SZE, who lives in New York, was born in China and educated in England, France and America. Her paintings have been exhibited in London, Paris, New York and elsewhere in the United States. She is the author of *Echo of a Cry, Silent Children*, and *The Tao of Painting* (Bollingen Series XLIX, 1956), on which this book is based.

THE WAY OF
CHINESE PAINTING

ITS IDEAS AND TECHNIQUE

*With Selections from the Seventeenth-
Century* Mustard Seed Garden Manual
of Painting

BY MAI-MAI SZE

VINTAGE BOOKS

A DIVISION OF RANDOM HOUSE

New York

PLATES:

LANDSCAPE - *Courtesy of the Smithsonian Institution, Freer Gallery of Art, Washington, D. C.*

BAMBOO IN THE WIND - *Courtesy, Museum of Fine Arts, Boston, Massachusetts.*

CALLIGRAPHY - *Courtesy of the Smithsonian Institution, Freer Gallery of Art, Washington, D. C.*

Detail from EARLY AUTUMN - *Courtesy, Collection of the Detroit Institute of Arts, Detroit, Michigan.*

COVER:

Detail from BREATH OF SPRING - *Courtesy of the Smithsonian Institution, Freer Gallery of Art, Washington, D.C.*

There have always been good and bad paintings . . .
in art, however, the terms ancient and modern have
no place.

Hsieh Ho, A.D. 500

To me there is no past or future in art. If a work of
art cannot live always in the present it must not be
considered at all. The art of the Greeks, of the Egyptians, of the great painters who lived in other times,
is not an art of the past; perhaps it is more alive today than it ever was.

Pablo Picasso, 1923

In respect of art, we are the first to be heirs of all the
earth. . . . Accidents impair and Time transforms,
but it is we who choose.

André Malraux, 1950

CONTENTS

LIST OF PLATES

Freer Gallery of Art, Washington, D.C.
9.96 in. x 10.7 in.; ink and tint on silk; by Yen Tz'u-yu (XII-XIII
centuries); Sung period

Yen Tz'u-yu was a member of the Southern Sung Academy during the reign of Emperor Hsiao Tsung. His signature on this
album-painting is written on a rock in the lower right corner.
The name also appears formally on a label on the mounting at
the top, right.

Museum of Fine Arts, Boston
29.63 in. x 21.39 in.; ink on paper; by Wu Chen (1280–1354); Yuan period

Wu Chen of Chia-hsing in Chekiang was one of the six Great
Masters of the Yuan period. Among the names he used was Mei
Tao-jen, "Taoist of the Plum Flower," which he signs at the end
of his poem on the right portion of the painting:
"Bamboo, without mind, yet sends thoughts soaring among the
clouds. Standing on the lone mountain, quiet, dignified, typify-
ing the will of a gentleman.
Painted and written with a light heart by Mei Tao-jen."

Freer Gallery of Art, Washington, D.C.
72.26 in. x 36.05 in.; ink on paper; by Ch'en Hsien-chang (1428–1500);
Ming period

Two lines of fourteen characters written in *ts'ao shu* (grass style),
translated by Mr. A. G. Wenley as follows:

"Wherever the light of body tread on steaming mist,
There the countless years of pine pitch at Stone Cave. *Po-sha.*"

Ch'en Hsien-chang came from Po-sha, near Canton, and so was also known as Ch'en Po-sha. The couplet alludes to a story in the iv-century Taoist work on alchemy, the *Pao P'u Tzu.* A certain man was cured of leprosy after taking pine pitch prescribed by a Taoist sage; it also made him immortal and he was said to have appeared youthful at the age of one hundred and ten.

IV   DETAIL FROM THE SCROLL

Early Autumn   PAGE 124

Detroit Institute of Arts
The painting on the scroll: 47.25 in. x 10.56 in.; color and ink on paper;
attributed to Ch'ien Hsuan (1235–90); Late Sung–Early Yuan period

Ch'ien Hsuan of Wu-hsing in Chekiang belonged to the end of the Sung period, though the custom of placing a painter by the year of his death classifies him as a Yuan painter.

A reproduction in color of the whole painting appears in Volume 1 of *The Tao of Painting.* A detail cannot fully depict the extraordinary evocation of an autumn scene at the edge of a pond or river bank: dragonflies, frogs, grasshoppers, bees and other insects among grasses, plants and lotus leaves in a light autumn mist, suggesting a moment pulsating with life and passing in a movement like that of a wave through the long horizontal composition. Over fifty years after the picture was painted, the mood was caught and described in an inscription which is mounted, with seven others, on the scroll with the painting, written by the eminent Yuan critic and painter, K'o Chiu-ssu. It reads:
"With gamboge from Yen-ch'i (Ch'ien Hsuan) smoothly paints the red and yellow (tones of autumn). (The scene) suggests the Ten Brocades Bank of the Tiao River. (To perceive) Great Power (of the spirit) one must look beyond color and appear-

ance. That of the artist, here, seems almost to mold the *Yin* and *Yang* (nature itself). One pond of lotus leaves shedding their garments. Two-tone song of frogs making music. (Likewise,) his lordship (Ch'ien Hsuan, in the autumn of his life) yearns to shed the cares of this troubled world.

Written by Tan-ch'iu, K'o Chiu-ssu, on the fifth day of the third month in the spring of the second year of Chih Cheng (1342)."

PREFACE

THE coordinating of inner and outer resources was often referred to by Chinese painters as "heart and hand in accord."
The phrase is one of many such axioms and serves well also to
describe the *tao* or "way" of Chinese painting. To take a close
look, however, at this *tao* of painting, it is necessary to examine
separately the two aspects, which are of course inseparable, "accord" in painter as well as picture being the result of a harmonious, complementary action of inner and outer resources.

Part One of this book attempts to explore certain beliefs and
ideas, rising from the heart-mind, which are key concepts of the
Chinese tradition and also of Chinese painting. It is this close
relationship between the *tao* of living and its *tao* of painting that
largely accounts for the continuity of Chinese painting, has conditioned its characteristically ritual disposition, and has given
the paintings meaning, substance and quality. Part Two pertains
to the training of the hand towards full control of the brush and
thus, eventually, brushwork that is completely free. It consists
of selections from the famous XVII-century handbook, the *Chieh
Tzu Yuan Hua Chuan* or Mustard Seed Garden Manual of Painting. This division of contents follows generally that of the two
volumes of *The Tao of Painting,* Bollingen Series XLIX, published in December, 1956, on which this book is based. Part One
corresponds substantially to Volume 1. The selections from the
Manual are made from Volume 2, which contains a complete
translation of the *Chieh Tzu Yuan Hua Chuan,* its text and over
four hundred pages of examples illustrating brushwork and the
elements of composition. A brief explanation is due about the

selection of text and examples, but a reader may wish first some
information about the Manual itself.

The *Chieh Tzu Yuan,* as it is called, consists of thirteen "books"
arranged in three parts. Part I, on landscape, appeared in 1679
and constituted the first edition. It contains five books: one on
general principles, with a section on the preparation and use of
colors; *Book of Trees; Book of Rocks; Book of People and Things;*
and a book of additional examples copied from parts of landscape compositions. In 1701, Part I was reissued with Parts II
and III, together making up the first complete edition. Part II
contains four books: *Book of the Orchid, Book of the Bamboo,
Book of the Plum, Book of the Chrysanthemum;* and Part III,
four books: *Book of Grasses, Insects and Flowering Plants; Book
of Feathers-and-Fur and Flowering Plants;* and two books of additional examples. Except for the first book, consisting entirely of
text, and the pages of instructions opening each book in Part II
and III, the rest of the Manual is composed of framed full pages,
the frames of fine black lines measuring about five by eight
inches; within the frames were printed the examples illustrating
brushwork with accompanying text varying in length from a
phrase to several paragraphs.

The considerable difference between the illustrations of the
first editions and those in later ones prompted the use of the
1887–88 edition for the complete translation. The copy of the
Chieh Tzu Yuan which was used for the translation and illustrations bears the imprint of the Ch'ien Ch'ing T'ang publishing
house and bookstore in Shanghai, which owned the manuscript
of the 1887–88 edition. Since this is a fairly late edition, the contents was checked with the examples and the Chinese text of
the K'ang Hsi (1679–1701) and Ch'ien Lung (1782) editions, reproduced in the complete Japanese translation of the Manual,
Zenyaku Kaishi-en Gaden, by Hoan Kosugi and Rentaro Koda
(Tokyo, 1935–36). The 1887 Shanghai edition was the first of the
many editions printed by a lithographic process. It was thus the
first for which the brushwork examples were drawn with a brush.
Earlier editions contained illustrations printed from engraved
wood blocks. The few specimens of the first editions, with their

several hundred pages of examples, many in color, are among
the finest collections in existence of early wood-block prints with
color; but rare and lovely as they are as wood-block prints, the
effect of stiffness and flatness necessarily resulting from impressions made from carved wood blocks makes them far from satisfactory as examples demonstrating strokes made by the soft
Chinese brush. The later edition, without color, while failing to
show a full range of ink tones, still offers better examples of
brushstroke forms and even brushstroke vitality, which are factors of primary importance in Chinese painting.

The title of the Manual was taken from the name of the home
in Nanking of its publisher, Shen Hsin-yu. His father-in-law, Li
Yu, wrote the preface to the first edition and has since often
been credited as the author. There were, however, three authors,
three brothers surnamed Wang, originally from Hsiu-shui in
Chekiang. They compiled the Manual and also prepared the
hundreds of illustrations. Wang Kai, whose *tzu* or formal name
was An-chieh, was the general editor of the whole work and the
sole author and illustrator of Part I. In the Manual he uses the
pseudonym or studio-name Lu Ch'ai, Master of the Ch'ing Tsai
T'ang, which may have been the Wang home or a fictitious
headquarters. Wang Shih (*tzu* Mi-ts'ao) and Wang Nieh (*tzu*
Ssu-chih) prepared Parts II and III with the help of two other
painters, Wang Chih and Chu Sheng. They seem to have been
particularly well equipped to produce a handbook such as the
Chieh Tzu Yuan. No other work of its kind is comparable in
scope, content and arrangement. The Manual became the most
widely used handbook of painting in China, published in many
editions and innumerable reprints. In scholarly circles, however,
it was long ignored, perhaps because it was a manual and, in
their eyes, merely a guide for beginners. In recent years it has
been hailed by Chinese art critics as a uniquely important work.
There is point to both attitudes. For on the one hand, no manual of painting can be entirely adequate; there are elements that
cannot be reduced to rules and formulas. On the other hand,
the *Chieh Tzu Yuan,* intended as a manual, succeeds also as a
unique summary of the ideals and standards established by the

masters of Chinese painting. For the present purpose it offers
the advantage of approaching the *tao* of painting through the
stages of apprenticeship.

In making a selection from the text and pages of brushwork
examples in the Manual, the aim has been to preserve on the
smaller scale the proportions of the original, to keep self-contained each of the ten books dealing separately with the various
subjects, and to retain intact the sequences of pages dealing with
the main steps in technique. This aim and the results are entirely different from that of recent Chinese abridgments, which
have either concentrated on the books of landscape, with little
or no text, or have offered a random and relatively small selection from all of the examples, drawing heavily on the *Book of
People and Things* and among the examples of flowers, and omitting most or all of the text. None of these abridgments have in
any way been used for the present selection.

As to the selections from the text of the Manual, the opening
book on the fundamentals of painting remains almost complete;
in fact, parts of the notes on colors at the end of the original
Manual are incorporated in the earlier section on colors. Five
short sections of mainly historical notes are omitted from this
first book and significant points in them summarized in footnotes.
On the whole, however, footnotes throughout the work have
been quite drastically cut or omitted, although the essential references are of course retained. Sentences in the first book and
sections in Parts II and III are omitted which consist largely of
laudatory lists of names no longer significant or now unidenti-
fiable. The presence of these names represented an enlivening
of the tradition. Sufficient evidence of this practice remains, however, since the masters and critics are still mentioned in one way
or another, and the outstanding painters are discussed or represented among the examples in the various books. In Parts II and
III, some of the rules phrased for memorizing by chanting which
repeat points in the instructions are omitted; in one or two
places, where fresh points are made, sections are retained; certain sample passages, though partly repetitious, are kept because
they help to give an idea of the method and tone of the Manual.

Since the lists of painters have been mentioned, a word should perhaps be said about Chinese names and how they are rendered in these pages. For there is the picturesque, and also confusing, custom of acquiring one or more names additional to that given at birth: a painter, for instance, might use and be referred to by his given name, his *tzu* or name assumed at the age of twenty, a pseudonym, nickname, or title; at times, by only a part of one such name. In these selections from the Manual, it seemed advisable to use consistently the full name by which a painter is now generally known and to give other names, when possible, in the Index. The exception is in Li Yu's preface to the first edition, in which his more informal use of names is an essential part of the tone of his contribution and which is short enough to keep intact. To use a formal name and drop a pseudonym such as Monk of the Bitter Melon, or Red Trousers, is somewhat disappointing but in the present circumstances makes identification easier and saves space.

As to the selection of brushwork examples, the first consideration has been to keep each book self-contained and, if possible, with at least one example of each of the subjects or aspects of a subject treated in the book, including text and, of course, the main steps in technique. Omissions have been made mainly from pages of groups of examples. It seemed preferable, for instance, in the *Book of Rocks,* to omit several pages showing the styles of various masters in drawing mountain peaks, retaining five as sufficiently representative, in order to include other examples, also copied from the works of masters, that demonstrate specific types of brushstrokes used in painting rocks and peaks. Selections have also been freely made from groups of examples, such as the figures in the *Book of People and Things,* single examples being taken from pages of figures of the same category and size and placed together on a page.

To fit the smaller dimensions of these pages and to present the translation of the instructions and comments on the same page with the brushwork examples, the illustrations in the Manual have of course been reduced. By removing the frames around the examples and omitting the Chinese text, some space has been gained. Most of the examples are reduced to approximately two thirds of their original size; a number are only slightly smaller than in the original Manual, a few the same size.

Although it will probably not matter to the general reader, it should be noted that for practical reasons all accents in the romanized Chinese words are omitted. Terms and expressions of Chinese painting are, however, italicized, and the Chinese forms of key terms are given in the Appendix. Parentheses are used to indicate the Chinese terms and expressions or their equivalents in English, and to give dates, modern names of Chinese provinces, and other such clarification. Parentheses are also used instead of brackets in the Manual to interpolate English words in the translation of terse Chinese phrases that appear frequently in the instructions and comments, and to indicate the position of an illustration on the page. In the discussion of Chinese thought, Western terms are generally used, such as "Neo-Confucianism" instead of its Chinese name *Tao hsueh chia;* and although there are differences, "Zen" is used instead of the Chinese *Ch'an,* since that school of Buddhism is better known in the West by its Japanese name.

During work on *The Tao of Painting,* help and encouragement were generously given from many quarters. Acknowledgments made in detail in that work can be made only briefly here, though with no less appreciation. As may be seen in the notes and the list of references, I am greatly indebted to scholars in various fields of Chinese studies, and to their treatises, translations and compilations. It was largely due to the late Dr. Ananda K. Coomaraswamy that the initial attempt was made to translate the *Chieh Tzu Yuan.* In the translating, Mrs. Wei T'an-huei, Miss R. T. Pan, and Mr. An Fu helped in the rendering of some passages, parts of which appear in the present selections. Mr. C. F. Yau and Mr. F. S. Kwen have over many years given me much information about the tradition in Chinese painting; and Miss N. Rambova, on the symbolism of the art of the ancient Middle East. In including three paintings and a detail of one from the group of paintings reproduced in *The Tao of Painting,* acknowledgment is again made to the Freer Gallery of Art, Washington, D.C., the Museum of Fine Arts, Boston, and the Detroit Institute of Arts for permission to use them. To Mr. A. G. Wenley, Director of the Freer Gallery of Art, a word of special thanks: for the information about the album painting and the large scroll of calligraphy in the Collection, for allowing me to include in the description of the plates his translation of the calligraphy, and for looking through the original manuscript. It should, however, be added that in making the present selection from the Manual, the responsibility is solely mine. I should like also to thank Mr. Paul L. Grigaut, Curator of Oriental Art at the Detroit Institute of Arts, for enabling me to have photographs of details of the *Early Autumn* painting in order to include one in black and white to represent the reproduction of the whole in color that appears in Volume 1 of *The Tao of Painting.* The rendering of Wu Chen's inscription on his painting *Bamboo in the Wind* is based on Mr. Kojiro Tomita's translation in *The Pocket Book of Great Drawings,* edited by Paul J. Sachs. For permission to quote from *Four Quartets* by T. S. Eliot, grateful acknowledgment is made to the author, to Harcourt, Brace & Co., New York, and to Faber & Faber, London.

Finally, I should like to express my appreciation to the editors of the Bollingen Series for permission to present *The Tao of Painting* in this version and for their continued interest in the book.

New York   *M. S.*
April, 1959.

PART ONE

THE WAY OF CHINESE PAINTING

CHAPTER ONE

THE CONCEPT OF TAO

IN the vast literature of Chinese painting, there is continual reference to a *tao* or "way." It is not a personal way, nor the mannerisms of a school. It is the traditional Chinese *tao*. As one among several ways, one dialect in the universal language of painting, this *tao* is distinctive for certain fundamental concepts and for the manner in which they have long been represented by the Chinese brush and ink. The great unifying aim has been to express *Tao*, the Way—the basic Chinese belief in an order and harmony in nature. This grand concept originated in remote times, from observation of the heavens and of nature—the rising and setting of sun, moon, and stars, the cycle of day and night, and the rotation of the seasons—suggesting the existence of laws of nature, a sort of divine legislation that regulated the pattern in the heavens and its counterpart on earth.

Among the schools of Chinese thought *Tao* has been described by many names; for these there are no exact translations, though their equivalents range from the abstract First Principle to the mystical Cosmic Mother and Primal Source, depending on the frame of interpretation. *Tao* has always evoked feelings of deep reverence, the more profound, perhaps, because of its inscrutable nature. The *Chuang Tzu* observes that "*Tao* cannot be conveyed by either words or silence. In that state which is neither speech nor silence its transcendental nature may be apprehended."[1] Painting might be described as a manifestation of "that state which is neither speech nor silence," and Chinese painting, at its

[1] Tr. Giles, *Chuang Tzu: Mystic, Moralist and Social Reformer*, p. 351.

best, with its swift brushstrokes and wonderful power of suggestion, was a particularly effective means of communicating aspects
of *Tao*.

To express *Tao,* a pattern or "way" of training and discipline
was established that made specific demands of the painter in
scholarship and character, besides technical skill. Knowledge of
this *tao* of painting being indispensable, Chinese painters and art
critics have found the topic of absorbing interest, and the records
are filled with their comments on it. Characteristically, their essays
on the *tao* of and the *Tao* in painting were largely quotation and
paraphrase of earlier writings. Their comments, displaying occasional flashes of intuition, scrutinized and sought to clarify the
various ideas about *Tao*. Originality of interpretation was never
applauded; it was neither expected nor encouraged, for intellectual comprehension of the concept was merely a step toward the
complete attunement necessary for successful results. And
throughout the course of Chinese painting the common purpose
has been to reaffirm the traditional *tao* and to transmit the ideas,
principles, and methods that have been tested and developed by
the masters of each period as the means of expressing the harmony of *Tao*.

The process of transmission was not as rigid as it might seem.
The Chinese tradition, ancient and deeply respected, has given the
impression of being massive and fixed. It has a monumental aspect but its prime characteristic is adaptability. It is not inflexible, or it could never have survived. Over long centuries, there
obviously were many changes and inevitably the outlook of each
generation has differed, slight as the differences may seem to us
today. In painting, particularly, the factor of personality has always been considerable: the influence of dominant painters and
critics in each period tended to change aspects of the traditional
tao; and, in actual practice, the ink and the soft Chinese brush
being extraordinarily sensitive, the personal touch could not fail
to be revealed in each brushstroke. Each generation might be
said to have used the tradition in its own way, modifying it to
suit its needs. There were, of course, lapses as well as moments
of great vitality, but the ebb and flow was sustained by the common acceptance of the traditional *tao*. It was the underlying *Tao*

that inspired Chinese painting to creative heights. The peaks came at those times, as in the T'ang era, when the impact of outside influences challenged the validity of the Chinese tradition, or when war, turbulence, and extreme distress forced the human spirit to draw upon resources rooted deep in the tradition. When, however, a period settled back and merely aped the past, the results often were monotonous; and tradition was a prison of the spirit.

Chinese painters and art critics did not overlook the disadvantages patent in a long and firm tradition. In their writings they repeatedly warned against set habit and imitation, particularly in brushwork, which could result only in lifeless pictures and therefore in denial of *Tao*. They were quick to discern such symptoms in works even of the masters, and they recorded these faults as faithfully as they praised achievement. On the other hand, the paintings that succeeded in expressing some aspect of *Tao* and the numerous works done in the styles of past masters that managed to catch the spirit of the originals show the strength and advantage of the long tradition. The outstanding painters never seemed to find conventions restrictive, such as the codifying of brushstrokes, the sets of methods, and the classification of subject matter. Their works prove rather the advantages of a unique idiom of brushstrokes and an accepted symbolism, which enhanced their opportunities of expression. There were, of course, individualists in every period, but the weight of tradition during years of preparation seems to have led them through the kind of experience recorded by Shih T'ao. In his essay *Hua Yu Lu* (Notes on Painting), Shih T'ao noted that he had painted and written for many years, declaring his independence of orthodox methods, until one day he suddenly realized that the way he had thought his own was actually "the *tao* of the ancients."

Training in brushwork and knowledge of the symbolism embodying the ancient beliefs and concepts were part of the traditional education of a scholar. Up to modern times, this discipline consisted of the reading, memorizing, and study of the classics of history, religion, and philosophy; in the process, one learned to handle the brush with ease. The preliminary steps required many diligent years and account for two important features of Chinese painting. The first is the close relationship between painting and calligraphy: in both arts the same soft, pointed brush is used, with a consequent emphasis on high standards of brushwork. The second feature is the traditional view that painting is not a profession but an extension of the art of living, for the practice of the *tao* of painting is part of the traditional *tao* of conduct and thought, of living in harmony with the laws of *Tao*. In such circumstances, painting in China has usually been an expression of maturity: most of the great masters first distinguished themselves as officials, scholars, or poets, and many were expert calligraphers, before they turned to painting. Some, though they painted, preferred to exhibit their brush skill in calligraphy; some excelled in painting as well as in other fields—for example, Chang Heng, astronomer and poet, was a painter of repute; Wang Wei (*tzu* Ching-hsien), calligrapher, musician, and medical man, painted and moreover wrote one of the most perceptive essays in the literature of Chinese painting; and the famous Su Tung-p'o, a rare and genial personality, was eminent as official, scholar, poet, art critic, calligrapher, and painter of bamboo.

In acquiring the education prescribed by the *tao* of painting, a painter underwent rigorous intellectual discipline and intensive training of memory. The ancient wisdom molded his character and nourished his innermost resources. In writing with brush and ink, he acquired sensitivity and control of the medium, and, because of the nature of Chinese writing, the finest training of hand and eye. Writing Chinese characters also developed a fine sense of proportion, which, in painting, was evident in the arrangement of a composition and its details, in drawing with the brush, and, more subtly, in the exercise of taste and discrimination. Such a sense is a form of that sense of fitness, so prominent in every aspect of Chinese life, which Confucius rated one of the Five Cardinal Virtues. He used the ancient term *li*, generally translated "ritual," although its significance lay rather in the motives and ideas underlying ritual. Essentially, the sense of fitness is knowing what to do and how to do it, suitable to the occasion, with the implication that, in performing a rite or behaving ceremoniously, one understands the meaning and purpose of the ritual approach.

It was inevitable that ritual conduct gradually lost a great deal
of its original meaning as more and more attention went to elabo-
rating the performance. Since Confucius in his day deplored such
loss of meaning, it is hardly surprising that, in later periods, the
original motives were generally neglected. But painting and every
other phase of Chinese life continued to be governed by the value
of the ritual approach. It is worth noting, therefore, that the original purpose of ritual was to order the life of the community in harmony with the forces of nature *(Tao),* on which subsistence and
well-being depended. It was not only pious but expedient to per-
form regularly and properly the rituals of worship, propitiation,
and celebration. These were acts of reverence. They were also
literally attempts to bring heaven down to earth, for they were
patterned on the rhythmic transformations in the skies and in nature, in the hope that a like order and harmony might prevail in
society. Men had observed that there is a dignity, an eminent
propriety, in that pattern, and they firmly believed it beneficial
to emulate it and thereby acquire a like dignity, grace, and harmony. Hence the conviction that individuals and society are better off when they have some signposts of belief and ritual and
moral conduct. The *Li Chi,* the ancient Book of Rites, declares
that the rules of ceremony (*li*) originated in the *T'ai I* (Great One,
Monad, or Primal Unity), an early term for what later was also
called *Tao.* The *Li Chi* explains that while rules "have their origin in heaven, the movement of them reaches to earth. The dis-
tribution of them extends to all the business of life. . . . They
supply the channels by which we can apprehend the ways of
Heaven and act as the feelings of men require. It was on this
account that the sages knew that the rules of ceremony could
not be dispensed with." [2] Rules of propriety, contributing to a
mature sense of fitness, were, in the words of the *Li Chi,* "instruments to form men's characters, and they are therefore performed
on a great scale. They remove from a man all perversity, and increase what is beautiful in his nature." [3] The *Tso Chuan* commentaries for 517 B.C. give the following relevant explanation: "Cere-

[2] Bk. VII, Sec. IV, 4, 5, 6 (tr. Legge).
[3] Bk. VIII, Sec. I, 1.

monials constitute the standard of Heaven, the principles of
Earth, and the conduct of man. Heaven and Earth have their
standards, and men take these for their pattern, imitating the brilliant bodies of Heaven and according with the natural diversities
of Earth."[4] Other communal and individual activities were also
regarded, no less than ceremonials, as acts of worship and sacrifice (in the original sense of *sacrifice:* "making sacred"). The
solemn responsibility of such acts, accompanied by the reassur-
ing conviction that thereby the state, community, and individual
participated in the Way of Heaven and received its benefits, gave
life meaning and every detail importance. This point of view,
which influenced Chinese life in every period and prevailed long
after the original significance of ritual was dissipated, is well illustrated in the course that painting followed. Painting began in the
service of religious ritual and custom: the careful decorating and
"making sacred" of ceremonial vessels and implements with celestial patterns and symbols of the sun, moon, stars. And even when,
in subsequent periods, the function of painting was enlarged beyond the religious, it continued to express the harmony of *Tao* as
reflected in nature on earth. In other words, painting, like every
other activity in Chinese life, retained most of its character as an
act of reverence long after its original motivations had become
obscure. The concept of *Tao,* the ideal of conduct and thought
expressive of *Tao,* continued to be of fundamental importance,
governing technique, theory, and the attitude of the painter.

Since *tao* and the *Tao* are key terms, it may be useful to look
more closely at the character *tao* and at some instances of its use
and connotation in Chinese thought.

In Chinese, a single character or a combination of two or more
characters to form a word depicts an object, act, or thought with
a vividness possible only in pictographic writing. Associated ideas
contribute overtones of meaning and greatly enlarge the import
of the words. The choice of *tao* (road, path, or way) and not another character denoting a path or way must therefore have been
based on ideas intrinsic in the pictograph. Beyond its general
meaning, *tao* by extension means "method, principle, standard,

[4] Tr. in Fung Yu-lan. *A History of Chinese Philosophy*, I, p. 38.

or doctrine." It is made up of two pictographs: *ch'o,* representing a foot taking a step, and *shou,* a head.[5] The use of *tao* in the simplest sense of "path" can easily be deduced from *ch'o* (foot). The "head" might have represented merely the man walking along the path, although even the earliest known use of the character contains the idea of *thought,* for following a path implies thinking about and choosing the particular path.

There is evidence that the combination of *shou* (head) and *ch'o* (foot) symbolized the idea of wholeness, that is, spiritual growth. One aspect of the character *tao* thus represents an *inner* way, an integration of character with deep and complex psychological connotations (as to soul, mind, and emotions). Dissection of the *ch'o* (foot) pictograph supports this meaning of *tao,* for it is composed of *ch'ih* (to step with the left foot) and *chih* (to halt).[6] Step-by-step progress requires care and deliberation and, by extension, careful and deliberate conduct or behavior from an inner motivation. The *left* foot also lends emphasis to the inner aspect. We find the explanation of this in the ancient polarity theory of the *Yin* and the *Yang: Yang,* as the Male Principle, represents also the sun, light, activity, the positive, the right; *Yin,* as the Female Principle, represents the moon, darkness, quiescence, the negative, the left. The *Yang* force radiates outward, like the rays of the sun, while the force of the *Yin* turns inward and is an inner activity.

As to the *shou* (head) pictograph and the combination of *shou* and *ch'o* (foot), a sentence in Appendix V of the *I Ching* (Book of Changes) likens heaven to the head, heaven being synonymous with total harmony;[7] in Chapter III of the Taoist *Huai Nan Tzu,* the Way of Heaven is spoken of as circular, the Way of Earth as square;[8] and the encyclopedia *T'u Shu Chi Ch'eng* contains this statement: "The head of man corresponds to Heaven, being round like Heaven and uppermost, the foot to Earth, being

[5] See Appendix for modern and old forms of the Chinese characters for *tao* and other key terms.

[6] Giles, *A Chinese-English Dictionary,* Nos. 2013, 1837; and Wieger, *Chinese Characters,* pp. 163, 263.

[7] Appendix V, Ch. IX, 13 (tr. Legge).

[8] III, l, v (tr. in Forke, *The World-Conception of the Chinese,* p. 52).

square like Earth and below."[9] The idea of wholeness, literally from head to foot, of total harmony, like Heaven and Earth, is therefore the goal illustrated in the composition of the character *tao,* and *tao* is primarily an inner way toward achieving this aim.

The "head" symbol appears significantly in many Chinese words. The idea of integration is illustrated, for instance, in the way a head is indicated in *ta* (great, greatness). Compare with this the deliberate omission of it in *jen* (man). Both words are shown in the Appendix. "Man" is symbolized by a pair of legs, whereas "greatness"—by extension, wholeness, and in accord with *Tao,* is depicted by a figure complete with a body, legs, outstretched arms, and, above all, a head. The idea connected with the attainment of the head may be observed in the title of the Confucian classic, the *Ta Hsueh,* usually translated "The Great Learning," which, however, from its theme and contents, may well be rendered "the learning of greatness (wholeness, or full maturity)."

The *ch'o* (foot) pictograph in the character *tao* is similar in form to a boat with a tall prow. Taking into account the association of Heaven with the sun and the head, and the concept of integration as equivalent to harmony with *Tao,* it calls to mind representations of the ancient Egyptian barge of the Sun God. According to the myth, the Sun God sailed through Night into Day—by another interpretation, along the River of Life from West to East—to emerge at the point of sunrise and godhood.[10] In gaining his godhood—completing his integration—he shed his animal's head and acquired a human head, his god's head. Man's efforts toward integration, conceived as a *tao* in accord with *Tao,* closely parallel the progress of the Sun Barge. The points of view differ in an interesting way: the ancient Egyptians believed in godhood achieved after many lives, while the Chinese referred to the goal of "sageliness and kingliness," the ideal of "the noble or great (whole) man," as the aim of life, the life they were living, the only one they could be sure of.

9. Tr. Forke, p. 77.
10. Budge, *The Gods of the Egyptians,* I, pp. 296, 505; II, pp. 99 (fig.), 105.

This goal of "sageliness within and kingliness without" summed up the early Chinese idea of "greatness" and stressed the necessary balance between the development of one's inner resources and the evidence of this in every activity. "Sageliness" or wisdom was an inner achievement. "Kingliness" was derived from the ancient conception of kingship as the office and function of the man who served as the connecting link between heaven and earth: on the one hand, interpreting and transmitting the Way of Heaven to earth, and on the other, offering earth's worship and sacrifices to heaven. The ideal ruler was the virtuous, whole, and perfectly balanced man, and kingliness the practice of these attributes.

The concern to achieve harmony with *Tao* was so intense in early Chinese society that it produced an outlook focused on Heaven, an attitude fixed on eternity and guided by eternal values. Remnants of this outlook are still evident throughout Asia: for instance, the attitude that time, and in particular clock time or man's time, is inconsequential. The focus on eternity, however, gradually diminished to the scale of man and became set as the human yearning for immortality.

The basis of the idea of immortality was the belief in the harmony and oneness of nature. The search for the secret of postponing or if possible banishing death became the directing idea in ancient and modern Taoist alchemy. Those given to alchemical practices interpreted passages in the *Tao Te Ching* dealing with the immortality of *Tao,* together with other passages about man's obligation to conform to *Tao,* to mean that life could and should be prolonged. According to their ideas, the distinction between soul and body was qualitative, the soul being the finer essence and by nature immortal, the body the coarser, and death merely a separation of the two. The problem was to bring the body to a state similar to that of the soul, so that it might share the attributes of *Tao*. This they attempted through diet, exercises, and breathing, and the imbibing of tinctures of gold, jade, and other substances associated with purity and power. The main motive was to attain *Tao* and, in so doing, to prolong life. But the original philosophical ideas about *Tao* were gradually obscured by the inordinate zeal put into the transmutation of metals and other substances in the search for the elixir of life.

The yearning for immortality may also have been associated in some way with the *shou* (head) pictograph. A recent study has pointed out that a primary form of the character, found in an inscription on a bronze vessel of about 1000 B.C., shows quite clearly an animal's head, "presumably a deer head."[11] In the records of ancient beliefs, animals were used to symbolize certain powers of nature and celestial and calendar signs. And such animals as the deer must have been, in early times, more clearcut emblems of immortality. Popular belief still associates the deer with the wish for everlasting life, and it has long been known as the only animal able to find the *ling chih,* the plant of immortality. According to legend, the fabulous unicorn resembles the deer in its traits, and has a deer's body. Its head is a dragon's and one horn grows not from the forehead but from the back of the head; it has a lion's tail, an ox's cloven hoofs, and sometimes wings at its shoulders. It is one of the four supernatural creatures and, as such, possesses cosmic power; its rare appearances herald the birth of a hero or a sage. A unicorn, we are told, was seen just before the birth of Confucius. These bits of popular legend, relics of ancient beliefs now forgotten, heighten the meaning of *tao* as primarily an inner way, in accord with *Tao,* through which men may partake in some measure of the superhuman and magical powers of the universe.

The concept expressed by the character *tao* is one of the oldest in Chinese thought. It has been shared by all the schools, with variants of interpretation. Lao Tzu and Chuang Tzu made *Tao* the central theme of their theories—indeed, so consistently that their followers were called *Tao shih* (scholars of the *Tao:* Taoists). For the same reason, the concept of *Tao* has usually been identified as a Taoist concept. But it is a concept—and a term—at the heart of all Chinese thought. Describing the importance of *Tao,* the author of the last chapter of the *Chuang Tzu* (who was not Chuang Tzu himself; his identity has been lost) speaks of its pervading influence in the Six Classics (*Ching*): the

[11] Karlgren, *The Chinese Language,* p. 23.

Shih (Odes, Songs, or Poetry), the *Shu* (History or Records), and *I* (Changes), the *Li Chi* (Rites or Rituals), the *Yueh* (Music; later included in Rites), and the *Ch'un Ch'iu* (Spring and Autumn Annals). Commenting on the existing interpretations of *Tao,* he remarks that they "did not know *Tao,* nevertheless they all had a certain acquaintance with it."[12]

The sense in which *tao* was used before the time of Confucius may be inferred from some of its occurrences in the *Shih Ching, Shu Ching,* and the *I Ching,* which contain information about the customs, rituals, and beliefs of a very remote period.

In the *Shih Ching, tao* is simply "road or path" and "way" of telling; it is also used in the sense of "plan": "The husbandry of How-tseih (Hou Chi) proceeded on the plan of helping the growth."[13] In the *Shu Ching, tao* is, similarly, a "way" of action; it appears also in a reference to the Decree of Heaven, with the meaning of the "right way" and hence the Way or *Tao:* "Thus did they receive the true favoring decree from Heaven; and thus did great Heaven approve their ways."[14] "The mind of man is restless, prone to err; its affinity for the right way is small."[15] In the oldest parts of the *I Ching, tao* is used in the ordinary sense of "path or way" and also "inner way," as in the excerpts: ". . . treading his accustomed path. If he go forward there will be no error. . . . Tread the path that is level and easy," and ". . . its subject moving right in the center . . . and yet returning alone to his proper path."[16]

To Confucius (551–479 B.C.), Mencius (c. 372–289 B.C.), and the Confucian schools, *tao* was primarily an ethical ideal and standard, the *tao* of man, and its goal was "sageliness within and kingliness without." In the *Lun Yu* (Analects), *tao* is "the way of the ancients," "the way of the Former Kings."[17] To Con-

[12] Tr. Giles, *Chuang Tzu,* p. 447.

[13] *Shih Ching,* Vol. II, Part III, Bk. II, Ode 1 (tr. Legge, p. 469). Hou Chi was a Minister of Agriculture, deified as the Harvest God and venerated as an ancestor of the Chou dynasty.

[14] *Shu Ching,* Vol. II, Part V, Bk. XXIII, 5 (tr. Legge, p. 567).

[15] Ibid., Vol. I, Part II, Bk. II, 15 (p. 61 n.): on *hsin tao* (way of the heart).

[16] Tr. Legge, pp. 79, 108. In the Appendices of the *I Ching,* a later addition, *tao* became the metaphysical *Tao.*

[17] The ancestor-emperors Yao and Shun, who were believed to have achieved sageliness and kingliness.

fucius, this *tao* was the *Tao*. It was "the way of good people" and of the *chun tzu,* "the noble man"; it was therefore "the way of virtue," which consisted of conduct exhibiting *jen* (Goodness), the foremost of the Confucian virtues. The character *jen* is composed of "man" and "two," referring to human relationships; it signifies a compassionate and altruistic attitude, and action accordingly. The main concern of Confucius—compare the view expressed by Socrates in the *Phaedrus*—was this *tao* of man; he would not discuss the *Tao* of heaven,[18] although he mentioned it with respect and characteristic caution.

Confucius did not, however, lack religious feeling. His concern that men should understand and properly observe *li* and his interest in the development of moral character suggest a deeply religious nature. In early Chinese life, as in other ancient civilizations, no separation existed between religion and philosophy nor between religion and culture. All of life was religious. Religion included philosophy and art; it was the basis of social conduct and political action; it embraced astronomy, divination, and alchemy.[19] The religious practices of prognostication and magic contained the origins of science. One branch of divination was astrology, regarded as an important part of astronomy, from which it was not differentiated; and much of the practice of magic was actually a chemical procedure that contained the beginnings of the science of chemistry. Most of Chinese philosophy might be said to be psychology, being concerned with the mind, emotions, and character—the development of the whole personality. Chinese thinkers, however, approached the problems of psychology from an ethical point of view, treating man as a thinking, feeling, and potentially "good" self; *jen,* as we have seen, is an attitude and kind of conduct essentially social, moral in focus, and guided by religious concepts. "The way of the ancients" was therefore religious, philosophical, psychological, cul-

[18.] *Lun Yu* V, 12.

[19.] "If we look upon magic, religion, and philosophy as ways of dealing with the same anxieties, we shall not be surprised to find these three sometimes overlapping, and shall not necessarily put the consolations of magic on a lower footing than those of philosophy or religion."—Waley, *Three Ways of Thought in Ancient China,* p. 77.

tural, and socio-political. Progress in following this *tao* was judged by the effects of "self-cultivation" shown in the relationships in the family, clan, village, and state. This, the Confucian focus, was the *tao* of man, the life each person had to live. To follow this *tao* was indeed a whole life's endeavor and merited all of one's attention and concentration. Hence Confucius would not concern himself with the world of spirits: "When you do not yet know fully about life, how can you know about death?"[20]

The Confucian *tao* was a lofty ideal, and Confucius' opinion of man's capacity to achieve it can be described only as gloomy. When he told his followers, "set your heart on the *tao*," he meant the same thing as when he told them, "Subdue one's self and recover the ritual disposition; this is *jen*."[21] "To subdue one's self" was to act morally, subduing egotism. "To recover the ritual disposition" meant to behave according to the beliefs embodied in rituals (*li*). In the *Lun Yu*, Confucius is reported to have pointed out that often those who sought learning did not seek learning about the *tao*, that those who sought the *tao* were not always able to "subdue themselves and recover the ritual disposition," and that those who could subdue themselves might lack an understanding of ritual.[22] Moreover, if after the age of forty or fifty a man had still not heard the *tao*, there was nothing to be respected in him.[23]

Mencius referred to *tao* as "the kingly way" and "the way of morality"; to him *tao* was the conscience. Man's nature was "what Heaven has given to us." And "he who has completely developed his mind knows his nature; knowing his nature, he knows Heaven." "If a man knows Heaven, he is not only a citizen of society but also a citizen of the universe."[24] He is a great man, the truly adult and whole man. The ideal of "a great man" is described by Mencius in another part of his work: "To dwell in the wide house of the world of man, to stand in the correct position in it, and to follow the *tao* of it; having obtained one's

[20] *Lun Yu* XI, 11.
[21] Fung, *The Spirit of Chinese Philosophy*, tr. Hughes, p. 21.
[22] *Lun Yu* IX, 29 (tr. in Fung, *Spirit*, p. 22).
[23] Ibid. IX, 22 (tr. in Fung, *Spirit*, p. 20).
[24] *Mencius* VI, a, 15; VII, a, 1; VII, a, 19 (tr. Fung, *Short History*).

ambition, to practice one's principles for the good of the people;
when that ambition is disappointed, to practice them alone;
when riches and honor cannot make one swerve, and power and
force cannot make one bend; these are the characteristics of the
great man."[25]

In contrast to the somewhat austere moral *tao* of Confucianism, the sublime metaphysical *Tao* of the Taoist philosophers
is as refreshing as the cool, clear water Taoists liked to use as a
symbol. The two interpretations do not conflict, however, but
supplement and reinforce each other. The Taoists enlarged the
tao into the concept of the Great *Tao,* which they describe by
many names—the Primal Unity and Source, the Cosmic Mother,
the Dark and Mysterious, the Unfathomable, the Formless Form,
the Infinite and Ineffable Principle of Life, the One, etc. It resembles the Macrocosmos in the thought of other parts of the
ancient world, and, in many respects, the ancient Greek Logos.
In modern translations of the New Testament into Chinese,
"Logos" is rendered by *tao.* The Gospel of St. John is generally
the favorite of Chinese Christians, and, indeed, an opening line
such as "In the beginning was *Tao* . . ." would appeal enormously
to a Chinese reader. The *Tao* of ancient Taoist philosophy, however, being inexpressible—in fact, beyond intellectual comprehension—could not be defined, although it was constantly referred to.
Taoist writers sometimes listed what it is not, thus giving a hint
of what it is. The extraordinary compilation of Taoist thought
ascribed to Lao Tzu, and later given the title by which it is now
well known, the *Tao Te Ching* (Classic of the *Tao* and Its Power),
describes *Tao* in a variety of ways: "The *Tao* that can be called
Tao is not the eternal *Tao* . . . this which has no name produced
both Heaven and Earth"; "*Tao* is invisible and nameless"; "*Tao*
never does, yet through it all things are done."[26] ". . . formless
yet complete, it existed before Heaven and Earth, without shape
or substance, alone but all pervasive. It may be thought of as
the mother of all things. It has no name, but it is termed *Tao.*
. . . Man's standards are conditioned by those of Earth, the
standards of Earth by those of Heaven, the standard of Heaven

[25] Ibid. III, b (tr. in Fung, *Spirit,* p. 26).
[26] *Tao Te Ching,* I, XLI, XXXVII.

by that of *Tao*, and the standard of *Tao* is that of its own intrinsic nature."[27]

An important aspect of *Tao* is its state of perpetual motion, endless mutation, including what Taoists called the movement of "returning" to *Tao*. All things are parts of Being, Being itself is a part of Non-Being (the Primal Unity) and all things, as they come into being and develop, progress through a series of changes moving persistently toward a return to the state of Non-Being, the Source (*Tao*).[28] *Tao* often is described as great (*ta*); this meant, in effect, the completely whole—Wholeness or Oneness. *Ta* is also the process of moving forward and outward and returning inward in completion of the circuit. This circular or rather spiral course describes the effort toward achieving wholeness by the process of "returning" to or reuniting with *Tao*, as well as the process itself, which is the natural and inevitable way common to all things. The basically circular movement of *Tao* confirms the idea of heaven as round, symbolized by the circle; for *Tao* is Heaven's Way. And the combination of *shou* (head) and *ch'o* (foot) in the character *tao* not only symbolizes *tao* as an inner way, as discussed above; it also illustrates the circular, complete, and perpetual course of *Tao*, for a circle's beginning (the head) and end (the foot) are the same, and the movement around its periphery is unceasing. Furthermore, the two pictographs exemplify the Taoist idea of *Tao* as both unmoving and continually moving, and of *tao* as the way of "actionless activity": the head—beginning, "source," and thus *Tao* itself—is fixed and therefore motionless, while the step-by-step progress of the foot represents movement; *tao* as "path" or "way" also is both fixed and moving, for a path lies on the ground and thus is still, yet it leads somewhere and so has movement. This aspect of *Tao* was the basis of the old Taoist idea of *wu wei*, "actionless activity" or non-assertiveness. The Taoists emphasized *wu wei*, and the idea has come to be associated with Taoist theories, although it actually was part of the common ground of early Chinese

[27] Ibid., XXV. "Intrinsic nature" is taken from the translation by Ch'u Ta-kao. The last phrase is rendered in Fung, *History*, I, p. 224: "*Tao's* standard is the spontaneous."
[28] *Tao Te Ching*, XXV, XXVIII, XL.

thought, held by all schools, which differed only in how to use it and to what end. *Wu wei* follows quite naturally the basic Chinese belief in a patterned and ordered universe, in which every thing has its place and draws on a common source of life. When each thing functions according to its nature and thus in proper relationship to everything else under Heaven, it is engaging in an unforced and natural action (*wu wei*). This applies to heaven itself, since it is Heaven's Way. Heaven, be it said, is not God. In early Chinese thought there was *Shang Ti* or *Ti,* who might be described as a kind of Superior Being; but Heaven (*T'ien*), though worshipped and prayed to as the bestower of benefits and punishment, was not God. It is all-powerful and impersonal. The order of Heaven is *Tao,* and its unceasing activity is an eternal process unfolding effortlessly and naturally (*wu wei*) and not by command of any celestial lawgiver. Such a command would imply directed effort.

"Returning" to *Tao* applies to everything in nature. It is one of the ways of describing the totality of *Tao,* which contains everything in its encompassing harmony. Within this Oneness, Unity, and Circle of *Tao,* opposites whose tension and conflicts account for the continual cycle of change and movement in nature are united and blended, resulting in the "Identity of Contraries."[29] Thus *Tao* has been designated also as the Great Void, which contains everything. Such words as *hsu* and *k'ung,* both meaning "emptiness," assumed great importance in Taoist works. Space of any sort was regarded as filled with meaning since it was filled with *Tao,* in fact was *Tao,* an idea that inevitably had a profound influence on painting. It is pointed out in Chapter XI of the *Tao Te Ching* that the space between the spokes of a wheel make the wheel of use, the inner space and not the pottery of a pitcher is its essential part, and the space within four walls compose the usefulness of a room. "Emptiness" in this Taoist sense is the equivalent of *wu wei:* the cessation of all action and the suspension of thought, in order to allow freedom

---

[29] Giles' title for Ch. II of his translation of the *Chuang Tzu.* The phrase often appears in translations of Taoist works; it also appears in the rendering of the same idea in early Greek material. William Blake expressed the idea in the first line of Bk. II of his poem *Milton:* "There is a place where contrarieties are equally true."

of the inner activity of the spirit. The purpose of Taoist meditation, what they call "stilling the heart," is to empty it of all dis-
tracting thought and emotion; the "emptiness" opens the way
to a state of quiescence and receptivity, the ideal state in which
to reflect *Tao*. As the *Lieh Tzu* states: "To a mind that is still,
the whole universe surrenders."[30] A modern commentator has
observed that the course of *Tao* is not only circular motion but
also, on the one hand, the marking off of a sacred precinct, and
on the other, fixation and concentration. The enclosing circle
prevents "emanations" that, in terms of modern psychology,
"protect the unity of consciousness from being split apart by the
unconscious." "Turning in a circle about oneself" involves all
sides of the personality, and has the moral significance of "acti-
vating all the light and dark forces of human nature and, with
them, all the psychological opposites of whatever kind they may
be."[31]

The *Chuang Tzu* gives a fuller picture of the Taoist mind than
one finds in the aphorisms of the *Tao Te Ching*. As we know it
today, the book is the work of many hands. Whole chapters
were inserted in later periods. The first seven of the thirty-three
chapters, however, are believed to be the work of Chuang Tzu
(*c.* 369–286 B.C.), and the rest to have been added by his followers, so that the work may fairly be said to represent the thought
of Chuang Tzu and his school. It gives abundant samples of the
paradox and humor typical of Taoist expression. Although, in
some respects, the philosophy of the *Chuang Tzu* differs from
that of the *Tao Te Ching*, the concept of *Tao* was essentially the
same in both. From the *Chuang Tzu:* "*Tao* has its laws and its evi-
dences. It is devoid both of action and of form. It may be obtained, but not seen. Before Heaven and Earth were, *Tao* was.
. . . To *Tao* the zenith is not high, nor the nadir low; no point of
time is long ago, nor by lapse of ages has it grown old." "*Tao*
cannot be existent. If it were existent, it could not be nonexistent. The very name of *Tao* is only adopted for convenience."
"*Tao* makes things what they are, but is not itself a thing." "All

[30] Tr. in Waley, *The Way and Its Power*, p. 58.
[31] C. G. Jung, in his commentary to *The Secret of the Golden Flower*, pp. 101, 106.

that a fish wants is water; all that a man wants is *Tao*."[32] "The duck's legs are short, but if we try to lengthen them, the duck will feel pain. The crane's legs are long, but if we try to cut off a portion of them, the crane will feel grief. Therefore we should not amputate what is by nature long, nor lengthen what is by nature short."[33] The Taoist attitude might be summed up in these words at the end of the *Chuang Tzu:* "Adopt no absolute position. Let externals take care of themselves. In motion, be like water. At rest, like a mirror. Respond, like the echo. Be subtle, as though nonexistent. Be still, as though pure."[34]

Some remarkable similarities of idea and statement may be found between the early Taoist thinkers and the Milesian and Ionian philosophers. Many of the declarations attributed, for instance, to Anaximander and Pythagoras could be applied to *Tao*. Perhaps the closest resemblances are found in the fragments attributed to Heraclitus of Ephesus: "Listen not to me but to the Logos. . . . Wisdom is One."[35] "Beginning and end are general in the circumference of the circle." "The way up and down is one and the same." "This ordered universe, which is the same for all, was not created by any one of the gods or of mankind, but it ever was and is and shall be ever-living Fire." "Everything is on the move." "It is not possible to step twice into the same river." The existence of the cosmos "is maintained by tension or strife of Opposites . . . and out of this, harmony is created." "God is day-night, winter-summer, war-peace, satiety-famine." Knowledge of many things through sense-perceptions "will not itself give wisdom, only the co-ordinating soul can do that." And the individual soul could learn only by looking into itself: "I searched into myself." For above all, "the hidden harmony is better than the visible." The Taoists would also have agreed with Heraclitus that men's conjectures were like "children's toys" and appreciated his comment that "Nature likes to hide." This last fragment might well be applied to the Taoist elements in Chi-

[32]. Tr. Giles, *Chuang Tzu*, p. 76, 351, 291, 85.
[33]. Tr. in Fung, *History*, I, p. 229.
[34]. Tr. Giles, *Chuang Tzu*, p. 447.
[35]. Following excerpts gathered from Freeman, *Companion to the Pre-Socratic Philosophers*, pp. 104–28, and *Ancilla*, pp. 24–34.

nese painting. Their influence encouraged great subtleties of expression in few brushstrokes and eloquent rendering of atmospheric effects and space.

There were schools of thought other than the Confucian and Taoist, and all shared the common concept of *Tao*. Hsun Tzu (*c.* 298–238 B.C.) and his followers, for example, though they did not agree with the general premise that man was by nature "good" and declared that "goodness" had to be cultivated, believed in *Tao*. To Hsun Tzu, "Heaven has its seasons, Earth has its resources, man has his culture,"[36] and everything good and of value has to be gained through man's own moral and intellectual efforts. He said, "If we neglect what man can do and think about Heaven, we fail to understand the nature of things,"[37] and in so doing we forget our essential vocation. In a chapter "On Freedom from Blindness," he remarked on the interpretations of *Tao* among the various schools of thought, noting that their views represented only single aspects of *Tao,* and that "the essence of *Tao* is constant and includes all changes. It cannot be grasped by a single corner. Those with perverted knowledge who see only a single aspect of *Tao* will not be able to comprehend its totality."[38] And later, out of his Confucian background, he declared: "*Tao* is not the *Tao* of Heaven; it is not the *tao* of Earth; it is the *tao* of man"; it was the correct standard for ancient times and for the present, and "if you depart from the *tao* to choose your own inner standards, then you will not know what will lead to calamity or happiness."[39]

Among the Hundred Schools, there were many interpretations of the basic concept of *Tao*. Their differences were of emphasis on one or another aspect of *Tao,* and further examples are unnecessary. Mention should, however, be made of the thought of two important later groups, the Neo-Confucianists and the sect of Buddhism called *Ch'an,* for they exerted a strong influence on Chinese painting. The *tao* of Neo-Confucianism differed in many respects from earlier interpretations; moreover, certain related

[36] *Hsun Tzu* XVII (tr. in Fung, *A Short History of Chinese Philosophy*, p. 144).
[37] Ibid.
[38] Ibid., p. 184.
[39] Tr. in Fung, *History*, I, p. 290.

concepts were given prominence that were taken over into the theories of painting. Ch'an or Zen Buddhism,[40] which had much in common with Taoism, affected painting profoundly, in particular the work of the Southern Sung landscapists. First, however, a brief explanation may be useful in relating these later groups to what has been discussed.

Confucianism had suffered a decline after the time of Mencius. Its doctrines lost much of their vitality and appeal, despite efforts to bolster them by Confucians and their supporters, who were men prominent in official circles and whose motives were markedly political. An important crisis, far-reaching in its effects, arose at the time of the first unification of China (221 B.C.) under the Ch'in emperor Shih Huang-ti, who tried to make history begin with his reign by a rather futile attempt to destroy all evidence of the past—for example, his famous order for the burning of the books. The Han period (207 B.C.–A.D. 220), which followed, attempted unification in another way: not by force and violence but by scholarship and by editing of the kind at which Chinese scholars were particularly adept. The Han scholars set about rewriting and rearranging such of the literature and records as had survived the self-styled First Emperor's edict to make them fit their ideas of Chinese history.[41] Their labors consisted in drastic revision of the accounts of earlier periods; accordingly, the nonliterary evidence excavated in recent times, and whatever part of the records can be identified as trustworthy pre-Han evidence, give us more valid information about the foundations of Chinese life and thought than the Han records and works. Han Confucianism, for instance, developed into something very different from what Confucius had taught, something even farther removed from the *tao* of the ancients that he had sought to revive. Confucianism became an official religion; in the process, Confucius was canonized—in the eyes of many, deified. A lively controversy ensued between those who supported

[40] Ch'an Buddhism has come to be better known in the West by its Japanese name *Zen*, both terms being derived from the Sanskrit *Dhyana* (meditation), and it may be convenient to use here the more familiar term.

[41] Su Tung-p'o commented in his famous epitaph on Han Yu that "from the age of the Hans, the Truth began to be obscured." Giles, *Chinese Biographical Dictionary*, No. 632.

this revised Confucianism and those who tried to revive the pre-Ch'in form, and even though Han Confucianism had the support of the throne and officialdom, it was a long time before the kind of unification sought by the Han scholars was achieved. Meanwhile, the influence of Taoism had spread, together with that of Buddhism, which had been introduced from India in the I century A.D., or even earlier; and, by the time Confucianism was firmly re-established in the latter part of the T'ang dynasty (618–906), it had become colored with Taoist and Buddhist ideas and practices. In the Sung period (960–1280) it emerged as the Tao Hsueh Chia (School of Study of *Tao*), which, in the West, is called "Neo-Confucianism."

During the T'ang period, representatives of foreign religions were welcomed in Court circles. Buddhism enjoyed a popularity that extended far beyond the Court: its scriptures, translated into Chinese, grew to vast proportions, converts responded by the tens of thousands to its message of Enlightenment and Nirvana, and the number of its monasteries increased so rapidly that they had to be checked by imperial decree. Among its sects, the Zen emerged as the strongest in appeal and influence and contributed inestimably to Chinese thought and culture. It has, in fact, been claimed by modern Zen Buddhists that without Zen there would have been no Neo-Confucianist revival. At any rate, the solace offered by the doctrines of Buddhism, and in particular the peace of mind that the Zen monks and their followers seemed able to achieve, answered a deep need in the strife and upheaval during the decline of the T'ang dynasty, and Zen became rooted in Chinese life. By the time that Neo-Confucianism was being expounded, in the Sung period, Zen was the only Buddhist school of any consequence, and to the Neo-Confucianists it represented the essence of Buddhism.

Having much in common with Taoism, the teachings of the Zen masters were easy to accept and assimilate. Both were "wordless doctrines" in their emphasis on enlightenment through intuition and the spirit. Zen was as strongly opposed to dependence on classic Buddhist scriptures as the Taoists were to the literary bent of the Confucianists. This did not mean that the Zen masters did not propound the scriptures; there were, in fact, attempts to reconcile Zen with *sutra* learning in order to counter-act the abuses of Zen philosophy by ignorant and half-enlight-ened followers. As a xiii-century Buddhist writer remarked, "the harm from depending too much on the *sutras* and philosophical treatises is slight compared with the harm from positively ignoring them."[42] Both Zen Buddhists and Taoists stressed the difference between the state of no-knowledge after passing through a stage of knowledge and the state of no-knowledge of ignorance. Though there was intermittent dispute between the two groups, many of their concepts actually were similar and reinforced each other, often merging so that they were indistinguishable. It was said of Hui-neng (627–713), founder of the Southern School of Zen in China, that he was unique because "he did not at all under-stand Buddhism. He understood *Tao* and no other thing."[43] Be-fore him, in the latter part of the iv century A.D., Kumarajiva, the great Indian Buddhist teacher, had used Taoist terms in translating Buddhist scriptures into Chinese, and he and other Buddhist teachers as well as many of the Zen masters used Tao-ist terms in their oral discussions. The flash of Sudden Enlight-enment that was the Zen Buddhists' aim, and which they be-lieved could be attained by meditation, they called "the vision of *Tao.*" Among Chinese painters, this Taoist-Buddhist view had a powerful impact. This will be discussed more fully in con-nection with brushwork and the ideal of *tzu jan* (spontaneity or naturalness).

One of the chief contributions of Buddhism to Chinese thought was the doctrine of the Universal Mind, which assumed an im-portant role in Neo-Confucianist theories. Before its adoption, Chinese works had contained references to "mind" but not to "Mind." On the other hand, when Buddhism in China became Chinese Buddhism, evolving as Zen, the practical "this-worldli-ness" of Chinese thinking modified the "other-worldliness" of Indian Buddhism and made it more acceptable and more readily adaptable to the themes of Chinese thought. For instance, when Chao-shou, an early master of Zen, in the T'ang period, was asked about *Tao,* he is said to have replied: "Your everyday life,

[42] Suzuki, *Essays,* 3rd series, p. 44.
[43] Suzuki, *Essays,* 1st series, p. 39.

that is *Tao*"; in other words, the Zen ideal was a quiet, self-confident and trustful existence of one's own, and the main point was to experience life at each moment.[44] The close relationship between Taoism and Zen may be seen in this approach; in fact, Zen might be said to have, in turn, anchored the aspect of Taoism that tended to soar. Another side of Taoism assimilated so much from the more fanciful elements of Buddhism that it developed into the popular, superstitious Taoist religion *(Tao Chiao)*. It is important to note the distinction between this Taoist religion and Taoist philosophy *(Tao Chia)*. And it is also of importance that, despite its mystical elements, Taoist thought is eminently practical. A Western philosopher has observed that "Taoism differs from all the other species of speculative mysticism known to us because of the interest which the Chinese mystics, despite their occasional asceticism and their exaltation of the inner life, displayed in human society and the regulation of the State."[45]

The Confucianist Han Yu (768–824), statesman, scholar, and foe of Buddhism, was one of the commentators on the Confucian doctrines who contributed to the birth of Neo-Confucianism. According to him, *tao* was not what the Taoists and Buddhists called *Tao*. It was still the Confucian *tao*. He and his followers held that this concept had been passed down from the legendary emperors Yao and Shun, and its transmission had been interrupted after Mencius; they undertook to resume the transmission of the Confucian *tao*.

The classics most important to the Neo-Confucianists were the Four Books—the *Lun Yu* (Analects), *Ta Hsueh* (Great Learning), *Chung Yung* (Doctrine of the Mean), and the book of *Mencius*—together with the *I Ching* (Book of Changes), in particular its ten appendices, the Ten Wings. Examples of the use and meaning of *tao* in the *Lun Yu* and the *Mencius* have already been given. The opening sentence of the *Chung Yung* presents an interpretation of *tao* similar to that of Mencius. The title of this classic denotes "practice of the Mean," for *yung* has the sense of "in ordinary use," and the form of the character *chung* might be described as a simple drawing of the Golden Mean with the main stroke exactly in the center.[46] The form has generally been interpreted as that of an arrow piercing the center of a target. At a deeper level of meaning, *chung* symbolized the whole concept of the Center, one aspect of which was the ideal of the Mean. The idea of the Center was held in common from earliest times among all the peoples of Asia; it is expressed, for instance, in two short verses in the *Mundaka Upanishad:*

> Taking as a bow the great weapon of the Upanishad,
> One should put upon it an arrow sharpened by meditation.
> Stretching it with a thought directed to the essence of That,
> Penetrate that Imperishable as the mark, my friend.

> The mystic syllable *Om* is the bow. The arrow is the soul.
> Brahma is said to be the mark.
> By the undistracted man is It to be penetrated.
> One should come to be in It, as the arrow (in the mark).[47]

The character *chung* has also been described as a representation of "the center of the four quarters" and an extension of the *Chi*[48] (Ridgepole of the Universe), an interpretation that lends weight to the concept of the Center and also exemplifies the ancient attitude about numbers and their application as symbols of cosmic structure and power. Such ideas associated with numbers, wholly distinct from their quantitative use, were common in the past among all peoples. They derived from the use of numbers in forming and recording ancient conceptions of the nature and structure of the universe, which made numbers the most sacred form of symbolism. The most familiar among the theories based on numbers in the West are probably those of the Pythagoreans; evidence of other and earlier theories, now lost to us, may be found in the dots and strokes on calendar stones and other sacred objects depicting the firmament, in the notches on bone knives and the motifs on painted pottery; in the decoration of ritual vessels, figures of deities, amulets, and virtually every

---

[46] See Appendix, Sec. II, for forms of *chung*. Legge translates the title "The Doctrine of the Mean"; some others are E. R. Hughes' "The Mean in Action," L. A. Lyall's "The Common Centre," and Ezra Pound's "The Unwobbling Pivot."

[47] Tr. Hume, *The Thirteen Principal Upanishads,* p. 372.

[48] Karlgren, "Glosses on the Ta Ya and Sung Odes," (*BMFEA* 18, 1946), p. 196.

object in the art of the ancient civilizations of the eastern Mediterranean, India, and South America, as well as China. The belief in the power of numbers has never completely disappeared; its remnants in the popular thinking today no longer have any profundity of meaning or any reference to the large concepts once symbolized by numbers, but they persist: for instance, in number games the world over and in superstitions about lucky and unlucky numbers.

Modern science, presenting its theories through mathematics, is still pursuing the very questions that preoccupied the ancient philosophers. Many statements of physicists and mathematicians of our day are marked by an element akin to the reverence of the great cosmological thinkers of ancient times. The mystery of multiple atomic particles is an aspect of the grand pattern that the natural philosophers of the past sought in their speculations. In presenting a new theory of the atom that envisages as many as six dimensions, in contrast to Einstein's theory employing four, an eminent physicist recently observed that "for hundreds of years we have learned that the great truths of nature are usually explained in classically simple ways. . . . The work we are doing is to attempt the beginning of understanding the existence of a great variety of particles and to reduce them to a more fundamental object or system that can make them appear as many different forms of a similar thing. . . . In an abstract sense I would suppose that certain groups of particles can actually be considered as different states of a more fundamental thing." [49] And one of the great teachers of natural history in our own day, who was described as the last of the Pythagoreans, wrote about the use and beauty of numbers in these words: "I know that in the study of material things, number, order and position are the threefold clue to exact knowledge; that these three, in the mathematician's hands, furnish the 'first outlines for a sketch of the Universe.' . . . The harmony of the world is made manifest in Form and Number, and the heart and soul and all the poetry of Natural Philosophy are embodied in the concept of mathematical beauty. . . . [Fabre,] in whose plainest words is a sound as of bees' industri-

---

[49] Professor A. Pais, in a speech at the World Conference of Physicists in Tokyo, reported in the *New York Times*, Sept. 21, 1953.

ous murmur, and who, being of the same blood and marrow with Plato and Pythagoras, saw in Number *le comment et le pourquoi des choses,* and found in it *la clef de voûte de l'Univers.*"[50]

In China, the persistence of classifying according to ideas about the potency of certain numbers has never slackened; indeed, it has become so firm a habit that some Western scholars have dubbed it a mania. It might seem so, except that the underlying ideas prove it no madness, nor even excessive enthusiasm. In the case of the character *chung,* it not only means "center" but is a drawing of "the center of the four quarters"; the long stroke through the square accents the fifth or central co-ordinating point (also the One) of what the Chinese have referred to as the Five Points. In Chinese astronomy the Five Points symbolize the division of the heavens into a central polar region and four peripheral regions; they thus marked off the basic structure of the universe and the total harmony of *Tao.* Geographically, the Five Points were represented by the Five Sacred Mountains in the provinces of Shantung, Hunan, Shensi, Hopei, and Honan, which compose the cradle of Chinese civilization. Their peaks, in lofty grandeur, symbolized the pillars of Heaven at the four corners and the center of the earth. The Five Points stood for the ideal of order and harmony of everything in nature (North, South, East, and West) under the vast dome of Heaven (the Zenith, the One, and also the Five). Thus, one aspect of Five was its symbolism also of the One and the Four—the manifestation of Heaven on the square of Earth—besides being itself the basic Five. And thus, too, *chung* (Center) was also the One, the Monad, Unity, and the Source *(Tao).* The ancient disks of jade were beautiful symbols of the One as the Source; they often had three nicks or notches on the outer edge, which lend an effect of perpetual rotation to the disks: the One in action, manifesting itself through the Three. The idea is elsewhere implicit in the concept of the Trinity. The symbol of the One and the Four as Heaven made manifest on the square of Earth was a common motif on early pottery, jades, and bronzes; it made the objects sacred and magically potent. Among clear examples, besides disks or flat rings of jade, are the backs of bronze mirrors on which the designs are quartered or in some similar way

---

[50.] D. W. Thompson, *On Growth and Form,* II, pp. 1096 f.

divided into four parts; the tubes of jade, varying in height, four-sided and four-cornered, of which the inner circular space or "emptiness" represented the One; and the three and four legs of pottery and bronze vessels which must surely have had a number significance besides serving as a stable base.

Imbued with the significance implicit in the idea of the Five Points, the number Five was held to be sacred and potent. It recurred in various basic classifications: the Five Planets, another indication of the framework of the heavens; the Five Elements, in reference to the nature of the universe; the Five Virtues, the basis of moral character and behavior; and other fundamental categories, such as the Five Tones, the Five Flavors, and the Five Colors.

Certain passages in the *I Ching* are of importance in explaining the significance of the Five. Of the numbers from one to ten, the odd pertain to Heaven, the even to Earth: five numbers belong to Heaven, five to Earth. Moreover, the sum of the odd numbers $(1 + 3 + 5 + 7 + 9 = 25)$ plus the sum of the even $(2 + 4 + 6 + 8 + 10 = 30)$ total fifty-five, which is the number of Heaven and Earth together.[51] Thus the Five of Heaven and the Five of Earth are reached in two different ways. The results are fittingly confirmed by the fact that the sum of the two Fives (and the sum of the two fives of fifty-five) is ten, the number regarded as complete and therefore perfect because it contains all the single and primary numbers and also is the sum of the four root numbers: $1 + 2 + 3 + 4$.

The range of numbers from one to ten is a universal basis of symbolism and of calculation, although no completely satisfactory explanation of its origins has been presented. One thinks at once of the ten fingers. But since numbers were regarded by all ancient peoples in these ways, the reasons for the basis of ten are probably to be found also in the symbolism of numbers. It is well known that the zero was of Indian origin and that in the religion and philosophy of India the concepts of the Center and the Circle have existed from remote times. The Arabic numeral for ten may have taken its form from Indian sources and have been based on similar ideas about the One and its encompassing

---

[51.] *I Ching,* Appendix III, Sec. I, Chap. IX, 49, 50 (tr. Legge).

unity and wholeness. Among the Chinese sources, the *Lieh Tzu*, in explaining a cosmogonic theory, states that "evolution in its transformations produces one, the changes of one produce seven, the changes of seven produce nine. Nine is the climax, it changes again and becomes one. With one, forms begin to change. The pure and light matter becomes the heaven above, the turbid and heavy matter forms the earth below. Their aggregation gives birth to man, and the vitalizing principle of heaven and earth creates all beings." [52] The One becoming the Seven represented the emergence of the *Yin* and *Yang* and the Five Elements; added to Heaven and Earth, of which they were the seven primary manifestations, the total made Nine. As a unit, therefore, Nine represented the universe, the whole, and thus the One, which was also symbolized by the ten, indicated in Chinese by the cross reaching out in four directions and in Arabic numerals by One alongside the Zero, the Circle of unity and wholeness.

The closely related concepts embodied in Five and Ten are represented by the forms of the cross in both the old and modern forms of the character *wu* (five) and in *shih* (ten) which are shown in the Appendix. The cross indicates the four directions or cardinal points and the center, thus the idea of totality and completeness—and perfection. The character *shih* retains today its original form of an upright cross with the four arms of equal length; it was, moreover, an emblem both of the sun, the central source radiating light and energy in all four directions; and of the Wheel, with its four main axes, signifying Eternal Law, movement, change, all that is implicit in the rotation of the Wheel of Life. The rim of the Wheel is invisible, and the character *shih* might accordingly be considered a Chinese analogue of St. Augustine's dictum that the nature of God is like a circle whose center is everywhere and circumference nowhere. The old form of *wu* (five) on oracle bones is a diagonal cross with a line above and a line below; it is identical in appearance with the Roman numeral for ten. The resemblance goes beyond form, for in both numerals the diagonal arms of the cross could be described as reaching out and touching all four corners of the universe or, microcosmically, of the whole personality. Likewise, the form of the Arabic numeral for ten,

[52] Chinese text and tr. in Forke, *World-Conception*, p. 35 n.

with its two symbols of One and Zero, side by side, represents unity and completeness, the totality of the One or Monad. To the early Chinese, totality and the ideal of concord was based on the idea of the harmony of Heaven and Earth, identified in one manner of interpretation with the Five. The upper and lower halves of the diagonal cross in the old form of *wu* also constitute two triangles, one pointing down, the other up. They may have represented the sacred mountains of Heaven and Earth, for the triangle form is a primary symbol of "mountain," as exemplified in the three triangles composing the original form of the character *shan* (mountain). The same triangular forms, denoting mountains, occur in the decoration of early pottery and bronzes. In terms of the Elements, the two triangles stood for the Element of Fire (Heaven, Sun, heat, light, the Male or *Yang* Principle) and that of Water (Earth, Moon, cold, darkness, the Female or *Yin* Principle). And the ancient sacrificial mounds at the south and north boundaries of community sites were counterparts of these triangles of Heaven and Earth.

The central point where the two triangles connect and where the arms of the cross intersect constitutes the axis upon which the Wheel of the Universe and of Life revolves, representing the core of creative power, analogous to *Tao*, static and at the same time radiating energy and life. Since this was a concept of very remote origin, held over a long period of time, it is probable that many expressions containing *chung*, usually translated "middle," actually connote "central or related to the Center." The designation of China as the Middle Kingdom *(Chung Kuo)* might well have originally contained the prayerful idea that the country would prosper as the "Kingdom of the Center" and partake of the creative and moral power of the Center. For according to the traditional view, the still, fixed central point, the *T'ai Chi* (variously rendered as the Ridgepole or Axis of the Universe, the Great Root, the Pole Star), is the support and point of reference of the whole of nature; in this sense, as the supreme motivating idea, it is representative of *Tao*. A Taoist work of the III century B.C. refers to *Tao* as the Center in these words: "Public affairs may be scattered to the four winds, but the essence is in the Center. The Sage clings to the essential, and thus the people of the

Four Quarters of the world will come to it of their own accord." [53]
The ideal was that everything should be in proper relationship to
the Center, in other words, in harmony with *Tao* and the whole of
nature. Confucius and his followers saw this aim mainly in terms
of man and his ethical development; in the *Lun Yu*, Confucius
said: "He who could put the Five into practice everywhere under
Heaven would be Good *(jen),*" [54] defining the Five as the Five
Cardinal Virtues that were analogous to the Five Points. He also
said: "He who rules by moral force is like the pole star, which remains in its place while all the lesser stars do homage to it." [55]
The Taoist way was through *wu wei,* non-assertiveness. To both
schools of thought, the right relationship to the Center was "true
action" as distinct from mere "doing."

The timelessness of the concept of the Center and its universal importance in sustaining the coherence of the metaphysical
tradition has been expressed in poetry of the modern West. These
lines from "Burnt Norton" could be describing *Tao* and the Taoist
idea of *wu wei:*

At the still point of the turning world. Neither flesh nor fleshless;
Neither from nor towards; at the still point, there the dance is,
But neither arrest nor movement. And do not call it fixity,
Where past and future are gathered. Neither movement from nor
    towards,
Neither ascent nor decline. Except for the point, the still point,
There would be no dance, and there is only the dance. . . .

This is the one way, and the other
Is the same, not in movement
But abstention from movement; while the world moves
In appetency, on its metalled ways
Of time past and time future. [56]

Returning to the classics of Neo-Confucianism, the *Chung Yung*

[53] *Han Fei Tzu,* Ch. VIII, 52, 54 (tr. Liao).
[54] *Lun Yu* XVII, 6 (tr. Waley, *Analects,* p. 210).
[55] Ibid. II, 1 (p. 88).
[56] T. S. Eliot, *Four Quartets,* pp. 5 f. In "East Coker," (p. 12) he refers to lines
from "The Gouernour," by his ancestor Sir Thomas Elyot: "In every daunse, of a
moste ancient custome, there daunseth together a man and a woman, holding each
other by the hande or arme, which betokeneth concorde." Movement, rhythm, and
"concorde" or harmony are also prime characteristics of *Tao,* manifested in a dance
through the couple, *Yang* and *Yin.*

opens with these sentences: "What Heaven confers on man may be called his nature, and acting according to this nature may be called *tao*. . . . No man can do without *Tao;* if one could do without it, it would not be *Tao*." The passage shows the blending of Taoist and Confucianist thinking. In the *Ta Hsueh, tao* is "the way of learning greatness or attaining wholeness." It is described in a key paragraph as follows: "Things have their roots and branches. Affairs have their ends and their beginnings. To know what comes first and what last is the *tao* of learning greatness." [57] Here we meet the sense of fitness in Neo-Confucianist terms. In the Appendices of the *I Ching, tao* is the *Tao* of Taoist philosophy and also the *tao* or principles that governed each thing, called by the Neo-Confucianists *li:* not the Confucian *li* (rituals) but *li* signifying "principle," sometimes also translated "reason," "essence" and "the fitness of things." [58] The character stands for the markings on jade, the grain of a piece of bamboo, the fibers of a muscle, or the threads of a fabric. Hence its meaning as a "natural principle." From the Sung period on, this *li* was a basic concept and term of Chinese painting.

To the Neo-Confucianists, *li* (principle) was only slightly less important than *Tao*. In reading their dialectics about *li*, one gains the impression that *li* was in fact another term for *Tao*, and that all their phrases describing the *li* (some examples of which are given below) were virtually exercises of the mind in search of *Tao*. With *li* they also stressed the *Ch'i* (life-breath or Vital Force) and the old cosmological doctrine of the *Yin* and *Yang*.[59]

The two main schools of Neo-Confucianism—headed respectively by Wang Shou-jen and Chu Hsi—each interpreted *li* in its own terms. Disagreement with both schools arose in the XVII and XVIII centuries, notably in the views of Tai Tung-yuan, but the interpretations of the two schools continued to be the more widely accepted.

Wang Shou-jen (1472–1528), Master of Yang-ming, chief expo-

[57.] *Ta Hsueh*, Part I, Ch. I, 3.
[58.] See Appendix, Sec. III, for the forms of the two *li*.
[59.] The concept of *Ch'i* was the basis of the First Canon of Chinese painting and is the main subject of the next chapter, in which the symbolism of *Yin* and *Yang* also will be examined.

nent of the School of the Mind, maintained that *li* was the Mind and that without Mind there could be no *li* (principles). He further states that "the mind of man is Heaven. There is nothing that is not included in the mind of man. All of us are this single Heaven, but because of the obscurings caused by selfishness, the original state of Heaven is not made manifest. Every time we extend our intuitive knowledge, we clear away the obscurings, and when all of them are cleared away, our original nature is restored, and we again become part of this Heaven. The intuitive knowledge of the whole is the intuitive knowledge of the part. Everything is the single whole." [60] This passage reveals some of the important contributions of Taoism and Buddhism to Neo-Confucianism: the doctrine of the Universal Mind, the all-inclusiveness of *Tao,* the value of intuition and knowledge gained through that faculty, and the idea that egotism *(ssu yu),* or what the Buddhists called "ignorance" *(avidya),* obscures a clear vision of *Tao.* The Taoist and Buddhist practice of meditation following exercises in controlling and regulating the breath—the human *ch'i* drawing on the *Ch'i* of the universe—was one of the means they believed helpful in emptying the heart of distractions, selfishness, and ignorance (what Wang Shou-jen called "obscurings") in order to be able to reflect clearly the *Tao.* The simile of a pool or a mirror was often used to describe the necessary state of stillness and receptivity of the heart. It should be explained that in Chinese the "mind" is denoted by the character *hsin* (heart), and that in Chinese thought the heart was regarded as the seat of spiritual and moral intelligence and perception, its function being to think and also to control the emotions. Here, again, an early Greek concept offers an illuminating parallel, for the Chinese idea of the heart and its function was similar to Socrates' concept of the "soul," the work and function of which was "to know, to apprehend things as they really are and consequently, in particular, to know good and evil, and to direct or govern man's acts." [61] For *ssu* (to think; also, thought) was to Mencius "knowledge of goodness *(jen)*"; in the *Lao Tzu* it had the meaning of "inner and thus spiritual and moral power *(te)*"; and to the Zen Buddhists it was the equivalent of

[60] Tr. in Fung, *Short History,* p. 315.
[61] Taylor, *Socrates,* p. 139.

bodhi, "true wisdom and knowledge." The form of the character *ssu,* which is composed of a pictograph of "head" in the form of a skull placed above that of "heart," suggests that thinking is guided by the heart and originates from it and is more important intuitively than intellectually. This concept of the heart, which is further evidence of the degree to which Taoism and Buddhism influenced Confucianism, was found also in the Neo-Confucianist Chu Hsi's interpretation of *ssu* as "seeking within the heart."

Chu Hsi (1130–1200) was the most important of the Neo-Confucianists. His interpretations of the classics became authoritative and have been so accepted down to modern times. To him, *Tao* was "the all-comprehensive Moral Law pervading the universe." [62] Concerning the term *li* (principle), he explained that "as soon as a thing exists, *li* is inherent in it. . . . Even a writing brush, though not produced by nature but by man . . . as soon as [it] exists, *li* is inherent in it." [63] And to Chu Hsi this was true of all other kinds of things in the universe; each kind had its *li*. These *li* were eternal, for these principles of things existed before the formation of the physical universe. Thus the *li* were "above shapes." The physical world, that which was "within shapes," was given existence by the *Ch'i* (Vital Force). As Chu Hsi puts it: "In the universe there are *li* and *ch'i*. The *li* is *Tao* that pertains to 'what is above shapes,' and is the source from which all things are produced. *Ch'i* is the material (literally 'instrument') that pertains to 'what is within shapes.' " [64] From *li*, men and things received their natures; from *ch'i*, their forms.

Chang Tsai (1020–1077), Master of Heng-chu, whose thought was a strong influence on Chu Hsi's theories, declared that "the Great Harmony is known as *Tao*" [65] and described this Great Harmony as *Ch'i*, "the wandering air." Thus, by Sung times, *li* and *ch'i* were made equivalent to *Tao*. This juggling of principal terms and the ideas for which they stood was a vital characteristic of Neo-Confucianism and therefore of Chinese thought down to the present. It might be summed up as a variety of descriptions of

[62] Bruce, *Chu Hsi and His Masters,* p. 171.
[63] Tr. in Fung, *Short History,* p. 296.
[64] Ibid., p. 299.
[65] Ibid., p. 279.

Tao, expressing aspects of it and ideas of such dimension and consequence that the terms themselves seemed to take on some of the
potency, mobility and elusiveness associated with *Tao* itself. Reciprocal and interchangeable, they became synonyms of the
Primal Unity. They had long been in use, but the Neo-Confucianists raised them to pre-eminent positions in philosophic thought,
forming an intricate intellectual superstructure imposed on the
grand yet essentially simple idea of *Tao.*

CHAPTER TWO

THE FIRST CANON

PAINTING in China was never separate from the *tao* of living. Its main focus was, and still is, *Tao*, the Way, the cosmic order, or the course of nature, which was alluded to not only in the classics but frequently in discussions of painting as the ideal—the harmony of Heaven and Earth that everything should express. In painting, this aim of the fusion of spirit, that which pertains to Heaven, and of matter, that which pertains to Earth, relates both to the artist's own development and to the work of art, for successful results require the exercise of insight as well as technical skill, the ability to render the inner character as well as its external form.

The First Canon of painting, *Ch'i yun sheng tung,* is a terse statement of the idea that *Ch'i* [1] (the Breath of Heaven, the Spirit) stirs all of nature to life and sustains the eternal processes of movement and change; and that if a work has *ch'i* it inevitably reflects a vitality of spirit that is the essence of life itself. Man's spiritual resources are regarded as a direct manifestation of this creative power of Heaven. Through developing them, a painter not only nourishes that part of Heaven in himself but, possessing it, is capable of revealing it in his conduct and activity. In his painting, he can draw on these spiritual resources to express the same force in every other natural thing that he depicts; for the subjects of his compositions have always been predominantly from nature. The First Canon and the Second, which states that the brush is the means of creating structure, establish the aim and the means,

---

[1] See Appendix, Sec. IV, for forms and parts of the characters of the First Canon.

representing the ideal and its form, the spiritual aspect and its tangible expression.

The first two Canons are the most important of the Six Canons, formulated about A.D. 500 by the portrait painter, Hsieh Ho, in his *Ku Hua P'in Lu* (Record of the Classification of Painters). The principles had existed long before his time but in transmitting the *tao* of painting he formulated them as the Six Canons. With slight modifications they were accepted as and have remained the general standards of painting and art criticism. The First Canon is the metaphysical first principle upon which the other five are dependent. It is essentially a compact expression of the *tao* of living and had been applied to painting in the earliest essays on the subject that have survived, those attributed to Ku K'ai-chih, Tsung Ping, and Wang Wei (*tzu* Ching-hsien), from the IV and V centuries.

Ku K'ai-chih (c. 344–406) is probably the best known of the Chinese painters of antiquity. He is one of the most honored masters, and a number of anecdotes about his eccentricities have been recorded. Today Ku seems perhaps less remote than many other great "names" of Chinese painting whose works have not survived, for the main portions of a masterpiece in the British Museum, the *Admonitions of the Instructress in the Palace,* have been reasonably certified as his work after long investigation by experts. He is known to have specialized in figure painting; judging from the nine groups of figures in the *Admonitions,* his composition and drawing were masterly and his grasp of character extraordinarily fine. His aim, and likewise his criterion of figure painting, was the rendering of the character and "soul" of the subject. In his essay on landscape painting,[2] preserved in the records, the basic consideration was that paintings, besides being representations of natural scenes, should be expressions of spiritual significance. The few examples of his style in works attributed to him or in copies of his paintings testify that, by the IV century, painting had already reached a high level, and the three essays attributed to him suggest that he, like Hsieh Ho a hundred years later, was transmitting accepted attitudes and principles that had evidently been in existence long before his time.

Tsung Ping (373–443), a contemporary of Ku K'ai-chih, wrote an essay on landscape painting[3] that discussed with even stronger emphasis the aim of painting as the manifestation of the spirit residing in each and every form, and pointed out the balance and fusion necessary between the impression received through the eyes and the perceptions of the mind. Mind, as mentioned earlier, denoted by the character *hsin* (heart), was the organ through which an individual was believed able to receive knowledge of *Tao*. Tsung's essay made several allusions to passages in the Confucian *Lun Yu* (Analects) and showed signs also of having been strongly influenced by early Taoist teachings. It mentioned at one point the Dark or Mysterious Female Spirit (*Hsuan P'in*), the *Yin* source; and recommended meditation as a preliminary to wielding the brush.

Wang Wei *(tzu* Ching-hsien), who was born in 415 and died at twenty-eight, and so was a young contemporary of Tsung Ping, wrote some brief notes on painting[4] in which he too declared that paintings were produced not only by skill with the brush but also by exercise of the spirit. "The form of the object must first fuse with the spirit, after which the mind transforms it in various ways. The spirit, to be sure, has no form; yet that which moves and transforms the form of an object is the spirit "[5] If the painting did not reveal some indication of the spirit *(ch'i),* the forms were lifeless. At the beginning of his notes, Wang Wei made the significant statement that "painting should correspond with the *I Ching* [Book of Changes]." In his short work he did not amplify this remark, and probably there was no need to, for his reader would have been familiar with the reference. In the middle of the essay, however, he made an observation that virtually defined the relationship between painting and the *I Ching:* the human eye is limited and cannot possibly see all there is to see, but a painter by

[3.] *Hua Shan Shui Su* (Introduction to Landscape Painting), in the *Li Tai Ming Hua Chi,* Sec. II, Ch. 6.

[4.] *Su Hua* (Notes on Painting), in the *Li Tai Ming Hua Chi,* Sec. II, Ch. 1.

[5.] Tr. in Sakanishi, *The Spirit of the Brush,* p. 44.

means of a delicate brush can depict the whole universe, that is, the multiplicity of nature manifesting the divine spirit; for in painting a scene, when one succeeds in conveying the *ch'i* of each form, the result is an expression of the *Ch'i* that pervades the universe, and to do this, the painter has to transcend the limitations of the eye and delve into the secrets of nature. The aim of the *I Ching* is in effect this same kind of exploration and attempt to understand the mysterious processes of nature or *Tao*. Its diagrams and enigmatic explanations allow such a variety of interpretation that its contents have had value and significance in every century. Since many other painters and critics mentioned the importance of the *I Ching*, a clearer view of its relation to painting may help in understanding the First Canon.

The ideas underlying the diagrams of the *I Ching* were part of the great common ground of Chinese belief out of which the different schools of thought emerged. The original diagrams were the Eight Trigrams *(Pa Kua)*,[6] each composed of three lines, broken or unbroken, representing "the way of Heaven, the way of man, and the way of Earth."[7] One account of how they came into being is described in the commentaries as follows: "The Sage was able to survey all the complex phenomena under the sky. He then considered in his mind how they could be figured, and by means of the diagrams represented their material forms and their character. Hence these diagrams are denominated semblances *(hsiang)*."[8] The invention of the Trigrams is traditionally attributed to the legendary ancestor-king Fu Hsi (*c.* 3000 B.C.). They represent Heaven, Earth, Thunder, Wind, Fire, Water, Mountains, and Rivers. As the commentaries explain, "the names of the diagrams and lines are but small matters, but the classes of things comprehended under them are large. Their scope reaches far, and the explanations to them are elegant. The words are indirect but to the point; the matters seem plainly set forth, but there is a secret principle in them. Their object is, in cases that are doubtful, to help the people in their conduct and to make plain the recompenses

---

[6]. See Appendix, Sec. III, for diagram.
[7]. *I Ching*, Appendix III, Sec. II, Ch. X, 63 (tr. Legge).
[8]. Ibid., Sec. I, Ch. VIII, 38.

of good and evil." [9] The diagrams and signs that were the earliest writing, such as the scratchings on the Shang oracle bones and fragments, might be described as the first pictures, the prototypes of paintings. Some of the records have stated that the Trigrams were the origins of writing. And it has also been suggested that painting developed from the drawing of maps; *t'u* (map or plan) is a term still used in reference to certain kinds of pictures. The important point, however, is the close relationship that has always existed between painting and writing; and as for map drawing, it may have been an early stage of the kind of painting that aims to illustrate, and in which specific localities, scenes, and sometimes characters were identified. The object there was accurate representation. The symbolization of the early writing and of the *I Ching* diagrams, on the other hand, pointed the way toward the creative works that aimed at presenting aspects of *Tao* by expressing the *ch'i* in landscape forms or in plants, flowers, fruit, birds, and animals. The underlying purpose was the transmission of a spiritual influence. As Wang Wei noted, both kinds of painting existed; the ancients did not produce paintings only for the purpose of recording sites and districts and marking boundaries and watercourses.

In the Chou period, the Trigrams were transformed into hexagrams by doubling them; this increased the number of combinations to sixty-four. As the commentaries of the *I Ching* explain: "The way is marked by changes and movements, and hence we have the imitative lines." [10] A great variety of combinations could be derived from these sets of diagrams, and their interpretation eventually developed into intricate philosophical theories. A basic theme was that of the *Yin* and *Yang*, which were called the Two *Ch'i*, the Breaths of Heaven and Earth, or the *Yang*-Positive and *Yin*-Negative Forces of the *T'ai Chi* (Ridgepole of the Universe, Absolute), the *T'ai I* (Great Monad), or *Tao*.

We do not know in what period the *Yin-Yang* idea originated, but in the *Shih Ching* (Book of Odes) and the Chou record of rites and customs, the *Chou Li,* we find proof that, as early as the xi

9. Ibid., Sec. II, Ch. VI, 47.
10. Ibid., Sec. II, Ch. X, 64,

century B.C., the *Yin* and *Yang* were mentioned as the two primal forces, and the concepts were applied by analogy to the weather, the calendar, ceremonies, musical instruments, directions, and personal attributes.[11] The *Yin* and the *Yang* are discussed in the early Taoist texts, the *Lieh Tzu* and the *Huai Nan Tzu,* where they are made a basic element of Taoist thought, so that they appear to be Taoist concepts; the two texts elaborate at length on the pure and light substance of *Yang,* which rose to become the air of the heavens, and the clouded and heavy substance of *Yin,* which sank and settled to become earth. Numerous other comparisons follow, based on the *Yin* and *Yang.* The theory was, indeed, shared by all schools. The Confucian classic, the *Li Chi* (Book of Rites), mentions the *Yin* and *Yang* in these words: "The Great One separated and became Heaven and Earth. It revolved and became the dual forces. It changed and became the four seasons. It was distributed and became the breathing *(ch'i)."* [12] On the whole, however, the Confucianists did not give the theory much attention until the Neo-Confucianists, having recovered the idea from Taoism, discussed it in their commentaries of the *I Ching.* In Appendix III of the classic, there is to be found probably the most succinct, if somewhat enigmatic, statement of the *Yin* and *Yang* theory: "There is the Absolute which produced the Two Forms, *Yin* and *Yang;* and the *Yin* and *Yang* between them produced all things.... One *Yin* and one *Yang* constituted what is called *Tao.* That which is perpetuated by it is good." [13]

There is no exposition of the *Yin* and *Yang* theory in the body of the *I Ching,* but the concept is implicit in the terminology of the diagrams. Each is designated as a *yin* or a *yang* form, with lines that are either *yin* (a broken line in two equal parts) or *yang* (an unbroken single line), and the interpretations of the diagrams explain the fluctuations of the *Yin* and the *Yang.* Their essential oneness—in their conception as halves of the *Tao*—is demonstrated in the purpose of the *I Ching:* the work was traditionally consulted to bring about harmony on earth, patterned on the har-

[11] Forke, *The World-Conception of the Chinese,* pp. 163–70.
[12] Bk. VII, Sec. IV, 4 (tr. Legge).
[13] *I Ching,* Appendix III, Sec. I, Ch. V, 1, 2.

mony in the heavens, and idealized as the harmony of Heaven and Earth, the fundamental *Yang* and *Yin*.

The old form of *yang* represents the sun with its rays; of *yin,* a coiled cloud. To each was added the character *fu* (mound).[14] Thus, according to the definition in the *Erh Ya,* a dictionary of the Chou period, *yang* describes "the sunny side of a mountain" and *yin* "the side in shadow." *Yang* signifies the South (where the sun is at its highest), heat, dryness, fire, red, day, light, the sun, and spring-summer (which in early times was counted as one season); and *Yin* the North, cold, moistness, water, black, night, darkness, the moon, and autumn-winter. The essence of Heaven is *Yang* and that of Earth *Yin: Yang* and *Yin* stand for the upper and lower worlds, the spiritual and the material, the intangible and the tangible. *Yang* is the Male Principle, *Yin* the Female; they also indicate positive and negative, activity and quiescence, motion and rest, life and death; they also describe advance and withdrawal, expansion and contraction; and as the Two *Ch'i,* exhalation and inhalation, condensation and dispersal. They describe such pairs of qualities as full and empty, straight and crooked, hard and soft, round and square, light and heavy, outside and inside, left and right, high and low. The examples can be multiplied a hundred-fold.

The concept that *Yin* and *Yang* set into motion and sustain all of life is illustrated in the emblem of the disk of the *T'ai Chi,* in which the *Yin* and *Yang* are the light and dark halves, red and black or white and black, and the S-shaped line dividing them ingeniously depicts the constant rotation that is their prime characteristic and also that of *Tao.* The emblem is often placed in the middle of a circle made up of the Eight Trigrams of the *I Ching;*[15] the diagrams and their lines each are either *yin* or *yang,* and the whole figure is a clear affirmation of the fundamental idea of the *Yin* and *Yang.* Here we have a Chinese version of the World Egg symbol, found elsewhere in oviform and also as a circle. The *T'ai Chi* disk itself might be described as a view from directly above "the mountain" referred to in the definitions of the characters *yin*

[14.] See Appendix, Sec. III, for forms and parts of the characters.
[15.] See Appendix, Sec. III, for the whole figure.

and *yang,* so that the result is a stylized figure of its sunny and shady sides, symbolizing not only the idea of the primal forces of nature in action, but also, by analogy, the light and dark forces of human nature, of all living things, all conditions and situations. The mountain is a version of the central sacred point or peak of the Center, discussed earlier in connection with the Five Points, among which the point in the middle indicates the *T'ai Chi,* the core and fixed point of reference that represents one aspect of *Tao.*

The *Yin* and *Yang* were like the warp and woof in the fabric of Chinese life. They are discernible very early in two main aspects of ancient Chinese society, ritual and divination—the one concerned with the performance of rites on earth, the other seeking to understand the ways of nature and Heaven. They may be traced as they developed into the two main strands of Chinese tradition: the Confucian, standing for the regulation of conduct and the ritual approach, and the Taoist, distrusting any kind of ordering and relying on intuitive wisdom, representing an individual ritual approach based on awe and reverence in the presence of the seemingly magical forces of nature. The Confucian element in the tradition, in many respects a stabilizing influence, sometimes proved in practice to be inflexible and deadening; and the Taoist influence, contributing imagination, spontaneity, and humor to Chinese life, could also be erratic and destructively superstitious. In these extremes, they exemplified how a *yang* or a *yin* aspect could turn into its opposite, as a pendulum, after reaching its furthest point in a *yang* movement, swings back in a returning *yin* movement over the same course. The motion in each direction completes the full swing. One aspect alone could be only a partial view, for everything is both *yang* and *yin,* each capable of change and always changing, being one or the other according to the angle of interpretation. Confucianism, for instance, in its concern with character and moral development, exhibited a *yin* aspect, but its emphasis on ceremony and behavior was *yang;* in its ideal of individual integration and harmony contributing to the harmony of the state and the universe it was *yin,* but its achieving of this through set procedure was *yang.* In relation to Taoism, Confucianism represented the *yang* part of the tradition, yet in many instances, when the thought of the two schools merged and particularly in the development of Neo-Confucianism, it was Taoism (with Buddhism) that was the vivifying element, acting on the depleted and static (*yin*) forms of Confucianism. The *Yin* and *Yang* principle was, in fact, applicable to every activity, every thought, large or small, every facet and stage of their development. And it also pervaded painting. The T'ang critic, Chang Yen-yuan, wrote in his collection of essays on painting, the *Li Tai Ming Hua Chi*, that "by the *Yin* and *Yang* innumerable forms are fashioned and produced, order is brought into chaos by their mysterious influence, while the indescribable spirit alone is revolving."[16] Their effect on technique and the execution of a picture will be examined in the chapters on equipment and the elements of a painting; meanwhile, in following up Wang Wei's statement relating painting to the *I Ching*, the chief concern is with the idea of the *Yin* and *Yang* as a basic concept of painting.

The keynote of the *I Ching*, as its title indicates, is change. And according to the meaning of its diagrams in varying combinations, the changes represent the processes and mutations of nature, the unceasing activity of *Tao* through the complementary action of its dual forces, the *Yin* and the *Yang*. The commentaries describe this characteristic of the diagrams as follows: "Its (the *I Ching's*) method of teaching is marked by the frequent changing of its lines. They change and move without staying in one place. . . . They ascend and descend, ever inconstant. The strong and the weak lines change places, so that an invariable and compendious rule cannot be derived from them; it must vary as their changes indicate."[17] Wang Wei's view, which was fundamental to the *tao* of painting, held that paintings, in their language of brush, form, and symbol, should describe the ever-changing processes of nature and *Tao* just as the *I Ching*, through its diagrams and their interpretation, explained their pattern and movement.

In depicting a landscape or individual plants, flowers, animals, birds, and insects, painting describes the appearance of nature. At the same time, in drawing the forms, in rendering their relation-

---

[16.] Tr. in Sirén, *The Chinese on the Art of Painting*, p. 231.
[17.] *I Ching*, Appendix III, Sec. II, Ch. VIII, 53 (tr. Legge).

ship to other forms in the picture, in the choice of subjects and
the appropriate outward circumstances of season, weather, and
time of day, the painter is also using a symbol language to describe the presence of *Tao*. Certain flowers, for instance, are associated with certain seasons and are also symbolic of certain
human attributes; the details of their setting have to support
their particular meaning in their appropriate natural scene as
well as in the realm of ideas. A striking instance of the double
use of a symbol was casually mentioned by Wang Wei in enu-
merating things that could be depicted in a painting. He wrote
of drawing "a circle with a dot in the middle to represent the
dragon's nose." The figure of a circle with a dot is the original
form of the character *jih*[18] (sun) and is also a symbol of *Tao*,
and the dragon is the creature associated with the sun and the
power of Heaven or the spirit. Through the nose was inhaled
the breath, part of the *Ch'i* (the Vital Breath or the Spirit), and
the nose was also often used to signify the beginning—for instance, it was believed to be the first part of the infant to emerge
at birth, and the first peak of a mountain range to be painted
was called "the nose."[19] To represent the dragon's nose by the
sun and *Tao* symbol described with unusual emphasis both the
reception of the *Ch'i* and the emergence of the power of the
spirit; moreover, it represents the idea of the *Yin* and *Yang*, the
inhalation and exhalation, the flow outward and inward. It illustrates the peculiar effectiveness of using symbols that add to the
enjoyment of looking at a painting if the spectator understands
their meaning, which, however, would not interfere with the enjoyment should the meaning be unknown or overlooked. Sometimes symbols are simply associations; at other times they are
abstruse, difficult to grasp without knowledge of their background and of related symbols. They offer an elaborate and
subtle means of expression in addition to representing appearances. The eloquence of symbols rests in their wealth of suggestion, which helps to enrich the central motif of a picture.

In observing the way a bud opens into full flower, eventually
to shed its petals, and the conditions under which this process

[18.] See Appendix, Sec. II.
[19.] See Part Two, *Book of Rocks*.

takes place, the painter is exploring an aspect of *Tao*. He is able to understand *Tao* when he is thoroughly familiar with every stage of the process, can see it at each stage and as a whole as analogous to other manifestations of the way of nature around him, including himself, and can through his heart and mind become aware of the same pattern of movement and change beyond his own limited horizon, on the scale of the whole earth and, yet beyond, of the whole universe. In learning about the growth of a flower he is exploring a way of nature, and when he is able to transmit his understanding to paper he is explaining a secret of nature in the same way as the contents of the *I Ching*.

The cycle of growth, bloom, and decay of a flower illustrates the operation of the *Yin* and *Yang;* thus a painting of a flower at a given stage of development depicts either a *yang* or *yin* aspect of it. And, as one may see, for instance, in the *Book of the Plum* in the *Chieh Tzu Yuan* manual, the petals, stamen, calyx, stem, leaves, and other parts of the plant came to be interpreted as either *yin* or *yang*. While this may help the painter to keep in mind a basic principle, it also exemplifies the tendency to carry an idea to such extremes that its essence became diluted, with a consequent loss of meaning in the painting.

The main aspect of the *Yin* and *Yang* idea, important to painting and illustrated by the diagrams of the *I Ching*, is the idea of *Tao* in perpetual motion, in other words, of the constant interaction of *Yin* and *Yang*. This idea adds considerable meaning to the attention given to brushwork and the concentration on brushstrokes, for line is the painter's means of rendering movement. Besides rhythm and vitality of brushstrokes, movement can of course be depicted by the manner in which things naturally grow or exist—by the inclination of a leaf or the formation of a mountain peak. It can also be rendered by the arrangement of the composition; movement can be accentuated by contrast with large expanses of still sky or water, in themselves symbolic of *wu wei*, outer passivity with inner activity. Above all, a sense of movement representing the vitality of *Tao* can be made to permeate a painting when the painter himself possesses *ch'i*, the creative force of Heaven in the individual. Being of the spirit, *ch'i* is elusive and difficult to describe, as also *Tao,* its source. But without it a painting fails to express any aspect of *Tao.* Hence it was the subject of constant discussion among Chinese painters.

Being present in all things as an integrating element of *Tao, ch'i* is an important harmonizing factor in painting. It provides the underlying unity derived from the spirit that can give a painting greater cohesion and harmony than the most skillful arrangement of its forms. An understanding and effective rendering of the fluctuations of the *Yin* and *Yang* in a composition not only infuses life-movement but controls the design in a harmonious whole. Such results may be seen in a landscape painting filled with tempestuous forces or a painting of a raging dragon among clouds, possessed of power and grandeur and seemingly at the point of bursting out of the picture; yet the elements of such paintings are controlled, integrated, and harmonious.

In depicting the order of nature in its infinite variety and changing moods, and in laying them out as living forms in a world on paper, painting was regarded in early times as an art of magic. In delving into the mysterious ways of nature as the *I Ching* did, painting used much the same approach as divination. In its use of color it was akin to alchemy, for the simple range of colors in Chinese painting symbolized the Five Elements basic to the thought and practice of alchemy, and the methods of preparing colors resembled and perhaps derived from alchemical brewing and distillation. And something magical indeed happened when skill with brush could transmit the spirit to silk or paper. This was the literal aim of painting in the earliest times, when the subject matter consisted of deceased ancestors and figures of history, religion, and legend, created from imagination to decorate the walls of tombs and palaces. The purpose of such paintings is implied in the term for portraiture, *fu shen* (depicting soul), for they represent the spirit of beings that were believed able to influence and aid the living. Another early form of painting, the decoration of pottery for religious and secular use with symbols of the sun, moon, and stars, might be described as portraits of Heaven, made in the hope of evoking its beneficial influence. These pictures, and the creative works of subsequent periods that in their way depicted the harmony of Heaven and

Earth, were well described by the old term for the art of painting, *i shu* (magic skill; art of delineating the mysterious). Painters were often regarded as gifted beyond skill with brush, and thus were sometimes called Sages, since, as a T'ang critic put it, they were able through their creative powers to reveal the brilliance of the sun and moon, and to penetrate to the limits of Heaven and Earth.[20] The attitude that painting was a magic art never entirely disappeared; traces may be seen, for instance, in the later classification of the masters, when the categories of excellence were termed *shen* (the divine), *miao* (the profound or mysterious), and *neng* (the accomplished).

The element of magic in the *I Ching* applied to numbers, the significance of certain of which has already been discussed. The Three and Six of the lines of the Trigrams and Hexagrams, however, had analogies in painting. Numbers were basic to the formation of the *I Ching* diagrams, in the explanation, the Appendices, the commentaries, and the stalks of milfoil used with the *I Ching* in divination; a chapter in Appendix III is devoted to numbers, for, as it explains, "the goings forth and comings in of the lines are according to rule and measure."[21] The importance attached to numbers is seen in the opening phrase of the *I Ching: ch'ien—yuan heng li chen* (first, pervading, beneficent, and immutable), all being attributes of *ch'ien* (Heaven), which is represented by the First Hexagram, of six unbroken lines. The opening phrase also signifies One, Two, Three, and Four, the root numbers, a definition that is still recorded in modern dictionaries. The Trigrams and Hexagrams were based on the number Three, representing the ways of Heaven, Earth, and Man, often called in the commentaries the Three Powers. Three was regarded as the actively creative number. Of its power and function the *Tao Te Ching* states: "*Tao* is Oneness. The One produced Two. Two became Three and out of Three evolved the ten thousand things." Belief in the sacredness of the Three and the use of such designations as the Three Powers or Three Worlds were universal in the

---

[20.] Chu Ching-hsuan, in the preface to his T'ang Dynasty Records of Famous Paintings included in *Wang Shih Hua Yuan* (Wang Shih-chen's Collection of Writings on Painting).

[21.] *I Ching,* Appendix III, Sec. II, Ch. VIII, 54 (tr. Legge).

ancient world. The idea found expression in the writings under the name of Hermes Trismegistus, in the works of the Pythagoreans and other early Greek philosophers, in the Holy Cabala, in the works of the alchemists, and in Neoplatonic thought; it exists today in the Brahmanic and Christian Trinity; it is evident also in such sets of terms as "electric-magnetic-neutral" in physics and, in anatomy, the description of the plexuses as "thoracic-abdominal-pelvic." The three anatomical terms parallel the ancient explanation of the three centers in man, head-heart-navel, the centers also of his intellect-spirit-emotions.

The doubling of the three lines of the original *I Ching* diagrams to form the hexagrams is explained in the commentaries. Six thus stood for an intensification of power: the doubling of the Three Powers and the tripling of the Two of the *Yin* and *Yang;* moreover, it was the sum of the three primary numbers, One, Two, and Three. It was therefore held to be a particularly significant number to use in basic classifications. In the entry for *lu* (six) in Giles' *Dictionary* is the interesting note that it was "adopted as the standard of all dimensions by the First Emperor," he who exempted only a few works from the burning of the books, among them the *I Ching.* Six was used in many basic classifications, one of the chief being the Six Points (North, South, East, West, the Zenith, and the Nadir) that marked the whole of the universe, encompassing its roundness and depth, as distinct from the Five Points, seen looking up or from above. As the *Chuang Tzu* says: "The Six Cardinal Points, reaching into infinity, are ever included in the *Tao.*"[22] Other classifications using the Six were the Six Influences (*Yin, Yang,* wind, rain, light, and darkness), the Six Arts (ritual, music, archery, charioteering, calligraphy, and numbers), the Six Classics, the Six Disciplines, the Six Duties, the Six Virtues, the Six Organs of the Senses, and the Six Classes of Poetry, of Writing, and of Characters. In painting, there were the Six Canons (*Lu Fa*) formulated by Hsieh Ho.

It is tempting to suppose that Hsieh Ho patterned his Six Canons on the six lines of the *I Ching* hexagrams, but there is no evidence of it. The most that can be claimed is that he was

²²· Tr. Giles, *Chuang Tzu,* p. 280.

aware of the significance of Six as a basis of classification. A relationship has been suggested between the Six Canons and the Six Limbs of Indian painting,[23] although two such general statements of the principles of painting could have existed side by side without any direct connection. Both sets of standards, however, show the influence of Buddhist classifications, such as the Six Stages of Meditation (*Lu Miao Men:* Doorway to the Six Excellencies) and the version with six divisions of the Buddhist Wheel, the *Fa Lun* (Wheel of Law).

The character *fa* has the general meaning of "method, means, or rules." It is frequently used in rendering Buddhist terms in Chinese, such as *fa tao* (Way of Buddha) and *fa shih* (the teaching of the mysteries of Buddhism), and it is also used to stand for *dharma.* Hsieh Ho, like the scholars and intellectuals among his contemporaries, must have been familiar with many of the innumerable translations of Buddhist doctrines; he might have been one of those deeply influenced by Buddhist teachings. He could not have been unaware of the added authority lent his title, *Lu Fa,* by its inclusion of the term for *dharma.* This may even have contributed to the eminence accorded Hsieh Ho's Six Canons, for later modifications of the principles—such as the Six Essentials or the Six Important Points or the Six Qualities, which were more specific in their contents and of more practical value to painters—never achieved an equal prominence. *Fa* as *dharma* held, and still holds, great prestige in the realm of ethics and philosophy, and so also in that of painting, for *dharma* is "The Eternal Law and Doctrine," embracing "conduct, morality, law, function, character, principle, and habit."[24] The concept of *dharma* has been explained as "a development of the idea of *rta,* which denotes cosmic as well as moral order . . . the quality of deciding what is right . . . and practice and action to convert the elements now opaque to reason and make them transparent to thought."[25] According to a Zen Buddhist explanation, *dharma*

[23.] "Differentiation of types, canons of proportion, embodiment of sentiment and charm, correspondence of formal and pictorial elements, preparation of pigments," in Yasodhara's commentary on the *Kamasutra,* translated and discussed in Coomaraswamy, *The Transformation of Nature in Art,* pp. 12, 181.

[24] Ibid., Glossary, *s.v.* "dharma."

[25.] S. Radhakrishnan, tr. and ed., *The Bhagavadgita,* pp. 78, 155.

derives "from the root *dhri* 'to hold, to bear, to exist'; there seems always something of the idea 'to endure' also going along with it. The commonest and most important sense given to it in Buddhism is 'truth, law, religion.' . . . It is synonymous with 'virtue, righteousness,' not only in the ethical sense, but in the intellectual one also. In the latter case, it is 'truth, standard, category.' "[26]

The need to classify the principles of painting arose no doubt from the Chinese ideal of harmony and the strong sense that things should be ordered to facilitate its attainment. Confucian thinking and practice reinforced this view, and also the Taoist belief in the oneness of *Tao*. Hsieh Ho's Six Canons were included in all the important compilations on painting. They are, of course, quoted in a basic manual such as the *Chieh Tzu Yuan*.

In their original forms in Hsieh Ho's *Ku Hua P'in Lu*, each Canon consisted of six characters. Each was phrased in the familiar four characters followed by the two words *shih* (to be) *yeh* (so, such, thus)—"thus it is." While we are concerned here with the basic principles in the forms in which they have been best known since the IX century, the seemingly slight difference between the original and later forms is significant. The essence of the Canons does not change; but the shift of emphasis helps to clarify the terse phrases. Hsieh Ho's First Canon, for instance, in its original form reads: *i: ch'i yun sheng tung shih yeh,* which has recently been translated "First, Spirit Resonance which means vitality," suggesting that *ch'i yun* stands as the Principle with the rest of the phrase as explanation. As transmitted by the T'ang critic Chang Yen-yuan, the First Canon reads: *i yueh: ch'i yun sheng tung* (The first is called spirit-resonance or life-movement).[27]

In the opening pages of the *Chieh Tzu Yuan*, the Six Canons are presented as follows:

In the Southern Ch'i period Hsieh Ho said:
Ch'i yun sheng tung (*Ch'i* or Spirit revolving life stirs). Circulation of the *Ch'i* produces life-movement.

[26] Suzuki, *Studies in the Lankavatara Sutra*, p. 154.
[27] Translation of the two versions are from Acker, *Some T'ang and Pre-T'ang Texts on Chinese Painting* (pp. 4, 148), a study of three important sources, including the Chinese text and a translation of Hsieh Ho's work.

Ku fa yung pi (bone means use brush). Brush creates structure.

Ying wu hsieh hsing (establish thing write form). According to the object draw its form.

Sui lei fu ts'ai (following kind apply color). According to the nature of the object apply color.

Ching ying wei chih (fulfill plan arrange seating). Organize composition with the elements in their proper places.

Chuan mu i hsieh (transmit copy transplant writing). In copying, pass on the essence of the master's brush and methods.

The First and Second Canons established the basic metaphysical principle and the means of expressing it. The Third, Fourth, and Fifth Canons applied generally to drawing, color, and composition; and since Hsieh Ho was primarily a portrait painter, he probably formulated them with portrait (as well as figure, flower, and bird) painting in mind. The Third Canon was concerned with drawing in the sense of establishing the mass, shape, and particular essence of each object in a picture; *hsieh hsing* (to draw or write form) had this connotation as distinct from the representation of the appearance of things, which was termed *hsiang hsing* (formal resemblance) or *hsing ssu* (shape or outward form). Chang Yen-yuan, in the T'ang period, explained the relationship of the first three Canons: "The representation of natural objects requires likeness of shapes, but the shapes must all have structure (*ku fa*) and life (*ch'i*)."[28] Color was given its important place in the Fourth Canon probably through Hsieh Ho's interest in portraiture, along with flower and bird painting. In later periods, color was mentioned less prominently, and in some instances it was omitted from lists of principles. Color implied ink, as also did the brush, but ink was not separately listed until the development of ink monochrome painting in the period of the Five Dynasties. The Fifth Canon referred to something more than what we now understand by composition and design: in accord with the premise of Chinese painting that *ch'i* came first and created form, the idea that the elements of a picture should be placed in their proper and natural relationships was rooted in the concept of *Tao* and its total harmony, by which each object and aspect has its proper place in relation to others and to the Center, which was also the Whole. The Sixth Canon was con-

[28] Tr. in Sirén, *The Chinese on Painting*, Appendix III, p. 227.

cerned with the practice of copying,[29] an accepted stage in learning to paint; its purpose was to acquaint the student with methods and styles of brushwork while, in the process, he absorbed something of the intent and spirit of the masters. Through the underlying purpose of copying, the last Canon sums up the intent of the whole Six: to follow and transmit to posterity the methods and principles developed and tested by the masters, and so to sustain the *tao* of painting.

The Six Canons stood as general standards of painting rather than as practical advice to painters. Later, when landscape became the first and most important category of subject matter, painters and critics modified the six principles to apply to landscape painting. The First Canon remained the basic and indispensable principle, controlling the other five and applying to all kinds of painting. About five hundred years after Hsieh Ho enunciated the Six Canons, Liu Tao-ch'un formulated on their pattern the Six Essentials (*Lu Yao*) and the Six Qualities (*Lu Ch'ang*). In the *Chieh Tzu Yuan,* they are presented immediately after the Six Canons in phrases, in the Chinese text, as succinct as Hsieh Ho's. They are given here in a translation aimed at transmitting their meaning without attempting to keep the four-worded phrases:

First Essential: Action of the *Ch'i* and powerful brushwork go together.
Second Essential: Basic design should be according to tradition.
Third Essential: Originality should not disregard the *li* (the principles or essence) of things.
Fourth Essential: Color (if used) should enrich.
Fifth Essential: The brush should be handled with *tzu jan* (spontaneity).
Sixth Essential: Learn from the masters but avoid their faults.

First Quality: To display brushstroke power with good brushwork control.
Second Quality: To possess sturdy simplicity with refinement of true talent.
Third Quality: To possess delicacy of skill with vigor of execution.
Fourth Quality: To exhibit originality, even to the point of eccentricity, without violating the *li* of things.

[29.] *Mu,* to copy, often by tracing and later transferring; *fang,* free interpretation which could still be described as "in the style of"; and *lin,* to copy with the original before one.

Fifth Quality: In rendering space by leaving the silk or paper untouched, to be able nevertheless to convey nuances of tones.

Sixth Quality: On the flatness of the picture plane, to achieve depth and space.

The prominence of *li* reflected the Neo-Confucianist influence, and the requirement that the brush should have spontaneity might be ascribed directly to Taoist and Zen ideas. The First Essential combined the First and Second Canons of Hsieh Ho: *ch'i* and powerful brushstrokes naturally went together, representing the balance between the painter's inner resources and their outer demonstration, the fusion of the subjective and the objective. This was the goal referred to in the familiar phrase "heart and hand must be in accord"; it was "the harmony of Heaven and Earth." The First Essential also emphasized the importance of the brush in drawing and creating form, including the space surrounding and containing forms. Such space was the main concern of the Fifth and Sixth Qualities; it was a factor strongly influenced by Taoist ideas about the emptiness, the space, that is filled with *Tao*. The magnificent rendering of space in Chinese paintings, particularly landscapes, where often mountains and other features were deliberately placed and drawn so as to emphasize the space, was a direct result of Taoist ideas about the Great Void.

There were other variations of the Six Canons formulated in the Sung period, most of them concerned with adapting the principles to landscape painting. Among these were the Six Essentials of the X century painter Ching Hao. These deserve attention, since they were the precepts of a master of landscape painting and, moreover, were principles of painting in ink monochrome, made at the end of the T'ang era, that were later adopted by painters and critics of the Sung period, which marked the peak of achievement in landscape painting. Ching Hao's Six Essentials[30] contained the principles of landscape painting in six characters: first, *ch'i* followed by *yun* (rhythm), *ssu* (thought), *ching* (seasonal aspect), *pi* (brush), and *mo* (ink). The changes were in

---

[30] In his essay *Pi Fa Chi* (Notes on Brushstroke Methods), tr. in Sakanishi, *The Spirit of the Brush*, Sirén, *The Chinese on Painting*, and Waley, *An Introduction to the Study of Chinese Painting*. See Appendix, Sec. IV, VI, VII, for these Six Essentials.

what was considered important and the order of importance. Due, perhaps, to Neo-Confucianist influence, *ssu* (thought) was given third place, immediately after the two basic Essentials. Brush and ink were given place as two separate Essentials. The use of color became less important although it was implied in the principles on seasonal aspect and on ink. Hsieh Ho had not specifically mentioned ink, but by the Later T'ang period ink monochrome had come into its own; it reached heights in the landscape, bamboo, and flower paintings of the Sung period and the bamboo paintings of the Yuan. The development of ink painting was due to the rise and dominance of the school of gentlemen-painters, which was strongly influenced by Taoist-Zen thought. Its views and practices were copied and spread by the literati. Ching Hao's list is of special interest for a shift of emphasis and the expression of each principle by a single term. Particularly important was the modification of the first principle from *Ch'i,* the Spirit of Heaven, to *ch'i,* the spirit in man, a recognition of the personal element not found in Hsieh Ho's First Canon. In still another list of principles, the T'ang writer Chang Yen-yuan also gave prominence to *ssu* (thought) and *i* (idea), observing that "structure (*ku fa*), vitality (*ch'i*), and shapes originate in the directing idea and are expressed by brushwork."[31] He placed the principle of "seasonal aspect" fourth, in closer relation to the preceding principles than to those naming brush and ink. For him, brush and ink rendered the appearance of the seasons, but the idea of seasonal aspect involved an understanding of the rhythm and mutations of nature and required observation, knowledge, reflection, and an understanding of the *Ch'i.*

Among the many treatises on painting of the Sung period, the *T'u Hua Chien Wen Chih,*[32] by Kuo Jo-hsu, published at the end of the XI century, was one of the most influential both then and later. In quoting the First Canon, Kuo used *yun* (rhythm). Subsequently, either *yun* (rhythm) or *yun* (to revolve)[33] was used in citing the First Canon. In the original *Chieh Tzu Yuan,* the Jap-

---

[31.] Tr. in Sirén, p. 227.

[32.] For a translation with detailed notes, and including a facsimile of the Chinese text (XVII-cent. edn. of Mao Chin) see Soper, *Kuo Jo-hsu's Experiences in Painting.*

[33.] See Appendix, Sec. IV, for the two *yun.*

anese reprints, and the 1887 Chinese edition, *yun* (to revolve) is used. Both characters describe aspects of *Tao: yun* (to revolve) connotes, from more of a Taoist standpoint, the movement of *Tao* manifest in *Ch'i; yun* (rhythm, harmony), though in a sense also Taoist, represents a Confucian ideal closely related to the Confucian *li* (rituals) and *ho* (harmony). The use of *yun* (rhythm) may be taken as evidence of the Confucian viewpoint that dominated art criticism. This was inevitable, since the background and training of painters and critics were basically Confucian, and the results were both good and bad. The works, likewise the influence, of the gentlemen-painters showed the sublime creative effects possible as well as the deterioration brought about in later periods by the systematizing aspect of the Confucian mind. The Neo-Confucianist emphasis on *li* (principle) and the search for a rational explanation of the nature of the universe encouraged the tendency to order and to regulate. *Yun* (harmony), the term that was used of sound and form, including rhythm, connotes a constructive and creative sense of the harmony of the whole; but in application, owing to its emphasis on order and correctness, it had the power to stifle that most desired quality, *tzu jan* (spontaneity). This was evident, for instance, in the Ming interpretation of *yun* as "correctness," already implicit at the end of the T'ang period, when Ching Hao, revealing the Confucian aspect of his background, explained that *yun* (rhythm, harmony), "without visible contours, suggests form; omits nothing yet escapes vulgarity."[34] This *yun* lacks the larger focus contained in one of the meanings of *yun* (to revolve): "a circuit or period of time, a turn of destiny." Thus, *yun* (to revolve) stressed the metaphysical aspect of the First Canon, while *yun* (rhythm, harmony) came to be used in speaking of, for instance, the production of harmonious effects by the qualities of moistness and dryness and the varieties of ink tones. In this approach there may have been the wish to add meaning to the brush as the active *yang* agent complementing the passive *yin* quality of the ink. The danger lay in spoiling the spontaneous application of ink tones by trying to dictate their depth and their moistness for certain effects. But there always was a safeguard, for it is impossible to prescribe ink tones, and

[34] Tr. in Waley, p. 169.

any attempts to systematize ink technique amount to intellectual explanations that are powerless to govern the handling of ink.

We see another instance of the shift of interest to appearance in Kuo Jo-hsu's change in the Third Canon: instead of the phrase *hsieh hsing* (to draw or write form) he used *hsiang hsing* (formal resemblance). This illustrates the tendency among Sung academicians to stress faithful representation, one happy result of which was the precise, accurate, and in many ways superb paintings of flowers, animals, and birds by members of the Imperial Academy and the Emperor Hui Tsung himself. Less happily, these examples led many painters of the time, and later in the Ming and Ch'ing periods, to produce overelaborate and ornate works. In the Second Canon, Kuo made another change that shows Buddhist influence. According to the text that has been transmitted, in the phrase *ku fa yung pi* (brush creates structure) he substituted the more complicated form of *fa*[35] (means), which was used only with reference to Buddhist thought and practice. While the simpler, commoner form of *fa* was also, and indeed more often, used in Buddhist contexts, Kuo apparently was making a special point that *ku fa* referred to "inner structure," that which was established by the laws of nature as the essence or principles of things (*li*).

The modifications of Hsieh Ho's Six Canons were numerous, yet the changes in basic meaning were on the whole not great, representing mainly the particular interpretation of them by the painters and art critics of each period. In the First Canon, for example, *ch'i* pertains to the spirit whether it is interpreted as the *Ch'i* or as its reflection as the *ch'i* in each living thing. The aim of painting remained the harmony of Heaven and Earth, expressed through the harmony of the parts and the whole of the picture. As Kuo Jo-hsu said: "In a picture, the spiritual harmony originates in the exercise of the mind (*hsin*); its full exposition comes from the use of the brush."[36] The Second Canon, referring to the brush, is dependent on the First, since knowledge of the inner structure of the forms rendered by the brush depends on an

[35] See Giles, *Dictionary*, Nos. 3368, 3366.
[36] Tr. in Tomita, "Brushstrokes in Far Eastern Painting," p. 31.

awareness and a manifestation of the *Ch'i*. Indeed, all the other principles are dependent on the First.

In the First Canon, *sheng tung* (life-movement) is a direct result of *Ch'i yun* (circulation of the *Ch'i*), whether in its characteristic revolving movement or as an all-encompassing order and harmony. The key phrase, therefore, is *Ch'i yun;* this concept of the *Ch'i* in action governs all the principles and every work of art, down to each brushstroke.

Ch'i yun, literally describing the circulation of the *Ch'i*, has often been translated "Rhythmic Vitality." Rhythm as it exists in nature—in the vast circuit of the heavens and the cycles of the seasons—would partially describe the movement of the *Ch'i;* but it should not imply the limitations of a measured beat, which would be incompatible with the nature of the *Ch'i*. As, in the human body, it is not the breath that creates the sound of the heartbeat, though it may be intimately connected with the process producing the beat, so with the *Ch'i:* it is the breath or Vital Force that produces and permeates life and its movement, but is not itself the results it produces. The wind, a form of *ch'i*, stirring the leaves produces a rustle, but the rustle is not made by the wind but by the foliage. In describing the *Ch'i* in its eternal operation on a cosmic scale, the essence of the phrase *Ch'i yun* rests in the concept of the *Ch'i*, and to render it as "Rhythmic Vitality" is to omit the central point and to put the emphasis in the wrong place, for rhythm is only one aspect of the total action of the *Ch'i*.

Ch'i is an elusive term, one whose meaning can be sensed without difficulty but which no simple definition can cover. The fundamental fact that it has to be grasped through intuition indicates that an intellectual definition would fall far short. Its significance is perhaps best suggested by its literal meaning of "breath," if one remembers the ancient concept of breath as soul and spirit. The Sanskrit *prana,* the Greek *pneuma,* and the Latin *spiritus* have the same import as *ch'i,* likewise *ruah* in Biblical Hebrew and the term *nefesh,* described in the Zohar as the breath and substance of the Fourth Sphere, the world of physical existence. Many statements by the early Greek philosophers could apply to *ch'i:* Anaximenes, for example, declared that "just as our soul, being air, holds us together, so do breath and air encompass the whole world."[37] Aristotle in the *Physics* recorded that the Pythagoreans held that there was "boundless breath" outside the heavens and that it was inhaled by the world.[38] Aristotle himself spoke of metals as having two exhalations or vapors, one moist and one dry, which rise up through the earth,[39] a statement applicable not only to *ch'i* but also to the Two *Ch'i,* the *Yin* and *Yang. Ch'i* could also be described by the words of Genesis 2:7: "And the Lord God formed man of the dust of the ground, and breathed into his nostrils the breath of life; and man became a living soul." In our own times, a statement made by a modern French master is reminiscent of many of the attempts by Chinese painters, over the course of centuries, to explain *ch'i.* In an interview on his seventieth birthday, Georges Braque was reported to have said: "There is only one thing in art that is worthwhile. It is that which cannot be explained." In speaking of a quality in objects that has to be brought to life, Braque said, "all I have to do is look at it in a certain way. . . . You just sort of project a magic ray on to an object and bring it into the enchanted circle."[40]

The very sound of the character *ch'i* is like a breath. Its various pronunciations among the Chinese dialects all retain this characteristic; even the completely different Cantonese version, pronounced "hay," is like an exhaling of breath. This circumstance tends to add vividness to the traditional belief that everything has *ch'i:* Heaven and Earth, the sun and moon, day and night, the months, the hours, each has its *ch'i. Yin* and *Yang* are the Two *Ch'i,* and their complementary action is said to produce the Five *Ch'i,* or the atmospheric conditions of rain, sunshine, heat, cold, and wind. Weather is still called "Heaven's *ch'i.*" Men and things have *ch'i,* their breath as well as other forms of *ch'i*—disposition, capacity, temperament, constitution, complexion, expression, style, and manner. As air, *ch'i* also denotes circumstances and pervading influences, physical, moral, and metaphysical. Thus,

[37.] Burnet, *Early Greek Philosophy,* p. 73.
[38.] Ibid., p. 108.
[39.] *Metaphysics* III, Ch. 6, 378c.
[40.] *Time* (New York), July 14, 1952.

ch'i is "breath" or "air" in the specific sense and also in the sense of essence, soul, and the Vital Force. *Ch'i* is used today not only in all of these ways but in a number of modern coinages: *tien ch'i* (breath of lightning: electricity), *yang ch'i* (nourishing breath or air: oxygen), *tan ch'i* (colorless air: nitrogen), *ch'i yu* (oil air or power: gasoline), *ch'i kuan* (air tube: the windpipe, the bronchial tubes, and also steam pipes), and *ch'i shui* (air water: aerated water).

The character *ch'i* is composed of *ch'i* (vapor) and *mi* (rice or grain). It is supposed to have meant originally the spirits distilled from rice or the vapor rising from the fermentation of rice or other grain. *Ch'i* (vapor) also stands for "clouds," and its old forms closely resemble bands or ribbons of clouds. It is interesting, in the light of the significance of the number Three, that the original form of the character was made up of three wavy strokes, indicating clouds or vapors. The three strokes, the shortest at the top and the longest at the bottom, suggest the form of an ascending spiral, the sign of circulation upward and One-ward. An old form of *ch'i*[41] is explained as being composed of *jih* (sun) and *huo* (fire), a contraction of which is the *ch'i* meaning "to beg, to implore"—an illustration of how the symbols of the sun and fire combined in ancient times to represent a common attitude toward the primal source of life. The character *mi* (rice) has many forms through which it evolved to its present one; here it must suffice to point out that the character *mi*, in the form of an upright cross with four dots in the spaces between the arms, represents both the four cardinal points and four grains of rice. The character *ch'i* (breath), combining *mi* with *ch'i* (vapor), might thus be described as depicting the *Ch'i* distributing sustenance in every direction.

In the earliest records we find the idea of *ch'i*—both as air and breath and as the manifestation of the *Ch'i* that is *Tao*—representing the pervasive Vital Force that gives life and sustenance to all things under Heaven. The *Li Chi* (Book of Rites) speaks of the *T'ai I* distributing itself as "the breathing." The *Chou Yu* (Chronicles of the Chou Dynasty) attributes the de-

41. Karlgren, "Grammata Serica," No. 517, a, b, c. and Wieger, *Chinese Characters,* p. 241. See Appendix, Sec. IV, for forms of *ch'i.*

cline of the House of Chou to the fact that the rulers and the
people had become confused in their understanding of the order
of the *ch'i* of Heaven and Earth.[42] This was Mencius' *hao jan
chih ch'i* (vital breath or force), which he described as the factor
that becomes manifest in moral conduct. The Taoists based their
cosmogony on the mingling of the *ch'i* of the *Yin* and *Yang* and
their differentiation into the heavens and the earth and the ten
thousand things. Their ideas were taken over by the Neo-Confucianists, and Chang Tsai identified *Ch'i,* the Wandering Air, as the
Great Harmony, *Tao.* Chu Hsi incorporated these ideas in his
synthesis of the thought of all schools. Since the rising, floating,
expanding, and active qualities of the *Ch'i* were *yang* and the
sinking, settling, shrinking, and passive qualities *yin,* he interpreted them as aspects of one Breath, in confirmation of the
earlier view of the two breaths of the *Ch'i.* Chu Hsi's formula-
tion of the Four Fundamental Principles of the Cosmos were *Li*
(Principle or Order), *Shu* (Number), *Ch'i* (Breath as Motion),
and *Hsing* (Form or Matter).

The *Chi* in the First Canon of painting is thus the Breath or
Vital Force or Spirit of *Tao,* and it is also the *Yin* and *Yang* as
the dual forces of *Tao.* Concretely (if such a word can be applied to the spirit), *Ch'i* is manifest in men and things as breath
and soul and spirit. In painting, *Ch'i* is both the creative resources of the painter and the essential vitality—spiritual, divine,
and creative—that can be transmitted to a painting and perceived by the spectator. There was some dispute among Chinese
painters and critics as to whether a painter was born with *ch'i,*
or whether it was a quality that could be cultivated. They never
ceased to discuss *ch'i,* and to describe it assiduously without attempting to define it. Such is the way of Chinese writing. Nevertheless, the comprehensiveness of the term and the elusive nature of the concept allowed a freshness of vision and made way
for the element of the personal and original in a *tao* of painting
that is replete with sets of rules and methods and traditionally
exacts an anonymity for any part of the common effort to express *Tao.* That the meaning and importance of the concept did
not essentially change may be seen in a passage from the XVIII-

---

[42] *Chou Yu* I, 10 (tr. in Fung, *History,* I, p. 32).

century painter Chang Keng: "*Ch'i yun* may be expressed by ink, by brushwork, by an idea, or by absence of idea. . . . It is something beyond the feeling of the brush and the effect of ink, because it is the moving power of Heaven, which is suddenly disclosed. But only those who are quiet can understand it."[43]

[43] Tr. in Sirén, p. 215.

CHAPTER THREE

THE FOUR TREASURES: BRUSH, INK, INKSTONE, PAPER

THE materials of Chinese painting—brush, ink, inkstone, paper —are the same as the simple equipment on the table in a scholar's study. Always held in deep respect, they have long been called the Four Treasures of the Abodes of Culture. Each is dependent on the others, and all are highly prized. Each has a long history of development amounting to a pedigree. Each is also endowed with symbolic significance that has enveloped it in elaborate layers of meaning. Besides paper, silk has also been used for paintings, and, besides ink, colors; so that silk and colors should be included in discussing the materials of painting.

Tradition has ascribed the invention of the brush to Meng Tien, a general under the Ch'in emperor, Shih Huang-ti, who reigned about 221–209 B.C. During that period, the word *pi* (brush) was first used to designate the instrument; and the general, if he did not actually invent the brush, was probably among the first to use the term. It is likely that brushes were made and used much earlier, for the decoration on early pottery believed to belong to the Shang era (*c.* 1776–1122 B.C.) suggests that some kind of brush was used. An early book on ritual referred to funeral banners of silk on which names had been written,[1] and it must have been done with a softer and more flexible instrument than a sharpened bone or stone or anything like a stylus.

The character *pi*,[2] composed of *chu* (bamboo) and *yu* (brush, pen, or stylus), depicts a hand holding an instrument and writ-

[1] Creel, *The Birth of China*, p. 173.
[2] See Appendix, Sec. VII, for *pi* (brush) and *mo* (ink).

ing on a tablet. Indeed, it is a direct representation of a hand wielding a brush in its bamboo holder to write or paint. Brush handles for ordinary use are made of bamboo, although in the past they were sometimes made of jade, quartz, gold, silver, or ivory, and tipped with buttons or knobs of these precious materials, for presentation and special occasions. The plain bamboo handle has usually been the most satisfactory, since its main advantage is lightness, an important factor in the balance of the brush. Into one end of the hollow bamboo holder is inserted a tuft of hair or fur, fixed with a little glue. The shape of the tuft varies: it can be pointed or rounded, fat or thin, coarse or fine, needlelike or broad. In the course of developing the brush, a great assortment of hair has been used—sheep, goat, deer, sable, wolf, fox, rabbit, or weasel hair, and even mouse whiskers. There are accounts of fine brushes made from chicken down and of the hair of children, and of large coarse brushes made of bristles from a pig's neck. Sometimes, the hairs of different animals were combined in one brush point, such as the brushes of fox and rabbit hair used by O-yang Tung, of the T'ang period. Su Tung-p'o is said to have liked using brushes made with a few mouse whiskers in the center enfolded by sheep's hair. Another famous Sung master and connoisseur, Mi Fei, is recorded as having tried to paint with sticks of sugar cane, the ends of which had been sucked and squeezed dry. The T'ang critic, Chang Yen-yuan, mentioned a brush made of the fibers of mountain bamboo that could draw lines as sharp as sword cuts.

In modern times, the brushes used in writing and painting, though still of great variety, are more commonly made of the hair of goat, rabbit, and sheep. Some ten different sizes are available, but a painter is well equipped with four or five. The demands of Chinese writing and painting, as to variety and quality of line, produce exacting requirements in the shape, texture, point, and flexibility of the brush. Many seemingly minor details have been considered important, such as the belief that in choosing rabbit's hair for the brush the best time to pluck it from the rabbit is the autumn, when the hair is neither too soft nor too stiff. And there are personal considerations: a painter often has favorite brushes and comes to know them so well they seem to take on part of his personality; he finds that a particular worn brush is good, for instance, for drawing the jagged outlines of rocks in a kind of brushstroke that cannot be produced by any other brush. In short, the brush is the painter's or scholar's chief means of individual expression, capable of reflecting traits of character and temperament, and so, in effect, an extension of his personality.

The character *mo* (ink) indicates in its component parts the origin of ink. It is made up of the pictograph *t'u* (earth) under that of *heh* (black), the latter being a drawing of "fire from which smoke rises through an opening in the roof." The old form of *heh* clearly indicates the four flames of the fire issuing as four wisps of smoke through the round opening in the roof. Soot mixed with a little earth and water was probably the first compound of Chinese ink. Apparently the mixture was molded and dried into solid pieces, although it is not known when Chinese ink was first made into sticks. For many hundreds of years, however, sticks have been its customary form. To call it "ink" is therefore misleading, since ink is, properly speaking, a fluid and moreover contains an acid.

Chinese ink is made of carbon or soot, obtained by burning dry pine or fir wood in a kiln *(sung yen mo:* pine-soot ink), or by burning vegetable oils in an earthenware bowl *(yu mo:* oil or lampblack ink). The soot is then mixed with a little glue. The proportions vary: in recent times, the blend is commonly ten parts carbon to five parts glue; in ancient times, a recipe prescribed ten parts pine soot to three parts powdered jade and one part glue. Whatever the proportions, the mixture is molded and dried into a stick or cake. For use, this is gently rubbed in a little water on an inkstone to produce the liquid ink. This procedure still yields the best ink, although liquid ink is now made and widely used.

Lampblack for *yu mo* is made by burning vegetable oil, compressed from tung nuts, hempseed, wintergreen, rapeseed, or soybean. Great care and patience are needed in the various steps of burning, cooling, changing the water in which the bowl of oil stands, sifting the lampblack through silk gauze, and protecting it from moisture. Pine-soot ink is often referred to as "lampblack ink," although its ingredients and preparation are different. To produce it, resin is drained from a pine before it is cut down by drilling a small hole at the base. In this hole is placed a small lighted lamp; the warmth draws the resin downward and out. The pine is then felled and cut into pieces. Burning these logs takes several days. Furthermore, the kiln has to be allowed to cool before the soot or "lampblack" can be scraped out and collected. Then it is mixed.

There has been a great deal of experimenting with ingredients ever since the invention of ink, which must have been at least as early as that of the brush, probably even earlier. It is known that in ancient times a bamboo stick dipped into lacquer was used for writing, and that in the III and IV centuries round pieces of ink were made from a lampblack obtained from black lacquer and pine wood.[3] By T'ang times there were many ink makers, and the art of its manufacture was far advanced. Since those times, the best kind of ink by repute has been made from pine soot, a kind of *sung yen mo* that is also called *chiao mo* (glue ink). It is deep in tone and glossy, the degree of blackness and sheen depending on the species of pine and the method of preparation. This kind of ink was famous in the past, and the best variety was identified in the writings of several masters as the ink made in the Tung-o district of Shantung, which never lost its gloss and its jet blackness. According to the records, it was used up to Yuan times and was easily distinguishable from the mat black ink made in the Ming period, which in use gave the same effect as lampblack ink *(yu mo)*, lacking in depth as well as sheen.

The famous Tung-o ink contained glue made by boiling donkey hides in Tung River water, which apparently contained minerals that enhanced the quality of the glue. The glue, called *O-chiao*, had the color of amber and the glossiness of varnish. It was a valuable ingredient of ink of the finest quality. And all painters and critics who mentioned ink emphasized that only the best available quality should be used in painting. Kuo Hsi, in his essay on landscape painting, was one who said that, of the different kinds of ink, "one should use only those of high quality, not necessarily, however, the famous *Tung-ch'uan.*"[4] There were other good glues made from deer horns, the hides of deer, cows, and other

[3] Li Ch'iao-p'ing, *The Chemical Arts of Old China,* pp. 119 f.
[4] *An Essay on Landscape Painting,* tr. Sakanishi, p. 56.

animals, or fish skin. The prime requisites have always been that the glue should be as clear and clean as possible and used when freshly prepared.

The process of making ink sticks may be seen, then, to consist of burning or cooking, mixing, pounding, stirring, sifting, shaping, setting in molds, and drying. Inscriptions or decorations are often engraved on the sticks. After the ink sticks are finished and completely dry, they are rubbed with a piece of rough cloth and polished with wax till clean and smooth, and then wrapped in paper for storage.

Among the experiments in inkmaking there were procedures to make it mat, an effect desirable for certain purposes. To dull the ink, pulverized oyster shells were sometimes added, or powdered jade, although jade was put in principally as a gesture of respect to the ink. So much care and skill were given to the production of ink that ink sticks became objects of art, prized for the variety of their shapes, their decoration, their inscriptions, and the names of their manufacturers and the places where they were made. They were collected and venerated. Inevitably, works were compiled recording their development and variety. Old sticks and cakes have a unique fragrance, which in the past was often heightened by adding musk, camphor, pomegranate bark, or the like, as the ink was being made. Besides giving the ink a fragrance, these ingredients were believed to improve its color and brightness and to help preserve the sticks. Old ink was and still is treated like vintage wine. The *Chieh Tzu Yuan* gives advice about using old ink on old paper and new ink on new and gold-leafed paper, partly for the practical reason of absorbency but mainly out of a sense of fitness, for old ink on new paper was considered inharmonious, inappropriate and, moreover, wasteful.

Although a great variety of tones can be produced from one stick of ink, depending on the amount of water mixed with it, several kinds of ink are often used in the painting of a picture. As Kuo Hsi said, "one kind of ink is not sufficient; a single kind of ink cannot give the desired effect. . . . If only one kind is used, the effect is monotonous."[5] Ink is also often blended with a

[5] Ibid., pp. 56 f.

touch of color. The *Chieh Tzu Yuan* includes in its pages discussion and instructions on how to blend and use ink mixed with color; in particular, the brief section on Blending Ink with Color tells of this procedure for "painting forests in sunlight and shadow, the clefts and angles of rocks on mountains, and the tones of shadows in hollows" and that ink blended with color "enriched the venerable air of trees and rocks" and enhanced the "element of the mysterious, the dark and fertile dignity hovering over hillock and pool." The one color that the painter is warned never to mix with ink is vermilion. And it is significant that this section on blending ink and color contains one of the few direct references to *Tao,* one aspect of which is symbolized by red as the color of fire, the power as well as the purifying element of Heaven or the Spirit, which is of course pure and unadulterated.

Kuo Hsi may also be quoted on the subject of inkstones: he wrote that "those made of stone, pottery, earthenware, or fragments of a broken water jar may be used."[6] They do not have to be large but should have a flat area on which the stick of ink is rubbed; this slopes to a slight hollow at one end, where a little water is kept for liquefying the ink and freshening and diluting it in the course of writing or painting. Inkstones used to be made also of iron, jade, and quartz; and bricks and roof tiles served the same purpose. Tiles fashioned for inkstones in the Han period have long been highly prized by collectors. Enamelled pottery produced inkstones with nonporous surfaces, so that the ink stayed wet considerably longer. Stones of unusual color and veining were made into beautiful inkstones of many shapes and sizes. Some famous stones, crescent-shaped and scaled like a dragon, were designed by the T'ang emperor Hsuan Tsung. The Ch'ing period, in particular the reign of Ch'ien Lung, is notable for the variety and decoration of inkstones, shaped like lotus leaves, fruit, flowers, fish, and animals, the symbolic meaning of which added to their value and the pleasure they gave their owners.

Brush and ink needed silk *(chuan)* and paper *(chih)* of equally fine pedigree to serve as the means of their expression. From what is known of the making and preparation of silks and papers

[6] Loc. cit.

in China, there was a great variety of both, and as much attention and care were given to their production as to the development of the brush and ink.

The invention of paper is usually ascribed to Ts'ai Lun, of the Later Han dynasty, a prominent official under Ho Ti (A.D. 89–106). In the history of the dynasty, he is said to have made paper out of tree bark, hemp, or fish nets. Before paper, slips of bamboo or wood had served for writing; in Ch'in and Han times, pieces of silk were sometimes used. The oldest examples of Chinese paper known to us today are probably those discovered at Tun Huang by Sir Aurel Stein, which have been dated at about A.D. 151. These samples show that at a very early date paper was being made that was thin, white, and of good quality. Since then, paper has been made from bamboo, mulberry, hemp, corn and rice stalks, cotton, flax, silk cocoons, reeds, moss, and a kind of water fungus. Hemp, bamboo, and what is called the paper mulberry *(Broussonetia papyrifera)* are most often used. The quality of papers varies; surfaces are smooth or rough, weight is thin or thick, and tints range from white through yellow, blue, and gray to quite dark tones. The most famous paper was the kind called *Ch'eng Hsin T'ang Chih* (paper made at the Pure Heart Hall), a fine, thin, smooth sheet of high quality, considered by some authorities the best ever made in China. It was perfected in the Later T'ang period (A.D. 923–934) and used by the great painters of the Sung and Yuan periods. Between this fine, smooth paper and the coarse, absorbent kinds are papers of innumerable degrees of smoothness and roughness. Paper is washed in a weak solution of lye, sometimes sized with alum, sometimes left unsized for special kinds of writing and for some kinds of painting. Besides being named for the manufacturer or the place where they were made, papers are also named according to qualities of texture, tint, and weight. The different varieties are therefore too numerous to list. Some well-known kinds are Wild Goose White paper, Kuan Yin paper, Blue Cloud paper, White Jade paper, Cicada Wing paper, Ice and Snow paper, and Six Times Lucky sized paper.

Silk was used as a ground for painting at a very early date, in the form of banners such as were discovered at Tun Huang. The subjects on the banners were mostly Buddhist, for they were used in ceremonies in temples, tombs, and halls of worship. These banners were long and were hung vertically on walls. They are said to have once been displayed alongside frescoes, which as a form of painting were developed in Han times, flourished from Ch'in to T'ang times, and continued to be used, although not widely. Perhaps because banners were a more convenient form of representing deities and mythical figures, they began to take the place of frescoes in temples and halls. Banners, in fact, led to paintings in the form of scrolls, which developed in the T'ang period. Scrolls were at first as long and unwieldy as banners, but gradually they were made shorter and narrower. The vertical form continued to be used for figures and also for some landscape paintings, but in time the horizontal scroll was introduced and became very popular. During the Sung period, the form of album leaves came into use.[7] Both silk and paper were made into these various shapes and forms, silk being more effective for the meticulous kind of painting filled in with color, and paper being preferred for paintings done with freer brushwork and for calligraphy.

According to the *Chieh Tzu Yuan,* "up to the beginning of the T'ang dynasty, pictures on silk were painted on unsized silk," prepared by dipping the silk in boiling water. A sizing made of alum and glue was sometimes applied to the silk, and in the process the silk was beaten and smoothed until it was like "a silver board." The same methods, as used in later periods, are described in the detailed instructions in the Manual for stretching the silk on a frame, preparing the alum and glue, and applying it to the silk.

In the past, both fine- and coarse-textured silks were used for paintings, ranging in color from the purest white through porcelain blue, light gray, and beige to the kind that was dyed a dark blue and used for Buddhist subjects, for calligraphy in gold, and

[7] Types of scrolls and leaves: *li chou* and *kua fu* (both vertical hanging scrolls), *heng fu* (horizontal scroll), *shou chuan* (horizontal hand scroll), *p'ing t'iao* and *t'ung ching* (sets of narrow scrolls painted to be hung together, e.g., four scrolls of the seasons); also *tou fang* and *ts'e yeh*, album leaves and single small pictures, which includes *shan mien* (fan face) paintings, removed from frames and put on album leaves.

occasionally for flower paintings. The weaves varied from single-threaded to double-threaded,[8] some loosely and some closely woven. Chang Yen-yuan, in the T'ang period, wrote of Shantung silk, Wu silk, a white silk, and a foglike silk as fine, brilliant, and closely and wonderfully woven.[9] Some of the closely woven silks were made even smoother in the sizing process and their surfaces were like the finest paper. The pieces of silk were made in various widths; the *Yuan chuan* (Academy silk), woven especially for members of the Imperial Academy of Painting, came in pieces as wide as seven or eight feet.

The traditional mounting of paintings on silk or paper is an art in itself. By Sung times, scrolls were made in many sizes and proportions: both the vertical type, long and wide or smaller and narrower, and the horizontal type, comparatively narrow and in various lengths that could be unrolled and slowly inspected by sections. The quality and variety of the silk and paper called for increased attention to the mounting, which both protected the painting and served to set it off fittingly. A typical mounting[10] gives the picture the form of a scroll. The painting is fixed to a piece of paper or silk, called the *ssu hsiang* (four-sided inlay), which forms a border around the four sides of the picture; this in turn is set on a piece of silk, sometimes an elaborate brocade, which shows at the top and bottom of the *ssu hsiang;* the top portion is called *t'ien* (Heaven) and is a third again longer than the bottom part, called *ti* (Earth). Usually two strips of silk or brocade are attached to the top and bottom of the painting to protect it and keep it firmly fixed to the *ssu hsiang.* At the bottom of the scroll a wooden roller is attached, around which the whole scroll is rolled when the painting is not displayed, and which acts as a weight when the painting is hung; the knobs of this roller often used to be ornamented with jade, ivory, horn, or metal. At the top are attached two strips of silk called *feng tai* (wind bands) or *p'iao tai* (flapping bands) or *ching yen* (to

[8] See March, *Some Technical Terms of Chinese Painting,* Nos. 11, 12.
[9] Sirén, *The Chinese on Painting,* p. 232: tr. of *Li Tai Ming Hua Chi,* Sec. II, Ch. III.
[10] March, Sec. XII, lists the names and brief descriptions of the parts of a mounting; and p. 56, diagram of a mounting.

frighten away swallows), probably indicating their purpose, to wave away flies and birds. The mounting has a certain symbolism: the higher and larger portion of the brocade represents Heaven, the lower and smaller part Earth, and the four-cornered and -sided *ssu hsiang* the product of Heaven and Earth that is the painting. The two strips might have originally represented the *Yin* and *Yang,* since they were two in number, hanging loose, and associated (as indicated by their names) with the wind, a form of *ch'i.* In the association of the top part of the painting and the mounting with Heaven and the lower with Earth may perhaps be found the original reason for the direction of Chinese writing from top to bottom, in rows from right to left, for the right indicated what pertained to Heaven and *Yang,* the left what pertained to Earth and *Yin.* A painting of the vertical type is also "read" from top to bottom. When inscriptions are added to pictures, they are usually placed at the top not only because this space is available but probably because originally inscriptions consisted of thoughts related to Heaven and the Spirit. Paintings of the horizontal type are unrolled and read from right to left.

The idea of *Yin* and *Yang* may be observed in the interdependence of the Four Treasures: the brush is *yang* as the instrument using ink *(yin);* the brush is also *yang* in expressing an aspect of Heaven and the *Ch'i;* and the ingredients of ink—earth and soot mixed with water—including their qualities of blackness and darkness, are all *yin* elements. The brush, however, is *yin* in relation to the *yang* of the *Ch'i* and the painter's *ch'i.* Yet the ink stick is *yang* in its relation to the *yin* inkstone and also in mingling with water *(yin)* to make liquid ink: ink itself shows a *yang* aspect when paired with paper or silk, passive and *yin.* The inkstone is *yang* when considered with ink and water, since it is the means of their blending. The brush is, of course, *yang* in making its expression on paper, but paper also has an evident *yang* aspect in that it presented the painting. The fluidity and interchangeable aspects of the *Yin* and *Yang* are thus revealed in the various relationships among the Four Treasures, depending on how they are paired. And, in numbering four, the Treasures represent the material means (Four) of making manifest *Tao* (One). They are the painter's equipment to express aspects of the order and harmony of Heaven and Earth, and the aesthetic analogy of this unity of Heaven and Earth is presented literally in the mounting of the picture midway between the upper area, symbolizing Heaven, and the lower, symbolizing Earth.

The ideal of the harmony of Heaven and Earth extends also to colors. The Five Colors of Chinese painting are interpreted as corresponding to the Five Elements, although the tendency in recent times has been to disregard this association. The colors are red, yellow, blue (which includes green), white, and black. In the past they were of mineral or vegetable origin; in later periods some synthetic colors have been used. Recent research offers interesting information about the sources of pigments used in early painting. From azurite, malachite, and indigo, various blues and greens were obtained; from cinnabar, realgar, and orpiment, a number of reds and orange-yellows; and umber was derived from a kind of iron oxide called limonite.[11] A red of extraordinary brilliance was made from coral, and a pink-red was derived from a vine with red flowers and leaves, which in the past was also used in the making of cosmetics. A yellow was derived from the sap of the rattan plant. White was either of lead or of crushed oyster or clam shells. All these colors were water colors, well suited to the soft Chinese brush and more akin to ink than oil colors, which were tried though never widely used.

In their preparation for painting, colors are ground, distilled in water, and carefully mixed with a little glue. The T'ang critic, Chang Yen-yuan, mentioned a stag-horn glue from Yun (Yunnan), a fish glue from Wu (Kiangsu), and an ox glue from Shantung.[12] Numerous other kinds also were used. The *Chieh Tzu Yuan* suggests a good substitute for glue made by boiling the pulp of the soap bean *(Gleditschia sinensis);* it describes this as lighter and clearer than ordinary glue and particularly useful in the preparation of gold leaf for painting. The Manual contains a section in the opening book on colors, with directions for preparing them. The instructions for preparing the colors are in some instances de-

---

[11.] Uyemura, "Studies on the Ancient Pigments in Japan," pp. 47–60, gives information about chemical compounds of colors, their mineral and vegetable origins, names and some samples of various pigments.

[12.] Sirén, *The Chinese on Painting*, p. 232.

tailed, in others brief and perfunctory. They include useful tips: the juice of an apricot seed is good for wiping clean the parts of a painting where white has been used and has darkened; flicking a little ear wax into a kind of mineral blue or into ink with grains in it helps reduce the substance to the required consistency.

The Manual's introductory remarks on color are mainly concerned with pointing out the difference between colors as pigments and "color" as a quality—for instance, of literary style, of oratory, and of personality. It was proper for a manual of painting to give information on the preparation of pigments but the chief concern of the *Chieh Tzu Yuan* with the quality of "color" is significant for illustrating the ruling idea that real color was in the character of the thing depicted and could be rendered by the drawing and the ink tones. According to this view, colors are an adornment. Hence the familiar expression, repeatedly quoted, "If you have ink, you have the Five Colors." As Chang Yen-yuan expressed it, by revolving *(yun)* the ink, that is, through proper handling of ink tones, "one brings in the Five Colors . . . but if the idea is fixed on the colors, the forms of the objects will become deficient." [13]

The distinction between "color" and colors is analogous to the contrast between the spiritual and material. Since Chinese painting is dedicated to expressing in forms aspects of the harmony of *Tao*, ink tones and brushstrokes have more telling powers of suggestion than color, used, as it usually has been, as an embellishment. A critic writing in the K'ang Hsi period, at about the time the *Chieh Tzu Yuan* was being compiled, confirmed this view of his predecessors when he declared that "coloring in a true pictorial sense does not mean a mere application of variegated pigments. The natural aspect of an object can be beautifully conveyed by ink-color, if one knows how to produce the required shades." [14]

The manner of applying colors suggests that they have generally been considered an aspect of appearance and so only of the surface. They are used as tints, applied thinly and flat in light washes or filling outlined forms. Such treatment conforms with

[13] Tr. in Sirén, p. 231.
[14] Shen Chieh-chou, quoted by Taki, *Three Essays on Oriental Painting,* p. 66.

the aim that colors, when they are used, should be unobtrusive, in strong contrast to the boldness and movement of the ink line and the eloquence of ink tones. The Chinese painter's skill with ink is the result of the brushwork discipline of writing (which, no doubt, had a great deal to do with the preference for painting in ink). And the preëminence of ink monochrome painting was due mainly to the influence of the gentlemen-painters, whose literary background led them to stress the close relationship between painting and calligraphy and between painting and literature. The results they achieved in ink, through masterly drawing, subtlety of ink tones, and a refinement of thought and conception rare in painting, prompts one to wonder what might have been the result had Chinese painters given free rein to the genuine delight in color that is so striking in other activities in Chinese life. Be that as it may, color never was given full display in Chinese painting; and, actually, the rich potentialities of ink tones combined with the wonderful kind of abstraction possible through line proved more than adequate. Moreover, there was a persuasive factor in the association, so important to the Chinese mind, of ink with the idea of the *Yin* and *Yang:* brush and ink were *yang* and *yin;* ink was *yang* in relation to the *yin* of the paper; and all the ink tones displayed in a painting symbolized degrees of the blending of the *Yang* (Light) and *Yin* (Dark), which represented Heaven and Earth, the two primary powers. The *Yin* and *Yang,* as the two chief principles and forces, were prior to the Five Elements, on which the Five Colors were based; the Elements were, in fact, derived from, and their rotation was due to, the action of the *Yin* and *Yang.* This facet of the *Yin-Yang* theory must certainly have been a strong influence in determining the preference for ink over colors.

The Five Elements *(wu hsing),* water, fire, wood, metal, and earth, represent in Chinese thought a great deal more than their physical substances. Metaphysically they described the five main groupings or "essences" of the ever-changing phenomena of the universe. According to the *Shu Ching* (Book of History), water was conceived of as soaking and descending, fire as blazing and rising, wood as crooked and straight, metal as yielding and changing, and earth as sowing and reaping.[15] The Elements were considered to be in perpetual motion and to alternate so that one after another in turn was the governing element. In the *Li-yun* chapter of the *Li Chi* (Book of Rites), man is described as "the product of the forces of heaven and earth by the interaction of the *Yin* and *Yang,* the union of the animal and intelligent spirits, and the finest matter of the Five Elements," accounting for the many analogies between the Elements and the human body and its actions.[16] A statement relating the Five Colors to the Five Elements is found in a collection of ancient texts antedating the VI century B.C., the *Chi Chung Chou Shu:* "Among the Five Elements the first one, the black one, is water; the second, the red one, is fire; the third, the green one, is wood; the fourth, the white one, is metal; and the fifth, the yellow one, is earth." [17] The symbolism of colors and their association with the Elements are evident also in a description of an ancient octagonal altar, the sides of which were painted green, red, white, and black, standing for East, South, West, and North, and the enclosed area yellow, the color of earth.[18] Colors were, moreover, related to the seasons, the Five *Ch'i* (Atmospheric Influences of rain, sunshine, heat, cold, and wind), the Five Planets, and the Five Points marking the Five Regions of the heavens, each presided over by a supernatural creature and each associated with a number:

Wood	*Green* Dragon	East	Spring	Jupiter	8
Fire	*Red* Phoenix	South	Summer	Mars	7
Metal	*White* Tiger	West	Autumn	Venus	9
Water	*Black* Tortoise	North	Winter	Mercury	6
Earth	*Yellow* Dragon	Center		Saturn	5

To explore the range of these analogies in traditional Chinese thought would lead too far afield, but such examples as the Five Viscera, the Five Tastes, and the Five Sounds may be mentioned. Each organ, attribute, and quality in each set was regarded as being governed by its corresponding Element.

[15] Part V, Bk. IV (tr. Legge, pp. 325 f.).
[16] Tr. in Forke, *World-Conception,* p. 238.
[17] Ibid., p. 236.
[18] Laufer, *Jade,* p. 149.

Among the Five Colors, red and black were the most important, being associated with the primary Elements of fire and water. Other colors, however, were also sometimes associated with fire and water, according to the particular view of them: fire was generally described as red, but when its purifying aspect was dominant, it was thought of as white, and in its relation to the heat of the sun it assumed the sun's color, yellow. Water had an active as well as a passive aspect, so that, while black symbolized its stillness, red sometimes represented its active and penetrating quality. When, as the Element of the moon, its *yin*ness was emphasized, in contrast to fire as the Element of the sun, water was associated with white; but it was more often regarded as black, since that was descriptive of *yin* qualities. This fluctuation of associations was characteristic of the Five Elements, for they were in constant rotation and transformation: while one Element was at its height, another had subsided and a third was emerging, mutually producing and destroying each other in a never-ending cycle of change.

Therefore, depending on the standpoint of interpretation, red and black represented at times fire and water, and at other times Spirit and Matter, Heaven and Earth, and also the *Yang* and *Yin*, as in the *Yin-Yang* emblem. In very early times, colors were apparently used in this symbolic way, though in the painting of later periods they were applied according to natural appearance. In the earliest evidence that has been discovered, red and black were the only colors used. The symbolic significance is illustrated in the following excerpt from the Chou Dynasty Records of Rites, the *Chou Li:* "The herdsman uses russet animals for the *Yang* sacrifices . . . and black animals for the *Yin* sacrifices," [19] the *Yang* sacrifices being those offered to Heaven, the *Yin* to Earth. As pigments in painting, red and black were conspicuously the only colors used on the painted pottery excavated from prehistoric grave sites in Kansu and Honan, attributed to the Yang Shao culture (2200–1700 B.C.) of northern China.[20] The pottery discovered in the grave sites was decorated in both red and black; on the

[19] *Chou Li* I, 270 (tr. in Forke, p. 165).
[20] See Andersson, "Researches into the Prehistory of the Chinese" *(BMFEA* 15, 1943), "On Symbolism in the Prehistoric Painted Ceramics of China" *(BMFEA* 1, 1929), and *Children of the Yellow Earth,* p. 315, fig. 137.

pottery found in the dwelling sites of the same period, only black was used. It appears that red, the color associated with Heaven and the Spirit, and hence in ancient beliefs linked literally to the spirit world, was never used on the dwelling-site pottery; its color, black, was associated with Earth and Matter.

In his *Preliminary Report on Archaeological Research* in Kansu, Professor Andersson calls the characteristic pattern on this grave pottery a "death pattern." He also describes it as "two opposite rows of black saw teeth with an intermediate band of red." [21] In his book *Children of the Yellow Earth,* which contains an absorbing account of his discovery of the prehistoric village of Yang Shao Tsun, in Honan, he mentions with some reservation that the two rows of teeth in the "death pattern" might conceivably have represented "in the one case *Yang* and in the other *Yin,* the male and female principles opposing each other in an endless series of ritual marriage scenes." [22] Also in that book, in connection with the use of red on the grave pottery, he describes having seen the Yellow River "blood-red" from red-clay deposits, at the height of the season of crops. In ancient times, a year was divided into two seasons, of which the spring-summer season was that of the *Yang.* The sight of the red river at the ripe season must have suggested to the ancient Chinese a river of blood, a powerful manifestation of the life-stream, and could have found expression in the red line on the grave pottery. The red line, furthermore, being used only on grave pottery, could have referred not to life on earth but to another kind of life, or it could have represented the qualities of vitality and fertility that were valued in life and were accordingly represented on vessels for the grave, in line with the custom of surrounding the dead with what they needed and prized in life. The red line could also have symbolized the hope that in death the spirits *(shen),* which were held to be beneficent, would triumph over the ghosts or demons *(kuei),* bent on evil, which were believed to be of a lower category and to dwell in the lower and black regions. The distinction between the upper and lower ranges of mountains suggests still another meaning, which is supported by the meaning of the triangle forms in the old character

[21] Andersson, "Researches," p. 99.
[22] Andersson, *Children,* p. 318.

wu (resembling the Roman numeral X). The upper row of mountains might have represented Heaven *(Yang)* and the lower row Earth (*Yin*), with the implication that death was an ascent from one region to the other, a "crossing" of great and telling import. The vibrant red line, whether it represented a river, a road, or a way in a more abstract sense, would seem also to imply that death was believed to be a transition to a state higher and better than life on earth. Mention of a "Red Road" is made in a XIII-century astronomical chart engraved on stone in a Confucian temple near Soochow.[23] Although this evidence was of a relatively late period, its material was based on observations and explanations of a very early period, which are relevant to color symbolism. The Red Road (the equator) is described as encircling the heart of Heaven, wherein dwelt the central spirit or the spirit of the Center. Rotating day and night made Heaven turn from East to West, produced the four seasons, and equalized the *Yin* and *Yang*. The text goes on to describe the sun as the essence of *T'ai Yang* (Great *Yang* or positive principle) and the moon as the essence of the *T'ai Yin* (Great *Yin* or negative principle); the sun's path is termed the Yellow Road, that of the moon the White Road.[24]

Colors thus were endowed in ancient times with a significance far beyond their application as hues and were used to denote a wide range of meaning related to nature, the seasons, and the weather, to metaphysical theories, and to man physically and morally. Associated with natural forces, colors inevitably were also believed to possess magical powers. And while they came to be used simply as pigments describing an aspect of appearance, the ideas associated with them, their ingredients, and the methods by which they were prepared linked them with the early practice of alchemy. The relationship of colors to alchemy, and thus of painting and alchemy, is a vast subject of undeniable fascination, difficult to understand without knowledge of the background of alchemy and its symbolic language, which was purposely veiled in elaborate allusion. Here, mention can be made of only a few of the ways in which alchemy and painting were re-

[23] Rufus and Tien, *The Soochow Astronomical Chart,* containing reproduction of chart, Chinese text, and translation.
[24] Ibid., pp. 3 f.

lated, in order to suggest the closeness and intricacy of the connection.

The aims of both alchemy and painting, as of all activities of Chinese life, were focused ultimately on the concept of Heaven and Earth, or *Tao*. The alchemists occupied themselves in seeking an elixir or other means to prolong life. In this search, they probed into the ways and processes of nature, aiming to understand nature and to share its secrets of vitality, evolution, and harmony. The Taoists, who were particularly concerned with alchemy and whose philosophy was interwoven with alchemical ideas, became absorbed in prolonging life through broad interpretation of certain passages in the *Tao Te Ching* that were so abstract, so vague, as to allow for many varied renderings. The book of Lao Tzu maintains, for instance, in Chapters XXIII and XXVIII, that if an individual conforms to *Tao* he eventually acquires its attributes, chief among which is its eternal and unceasing activity. Elsewhere the work mentions that a man possessed of *Tao* not only will live long but will be exempt from danger and decay. Thus, *Tao* became the source and the secret of immortality. And thus certain practices of magic and necromancy arose, exploiting basic human fears and longings. These developed into organized cults, that, through play on superstition, vitiated the serious and thoughtful aspect of alchemy, the keenly observing, speculative, and experimental spirit of the beginnings of science. A distinction should therefore be made between the alchemists bent on exploiting their "secrets" to obtain court patronage and those who believed alchemy a way towards understanding nature in order to live more closely according to its laws. Whatever the modern opinion may be of these early alchemists—described in the Han records as those "who know how to sacrifice to the stove"—it was their experiments that led to such discoveries as Kaolin and other ingredients of porcelain and other ceramics, gunpowder, salt, dyes, lacquer, the alloys of silver and copper with lead, and the use of mercury for mirrors.

The brewing and distilling of immortality elixirs were therefore only a part of alchemical activity. The alchemists were deeply concerned with physical and mental discipline. They evolved a comprehensive regimen, regulating diet and prescribing exercises and proper breathing, that on the whole was sensible and salutary. "One should not desire to eat too much" [25] was a basic rule laid down in the *Pao P'u Tzu,* a work that took its title from the pseudonym of its author, a IV-century Taoist adept in alchemy, and contained an extraordinary fund of information and comment not only on the transmutation of metals, elixirs, rules of health, immortality, and asceticism, but also on government and politics.

As we have seen, Chinese painters and writers early established the aim of observing and exploring the secrets of nature as an indispensable part of learning to paint. They tried to express aspects of *Tao* in their works and to fill them with its unifying harmony. For many centuries, paintings were produced for a definite moral and spiritual purpose that might be described as the effort to conform to *Tao,* the Way. Even in later periods, when pictures were not regarded primarily as works of moral inspiration, painters continued to strive to express some aspect of *Tao,* and their lofty intention tended still to produce morally inspiring effects. The colors used in painting were derived from the basic ingredients of the alchemists' elixirs and were prepared in a similar manner. And it is notable that, whenever painters and critics wrote of the importance of health and a calm mind, of breath control, meditation, and practices conducive to good painting, they cited methods similar to those found in Taoist alchemical works. The insistence on clarifying thought and on stilling the heart before wielding the brush was a discipline also practiced by the philosophical among the alchemists.

The general term used to describe alchemy is *lien tan* (to melt or transmute the pill or drug); *tan* (pill, drug, red, elixir) is used also in a common term, *tan ch'ing* (to use red and blue or green), meaning "to paint" in the sense of applying pigments, as distinct from the more general term *hua* (to draw, to paint). There are several characters designating various reds, such as *hung, chu, tzu* and *yen chih,* but *tan* most likely is the oldest. The character, the modern and old forms of which are shown in the Appendix, may be seen to indicate a pill, represented by a dot, be-

²⁵· *Pao P'u Tzu,* Ch. VIII, quoted in Johnson, *A Study of Chinese Alchemy,* p. 52.

ing brewed in a caldron; and it probably illustrates the actual preparation of cinnabar, the favorite ingredient in life-prolonging concoctions, from which several reds used in painting are derived. The importance of cinnabar in alchemy may be seen in the following statement in Chapter II of the *Pao P'u Tzu:* "In the medicine of the immortals, of highest rank is cinnabar, next is gold, next is silver, next are the various species of the *chih,* and next are the five species of jade." [26] The *chih* is the plant reputed to be the food of Taoist immortals, and jade has always been prized for its purity. The inclusion of jade among the life-giving substances may offer one of the reasons for its use in burial customs, when pieces carved in symbolic forms were placed on different parts of the body, with the hope of preserving it from decay.

It is notable that cinnabar was placed ahead of gold and silver in the "medicine of the immortals." The belief in its magical powers was evident in prescriptions for refining it that are quoted in alchemical works, where one often finds such a phrase as *chiu chiu chin tan* (nine revolutions produce the philosopher's stone), which was shortened into a byword of alchemy, *chiu chiu* (nine nine), standing for "nine times fired at nine regular periods." The fact that cinnabar was red, and in preparation was subjected to the divine element of fire, further enhanced its value and meaning; it was referred to as the "divine cinnabar" and as the *Yang* ingredient. Moreover, it yielded mercury, called "the living metal" and "the soul of metals," and regarded as a *Yin* ingredient. From mercury was derived vermilion (according to an alchemical work, fourteen ounces from a pound of mercury). The process of manufacturing vermilion has been kept secret even into the modern period, partly no doubt for commercial reasons but also perhaps from the habit of secrecy characteristic of the old alchemists. In recent times, Chinese vermilion of the best quality has been made in Canton. The main steps in its preparation are, first, the heating of mercury and sulphur together in shallow iron pans, then pulverization, and finally separation in small quantities in a retort, where the black sulphide

[26] Johnson, p. 59.

sinks and the bright red powder gathers in the upper part; the red is then ground, washed, and dried.[27]

In alchemy, vermilion was called *she nu* (serpent woman or female serpent), a term for which no explanation is known. Another term in alchemical prescriptions was "cloud mother," which is not unlike its more familiar name "mother of pearl." "Masculine yellow" was realgar and "feminine yellow" orpiment. Gold was related to both the sun and moon, which were sometimes referred to as "The Golden Crow" and "The Golden Mirror."[28]

Owing to the purposely elusive language of alchemy, the recipes for the elixir are usually beyond a layman's grasp. One recipe, however, from the *Ko Chih Ching Yuan* (Mirror of Scientific Discovery), fairly direct in expression, names ingredients also used for pigments: "The elixir of the eight precious things . . . contains cinnabar, orpiment, realgar, sulphur, saltpeter, ammonia, 'empty-green' [an ore of cobalt], and 'mother of clouds' [a kind of mica]."[29] Orpiment, a sulphide of arsenic, provides painting with a soft yellow, and realgar has been described as "red as a coxcomb." The *Pao P'u Tzu* gives directions for preparing nine kinds of elixir; one contains not only cinnabar and orpiment but also alum and crushed oyster shells, both of which are among the materials of painting.

Colors were imbued with so much additional meaning that it is surprising they were regarded as secondary in painting. The manner in which they came to be used in painting, simply to add a tint of the natural color of objects with little reference to the elaborate symbolism of each color, relegated them to being merely a decorative aspect. The ideas associated with colors, even when they were recalled, were therefore outside of and apart from their use. And ink, with its *Yin* and *Yang* association and its wide range of subtle tones, admirably suited to suggesting the presence of *Tao,* clearly provided the stronger and more expressive medium. A recent study[30] contains a chapter on Goethe's

[27] Yan Tsz Chiu, "Chemical Industry in Kwang Tung Province," pp. 133–43.
[28] Johnson, p. 87.
[29] Martin, *The Lore of Cathay,* p. 64.
[30] Gray, *Goethe the Alchemist,* Ch. V.

use of alchemical terms and symbolism in his theory of colors that offers much interesting material on the concepts and symbolism of alchemy in the West. It shows how Goethe used the two triangles of the Star of David as a basis of arranging six colors: the upward-pointing (Fire) triangle, with red at the top and yellow and blue at the two lower corners; the downward-pointing (Water) triangle, with the intermediate yellow-red and blue-red at the two upper corners and green at the bottom. Goethe further carried through the symbolism of the triangles by explaining colors as activity and passivity of light, and elsewhere in the study he is quoted on the symbolism of the Circle and the Center, which were important points of reference in his works. Chinese alchemists apparently did not conduct experiments in optics and hence into theories of color in connection with the laws of light, or they too might have come to describe colors in terms of the activity *(Yang)* and passivity *(Yin)* of light. Then color in Chinese painting would have been as important as ink.

CHAPTER FOUR

THE ELEMENTS OF A PICTURE

JUST as ceremonial rites and individual conduct in Chinese life were originally patterned on the order and harmony of nature, *Tao,* in the hope that a like order and harmony might prevail in society, so it has been in painting: the classification of subject matter, the codification of brushstrokes, the sets of rules and standards, and the self-cultivation required of a painter evolved as an extension of the ritual attitude and procedure, and were formed to guide and facilitate the expression of aspects of *Tao.*

This motivating idea was a constant inspiration. Summed up in the First Canon, it has provided a unity of aim and a central theme. Its truth is so vital and so pervasive that it affects virtually every aspect of painting from the elements of the painter's character to the single brushstroke.

In striving for harmony with *Tao,* painters and critics have given weight to the complementary idea that everything should be in its proper place and should function accordingly. This stimulated intensive efforts to effect order in every possible way. That ordering fortunately could be flexible, for the chief characteristic of *Tao* was conceived to be movement and constant change, representing all the processes and mutations of nature. Hence the innumerable rules, methods and classifications, at first sight excessive, are upon closer study and in actual use quite general and remarkably elastic.

These conventions of the *tao* of painting summarize what has been regarded as the essential framework and type forms, or *fa,* the term discussed earlier in connection with the *Lu Fa* (Six Canons), used in the sense of *dharma* (law, discipline); it may be rendered "models and basic methods." The conventions supply the minimum means of statement and are therefore indispensable; after they have been learned, there remains a wide latitude for individual taste and touch. In general, the conventions have upheld a high standard of technique and quality. The idiom of painting they established can be used with great expressiveness or with more limited degrees of expression, depending on the painter; and experience in handling it has generally tended to sift the truly creative talents from the merely adept and imitative. The main principles and rules are set forth among the instructions in the *Chieh Tzu Yuan.* Some additional notes are necessary, however, since the Manual concentrates on instruction and refers to the background of painting only by quoting principles from the records and mentioning the names of many masters. And while the Manual is divided into books, each devoted to a subject, it does not discuss other classifications or the various sets of subject matter.

In Chinese painting, the classification of subject matter, loose and comprehensive though it is, is one kind of attempt to effect order. As will be seen from the examples below, no one set of classification has sufficed. In many instances, classes overlap or can be combined, and each has numerous subdivisions, of which several have developed into important independent subjects. Moreover, opinions have differed about both the contents and the order of importance. At one time in the Sung era, for example, there were at least three well-known classifications. Su Tung-p'o (1036–1101) referred to a set of four: Landscape; Figures; Flowers, Bamboos, Birds, and Fishes; and Architectural Pictures. The catalogue of the Imperial Sung Collection of pictures, *Hsuan Ho Palace Collection of Paintings,* dated 1120, made a more detailed classification of ten: Taoist and Buddhist Scenes, Human Affairs, Palaces and Houses (including ships and vehicles), Foreign Tribes, Dragons and Fishes (including crabs and shrimps), Landscape, Domestic Animals and Wild Beasts, Flowers and Birds (including butterflies and bees), Ink Bamboos, and Vegetables and Fruit. And the great painter and con-

88 THE WAY OF CHINESE PAINTING

noisseur, Mi Fei (1051–1107), put Buddhist subjects in the highest class, because of their moral influence; landscape second; and, third and last, flowers, grasses, and whatever goes with them, which he regarded as the subject matter of paintings intended merely for the amusement of officials. Generally speaking, however, there gradually evolved four principal classes of subject matter: Landscape *(shan shui),* Man and Things *(jen wu),* Birds and Flowers *(ling mao hua hui),* and Grasses and Insects *(ts'ao ch'ung).*

In the discussions of the categories of subject matter, there were two notable omissions: Buddhist paintings and portraiture. Despite Mi Fei's authoritative opinion and the fact that such masters as Wu Tao-tzu were famed for their works of Buddhist subjects, this type of painting was usually separated from the general classifications. At the court of Kublai Khan, in the Yuan dynasty, Buddhist paintings were called "Indian painting" and placed under the care of a special curator. Since the works of Chinese painters were, in a deep and important sense, "religious paintings," it was not because Buddhist pictures were religious works that they were considered separately but rather because their subjects, treatment, and symbolism set them apart. Buddhism introduced a new world of mythology into Chinese art. The stylized manner and ornamentation of orthodox Buddhist pictures also had a considerable influence. Zen Buddhism, however, had a totally different effect; it encouraged what might be described as impressionistic works in which ink tones and the vitality of brushwork were the most important factors, and color was on the whole unnecessary.

As to portraits, usually painted to order, they were traditionally considered picturemaking as distinct from art, therefore the work of artisans. Figures, however, had been among the earliest subjects of Chinese painting. Representations of emperors, heroes, sages, and religious and mythological characters on the walls of temples and palaces are mentioned in the records; on such murals, and later on long scrolls or banners, figures apparently were the sole subject matter, without setting or other details. As the scope of painting broadened, figures were more often incorporated into scenes as one of several other features of a picture. Such were the court and festival scenes, the tribute-bearing processions in a landscape, the figures of court beauties or paragons of female virtue, and the solitary fisherman or hermit in an appropriate setting. Character was not overlooked; for instance, in the painting the Museum of Fine Arts in Boston calls *Scholars Collating Classic Texts,* each figure is a unique personality. But while each face and figure had character, each was anonymous. In such works the treatment of clothes, headdress, and equipment was as important as that of the face, and the pictures belong in the *jen wu* category, distinct from portraits that aim primarily at likeness.

Besides figures, the classification of *jen wu* includes domestic animals and birds and man-made structures such as houses, pavilions, huts, bridges, trellises, and furniture. In many works, the background of *jen wu* places them in the landscape category. An entire book of the *Chieh Tzu Yuan* deals with this class of subject matter. It includes also a few examples of *chieh hua* (boundary painting), depicting elaborate structures drawn with a square and rule, which actually form a special and separate class.

The very large category of Birds and Flowers overlaps that of Grasses and Insects, and both contain many subdivisions. As the term suggests, *ling mao* (feathers and fur) describes both birds and animals, although it is generally applied only to birds. *Hua hui* (flowers and plants or flowering plants) covers all kinds of wood-stemmed shrubs and plants with flowers, as well as grasses and herbaceous plants. Fruit trees are included among wood-stemmed plants, since they have trunks and branches and also bear blossoms, whereas other trees belong in the landscape category, as may be seen in the *Book of Trees* of the Manual. Flower painting is said to have become a specialty in the T'ang period, when certain flowers and plants, sometimes with birds or animals, began to be important individual subjects. The Sung Emperor Hui Tsung was himself a distinguished painter of birds and flowers; his interest and patronage, of course, fostered enthusiasm for works of this class. The precise, naturalistic pictures produced under his personal supervision by the members of the Imperial Academy represent one manner of painting birds, animals, and flowers. The school of gentlemen-painters, with its scholarly bent, devoted to the close relationship of calligraphy, poetry, and painting, carried ink painting of the same subjects to heights of lyricism through extraordinary brushwork and subtlety of ink tones. This school's characteristically free handling of brush and ink was further encouraged by Taoist-Zen ideas about spontaneity and the flash of Enlightenment. These two main styles of painting birds and flowers—the academic and the lyrical—are analogous to the two styles of landscape painting traditionally designated as the Northern and Southern Schools.

Certain flowers, plants, birds, and animals became special and independent subjects, mainly because they happily seemed to represent ideal human qualities, auspicious omens, and beneficial influences. As might be expected, the wish for longevity has long been a favorite theme, likewise the wish for good fortune of all kinds; and many of these subjects represent such hopes, individually or in combination. In this attitude may be observed a relic of the magic role of painting in early times, for to prize a picture as a composition of symbols of desirable qualities or aims endows it with the potency of a talisman. While pictures have always been enjoyed as paintings, a great deal of attention has been paid to the symbolism of their subjects, which, when of interest and value, could give them significance beyond pictorial and aesthetic considerations. In time, such interpretations grew so elaborate, with so many ramifications, that few persons could have been acquainted with all of the symbolism. Today, knowledge of the details is even more fragmentary, and it is difficult to piece it together. Before looking at a few of the more widely known examples, some distinctions should perhaps be noted between this type of symbolism, which one may call secondary, and the primary symbolism, directly expressing the idea of *Tao,* the harmony of Heaven and Earth.

The simplest and purest expressions of the primary symbolism may be found in the forms and decorative motifs of the ancient bronzes and jades, and the signs that were the first Chinese writing. Probably the most familiar of these symbols is that of the circle or disk, representing the totality and eternal processes of *Tao.* In painting, landscape is the fullest possible expression of this total harmony, using scenes and natural features in place of the abstract and geometric symbols of the early art. The subjects in the other categories also express aspects of *Tao,* but the scope of such works is necessarily limited. Moreover, the incrustation of the secondary type of symbolism at times almost obscures a clear view of that central focus. In paintings of flowers, birds, animals, and other special subjects, the influence of the concept of *Tao* may nevertheless be discerned in the brushwork, the attention to appropriate setting, season and mood, and the importance given to the qualities of *chen* (trueness) and *tzu jan* (naturalness, spontaneity). Thus, both types of symbolism can coexist and mingle. Each adds meaning of its kind and increases enjoyment of the paintings. The situation is similar to what happened in Taoism when part of Taoist philosophy was reinterpreted, suffering distortion, and developed as the Taoist religion. For, on the one hand, there was the preoccupation with nature and eternal values, and the concern to live attuned to this grand harmony of *Tao;* on the other hand, there was a relaxation of this preoccupation and concern, a deterioration of high ideas and ideals into superstition, and wishful longing that relied on omens and magic formulas—the superficial activity and "trimmings" that travestied sincerely reverent attitudes and acts. Nevertheless, the fact that both kinds of symbolism may be used might be considered evidence of the harmonizing effect of *Tao.* It is, indeed, a measure of the power invested in the concept of *Tao* that, whatever the subject matter of a painting, the controlling idea has consistently held to this harmonious aim.

The way the two kinds of symbolism mingled is characteristic of Chinese painting, which acquired new subject matter and absorbed new techniques and other influences from outside without being deflected from its own *tao.* The horse and the lion, for instance, were among the subjects introduced from Central Asia, India, and other neighboring countries; a number of other animals and birds brought to the T'ang court as tribute or gifts were quickly adopted as subjects of painting and were interpreted, according to their habits and behavior, as symbols of ideals. The beasts and the one bird of the Chinese zodiac— namely, rat, ox, tiger, hare, dragon, serpent, horse, goat, monkey, cock, dog, and pig—have significance through being used as signs of the heavens and through other interpretations attached to them. And legendary and supernatural creatures—such as the four associated with the cardinal points, dragon, phoenix, tortoise, and unicorn—are also special subjects, individually and as a group. Symbolism based on a similarity between the sounds of words is of early origin and supplies a number of subjects: the character *fu*, for instance, means "bat," and another *fu* character happens to mean "happiness," so the bat became an emblem of happiness; likewise, two characters both pronounced *shih* stand respectively for "lion" and "scholar and teacher"; and *yu*, both "fish" and "fertility." There is a playful quality in this sort of symbolism that can produce delightful results, but it has led to a number of stereotyped themes and sometimes to a misplaced emphasis in estimating paintings. Literary associations tended occasionally to overshadow the painting itself; for example, a picture of an animal or plant mentioned in the Book of Odes acquired significance mainly for its association with that classic. Often the original reference and meaning of a traditional theme has been forgotten, but the habit of esteem is so strong that the subject has continued to be used and admired. Among such themes are swallows with willows and sparrows with bamboos; the respective associations are lost. On the other hand, the familiar combination of the cock and peony is well known as two *Yang* symbols, and the crane and the pine tree are still a popular motif for longevity. The Taoist cult of immortality not only provided many subjects for figure compositions but also made many flowers, fruit, and animals emblems of longevity, such as the narcissus, bamboo, and peach, to name three that are included in the *Chieh Tzu Yuan*. Such are some of the associations of subject matter. It may be of interest to single out one, such as the dragon, for detailed consideration. Its interpretation shows extraordinary inventiveness and is rich in meaning closely related to the concept of *Tao*.

The dragon, as a symbol of the power of Heaven and of analogous ideas, is a composite being and a composite symbol. In the Chinese work on materia medica, the *Pen Ts'ao Kang Mu*, it is described as having resemblance to nine other creatures: "It

carries on its forehead horns resembling the antlers of a stag. It
has the head of a camel, the eyes of a hare, the ears of a bull,
the neck of a snake, the belly of a frog, scales like a fish, talons
like an eagle, and paws like a tiger." [1] Another description, to
quote from the records of painting, specifies (again, nine) "the
head like that of a bull, the muzzle like a donkey's, the eyes like
shrimps', the horns like those of a deer, the ears like an elephant's,
the scales like those of fishes, the beard like a man's, the body
like a serpent's, the feet like those of the *feng* bird [phoenix]." [2]
The second quotation, from a section specifically on dragons,
continues with a description of the male and female dragon: he,
"red as fire," has a strong, scaled serpent body with four legs
and a short tail, a thick head with deep-set eyes, flaring nostrils,
a beard, and horns; she has a body "like flat waves" and small
thin scales, a tail longer and stronger than the body, a head with
bulging eyes, a straight muzzle, and a curly mane. The similarity to the serpent comes out very clearly. It is notable that Chinese translations of Sanskrit Buddhist texts render the term *naga*
(serpent; also, a cobralike supernatural being) by the character
lung (dragon). [3] It has been pointed out that the python still
exists as far north as Fukien and that the dragon was probably
based on this reptile with the addition of the head, gaping mouth,
and canine teeth of some large carnivorous animal, the horns of
a deer, the barbels of a catfish, the scales of a carp, the dorsal crest
of an alligator, the legs of a lizard, and the talons of an eagle. [4] The
alligator of the Yangtze River has also been mentioned as a possible prototype of the dragon.

Actually, the origin of the dragon reaches so far back in time
that it might even have been some creature now extinct. Fossilized
bones, still used medicinally in powdered form and called "Dragon's Bones" and "Dragon's Teeth," are named advantageously
after a creature of just such a remote origin; that it might be
mythological enhances the potential benefits. It is not too fan-

[1] Quoted in Yetts' lecture, *Symbolism in Chinese Art*, p. 22.
[2] From the *Mei Shu Ts'ung Shu*, tr. in Sirén, *History of Early Chinese Painting*, II, p. 106.
[3] Eitel, *Notes and Queries on China and Japan*, III, p. 34.
[4] Sowerby, "Animals in Chinese Art," p. 4.

tastic to speculate that the harmless lizard, seen perhaps unexpectedly and startlingly magnified, might have contributed to the general conception of the dragon. Above all, however, it is a composite creature, as the descriptions show. Besides being serpentine, it has certain characteristics of the horse of myths, for it has at times been shown drawing the chariots of deities or of emperors across the heavens; and, from other well-known stories, the dragon has something of the fish. There is the tale of the carp that turned into a dragon at the Lung Men (Dragon Gate) of the Yellow River on the third day of the third month, which has served as the basis of the expression "passing through the Dragon Gate" in describing a scholar attaining his *Han-lin* degree, the highest literary achievement under the old system.

In spite of its ferocious aspects, the dragon has generally been regarded as a beneficent power, though severe in presence, with the majesty of law and high morality befitting the symbol of Heaven. This popular interpretation of the dragon is of very early origin: the opening verses of the *I Ching* on the *ch'ien* (first, originating, Heaven) hexagram describe the dragon slumbering in the deep, stirring, leaping forth, winging across the heavens, a vivid picture of the ruling and pervasive power of Heaven and, by analogy, of moral and spiritual strength. Many early representations of the dragon still exist, such as, on an urn of the Hsin T'ien period in Kansu (probably of the II millennium B.C.), "a snakelike animal with forelegs and horns." [5] Its form was conveniently and simply rendered by a spiral; and the "cloud and thunder" spiral motifs on ancient vessels and other objects were certainly related to the dragon through their form as well as through the association with the clouds and thunder that were so often its element and the signs of its presence. Early Chinese cosmology divided Heaven into Nine Regions, each ruled by a dragon, the nine of which symbolized the powers of the universe. This basic set of nine, and also the many aspects of power that had to be differentiated in depicting the dragon, probably accounts for the several varieties of the creature and for its many variant features in paintings and other art forms. When a single dragon, in the form of a spiral or in a realistic version, is a com-

[5] Andersson, *Children of the Yellow Earth*, p. 73.

posite symbol of the power of all nine, it usually indicates cosmic power as well as various analogies ranging from forces in nature to elements of the human character. And in representing all these various aspects, the dragon possesses a main characteristic, described in the *I Ching* and evident in nature itself: its constant movement, essential to it as a symbol of change. Indeed, the dragon was described as being capable of extraordinary transformations—"at will reduced to the size of a silkworm, or swollen till it fills the space of Heaven and Earth" [6]—and it had the gift of becoming invisible.

As a symbol of the *Yang,* the Heaven force, the dragon is also associated with the sun. As the rising sun, it represents the dawning of day and light, the season of spring, and the nourishing element of water. The glory of the sun was seen as reflected on earth in imperial power, which took as its color the golden light and as its badge the five-clawed dragon. As discussed in the first chapter, the number five is significant in showing "greatness or wholeness," totality, as circumscribed by the Five Points, which in turn express an aspect of the concept of the Center. Other dragons were shown with four claws, perhaps to stress the manifestation of the power of Heaven on earth, four being the number related to the earth. As to numbers, incidentally, the Nine Regions of Heaven provided the basis not only of the nine varieties of dragons but also of the nine similarities of the dragon to other animals, remarked above. And of the Four Quadrants, the Azure Dragon represented the first and Eastern Quadrant. Furthermore, descriptions in the records of painting specify that the body of the dragon should be divided into three sections, and paintings often showed only a part of each of the three emerging through clouds or water.

Legends describe the dragon dwelling in the sky, rivers, the sea, and wells, and marking the courses of rivers and streams. Many facets of meaning belong to this association with water. Rain is the life-giving element, and therefore clouds and thunder announce or accompany the dragon. In the *Chieh Tzu Yuan,* the instructions for painting clouds and sea billows appear on four pages treating these two natural features together and show-

[6] Kuan Tzu (VII cent. B.C.), quoted in Mayers, *Chinese Reader's Manual,* p. 142.

ing the similarity of brushstrokes and forms in painting them; the dragon is mentioned several times in the Manual as a force of nature and as the power of Heaven energizing man through his spirit.

The dragon is thus a symbol of the idea of *Tao,* giving it substance and vividly illustrating its main aspects. Painters who specialized in painting dragons and who wrote on the subject were strongly influenced by Taoist ideas and repeatedly used Taoist terms in referring to the dragon. In connection with the Taoist emphasis on *wu wei* (non-assertiveness), there is an aspect of the dragon that should be mentioned, namely, the power of restraint. There is evidence of this interpretation in representations of the *k'uei* (monster) dragon and the *t'ao tieh* (glutton) mask of a monster on ancient vessels, which are explained in the classic on bronzes, the *Po Ku T'u,* by Wang Fu, as exerting "a restraining influence against the sin of greed." [7]

The Azure Dragon, the Vermilion Bird (the phoenix), the White Tiger, and the Black Warrior (the tortoise) together symbolize the four cardinal points and the four seasons. The seasons are also represented appropriately by flowers, trees, and other plants. The books on the orchid, bamboo, plum tree, and chrysanthemum, composing Part II of the Manual, symbolize the four seasons. These were not, however, the only possible four; sometimes, for instance, the peony and lotus were used in literature and painting in place of the orchid and bamboo. The Manual's *Book of the Plum* mentions the crab apple, water lily, plum, and chrysanthemum as representing spring, summer, autumn, and winter in paintings.

The orchid, bamboo, plum tree, and chrysanthemum are also called the Four Gentlemen, symbolizing various qualities of the ideal gentleman, cultured, of pleasing personality and exemplary character. Under the influence of the gentlemen-painters and the literati, ink painting of these subjects attained heights of expressiveness. To *hua* (paint) flowers and plants came, in fact, to be described as to *hsieh* (write) these subjects. And the bamboo and the plum tree were favorites of the scholar-painters.

Bamboo was a perfect choice for these masters of the brush.

[7] Yetts, p. 3.

A work depicting bamboos is both a painting and a piece of calligraphy. To produce such a work, it is absolutely necessary to have a steady wrist and complete control of brush and ink, and to work in swift, sure brushstrokes without the least hesitation. Experience teaches the values of ink tones, the way of handling a dry or wet brush, and variety of brushstrokes. The bamboo plant, like the orchid, is interpreted as having all the ideal qualities of a scholar and gentleman. It represents the essence of refinement and culture. It is gentle and graceful in fair weather, strong and resilient under adverse conditions. Its suppleness, adaptability, uprightness, firmness, vigor, freshness, and even the sweet melancholy of the rustle of its leaves have been translated into qualities of mind, spirit, and character. Su Tung-p'o referred to bamboos as "those dear princely joints *(pao chieh chun)."* His passionate admiration seems to have been shared by painters and connoisseurs to the point that amounted to a cult of the bamboo. Certainly, among all the subjects in its class, bamboo offers in painting the most direct and effective communication of the vitality called *sheng tung* (life-movement) and the breath *(Ch'i)* of *Tao.*

The numerous associations with the plum tree illustrate how the primary and secondary symbolism existed side by side and did not interfere with each other. The application of the theories of the *Yin* and *Yang* and of numbers as derived from the *I Ching* is given concisely in sections of the *Book of the Plum* in the Manual. Each part of the plum tree and each phase of its development corresponds to laws of nature and *Tao.* The fact that it blossoms in winter makes it the perfect representative of that season, admirable for its fortitude. It was also popularly accepted, therefore, as representing venerable old age; its gnarled and twisted trunk and branches admired as characteristic of Taoist sages and hermits who retired to the mountains to live closer to *Tao.* As the emblem of winter, the plum tree symbolizes the end of the cycle of birth, growth, and decay; but, precisely for this reason, it is also a sign presaging the return of spring, of life and hope. It is relevant that its sinuous trunk has often been compared to a dragon's body. The connection with the return of spring and its associated benefits caused the design of the plum tree—or sometimes just a branch or sprig, often mistakenly called the "hawthorn pattern"—to be used for decorating New Year's gifts, to express appropriate good wishes. Such notions afford delight and, of course, they have proliferated; they might have completely submerged the primary symbolism but for the ideal, maintained through the whole course of Chinese painting and firmly established by the First Canon, of *Ch'i yun sheng tung* *(Ch'i* circulating produces life-movement). On this basic principle all others, and all the terms and expressions of painting, depend. Two of these terms are *chen* (trueness) and *tzu jan* (naturalness).

Chen is the term used frequently in Taoist and Buddhist works in discussing the spiritual, the pure, the divine, that which is held to be real. As it is yet another way of describing harmony with the laws of *Tao,* it stands as a key term of Chinese thought and painting. *Tzu jan* is an equally important Taoist term. The two are complementary and in many respects interchangeable, for what is true to nature is natural and spontaneous. And to achieve trueness and naturalness is, in effect, to be in harmony with *Tao:* what the Taoists describe as being one with *Tao.* The same idea is implicit in the Confucian goal of *ho* (harmony), which has the meaning also of "conciliation" and "blending." In reference to the individual, whether the aim is expressed as *ta* (greatness and wholeness) or as accord with *Tao,* one way to attain it is through the qualities of *chen* and *tzu jan.* In painting, these qualities apply to both an outer and an inner harmony. The accurate representation of flowers, plants, and all living things is essential, with careful attention to setting, season, stages of growth, and various conditions of weather and time of day; to accomplish this, the artist has to be a constant and alert observer, in time gathering a fund of detailed botanical knowledge. A unified composition is the aim, through technical means and through the gradual storing up of knowledge and experience. Above all, the essential and inner harmony of a painting is ultimately dependent on *chen* (trueness) and *tzu jan* (naturalness) in its elements and in the painter himself—or, as painters and critics so often described it, on the operation of the *ch'i* (spirit) in painting and painter. This elusive but indispensable prerequisite to harmonious results is thus rooted in the painter's own efforts toward self-cultivation, his spiritual and intellectual capacities as well as his technical skill and experience. Whatever the degree of his sensibility to the outer and inner aspects of the unity underlying nature's multiplicity, his state of awareness is not a passive receptivity but a positive affirmation, the equivalent of an act of worship. This is succinctly expressed in the literal meaning of *tzu jan,* "naturally and certainly yes," an affirmation echoed nearer our own time by Carlyle's Everlasting Yea.

The concern for trueness and naturalness accounts for the preference for painting flowers and plants growing in their natural setting rather than as a still life. It may be observed that the Western art form of still life and the term itself—even more pointedly, the French term *nature morte*—is contrary to the whole Chinese conception of painting. It may also be seen that, while aspects of *Tao* can be expressed in the painting of flowers, plants, birds, animals, and insects, the category of landscape offers the fullest possible expression of the unity of *Tao,* the harmony of Heaven and Earth. For, in landscape paintings with their panoramic vistas, views of mountain peaks and valleys, and scenes at various seasons, all depicting the forces of nature in sky, earth, and water, there is the opportunity to present everything in proper perspective, in relation to the infinity of *Tao* and in due relation to the rest of nature. The aims and lofty motives of Chinese landscape painters may be clearer, perhaps, if we follow the continuous thread of this idea of the harmony of Heaven *(Yang)* and Earth *(Yin)* as it wove through every aspect of landscape painting. It is impossible to enumerate all of the details of this intricate pattern, but one approach to understanding how the concept determined the aims and manner of representation is to note its expression among the main terms and some of the elements of landscape composition.

The term for landscape, *shan shui* (mountain-water), is in itself symbolic of the *Yang* and the *Yin.* From the evidence of the earliest beliefs, it is known that mountains were associated with Heaven and the *Yang* principle. According to decorative motifs on early pottery and bronzes and excerpts in the records, the sun

rises from behind mountain heights. Mountains also were represented by upward-pointing triangles, symbolizing the element of
fire and thus also the sun, heat, red, power, spirit, and literally
the fire of life. In early cosmology, mountains were described as
the pillars of Heaven, the central peak being also the *T'ai Chi*
(Great Ridgepole), the axis and the still center. Similarly, *shui*
(water) represents the *Yin* principle as the nourishing element,
both the depths and the source, and in its apparent stillness
possesses both motion and strength.

The application of the term *shan shui* to landscape painting
evokes whole sets of analogies to the *Yin* and *Yang* and lends
painting a worshipful attitude, making it a ritual act of reverence in praise of the harmony of Heaven and Earth. Although
the landscape form that is seen today in most Chinese works was
a development during the Five Dynasties and the Sung and Yuan
periods (roughly, x-xii centuries), it is a continuation of the earliest expressions of the worship of Heaven and Earth. In the beginning, when a year was divided into two seasons, the *yang* (spring-
summer) and the *yin* (autumn-winter), the great festivals of
welcome, celebrated later and up to the present time as the spring
and autumn festivals, were held on river banks and on mountains.
The festivities were like picnics, and two kinds of contests were
held, one in which the river was crossed in boats and the other
in which certain flowers were gathered on a mountain or hill.
The significance of the many details is not easy to unravel; it
seems clear, however, that the celebrations were ceremonial and
were associated with the worship of Heaven and Earth as symbolized by the two seasons over which they ruled. Mention has
already been made, in discussing the symbolic use of red and
black, of the mountains-and-river pattern on the early Kansu
pottery, which might be considered a very early form of landscape painting. An excerpt from the *Lun Yu* (Analects) gives a
Confucian interpretation of the analogy of human qualities with
these symbols of Heaven and Earth: "The wise man delights in
water, the Good man delights in mountains. For the wise move,
but the Good stay still. The wise are happy; but the Good,
secure." [8] There are also many popular sayings that point to the

[8] *Analects*, VI, 21 (tr. Waley, p. 120).

meaning attached to water and its symbolism, such as the four-character *yin shui ssu yuan* (when you drink water, reflect on its source).

The power of this concept of the harmony of Heaven and Earth, *Tao,* is evident in the later forms of landscape painting, where the natural features of scenery, painted with the aim of transmitting the *ch'i,* are accurately portrayed in the sense of *chen* (true) without being realistic in manner of presentation. Trees, rocks, mountain peaks and ranges, and other features of landscape are drawn with scientific accuracy. Observation taught the varied forms of rocks, the shapes of rounded or pointed peaks, the massing of mountains, the angles of slopes, the dip of gullies, and the spread of fields in a valley; it taught the details of characteristic habitats of trees and plants, and the way they grew under certain conditions; it taught the variety of brushstrokes that are necessary to render different kinds of grass and moss. These are among the requirements of *chen* and *tzu jan.* In observing setting, and seasonal and weather conditions, painters learned to watch the moods of nature. They represented these various changes in "Heaven's mood" (Heaven's *ch'i).* It was in this rendering of mood that the masters excelled; they used the unifying effect of a mood of nature for harmony of composition as well as to express the oneness of nature. This aim is expressed characteristically in a flat statement in the *Tao Te Ching* (Chapter XLII), "*Tao* produces Oneness," and was called by the painter Shih T'ao "*i hua* (One-painting or painting the oneness)."

The attention given to accurate representation is accompanied by an elaborate symbolism. This is not only a matter of reverence for traditional interpretations and a general fondness for an underlying meaning; the idea of a layer of symbolic significance is in accord with the belief in the living quality of trees, rocks, and all things in nature. Symbolism gives to each a living significance beyond its existence as a tree, a plant, or a rock. Or, as it might be described, each has appearance (the material, *yin)* and an inner vitality (the spirit, *yang),* the whole representing the harmony of the *Yin* and the *Yang,* the great vivifying unity of *Tao.*

Several kinds of trees have been named at different times as the Tree of Life, and many were associated with the seasons, months, and certain days. As in other ancient civilizations, tree cults in China of very early origin were based on the symbolization of life and death. Hollow trees were particularly significant, because emptiness was interpreted as being filled with spirit. The hollow mulberry tree *(fu sang* or *kung sang)* was often mentioned in early literature; it is probably the tree, depicted in the character *tung* (East), that is "climbed" by the sun each day as it rises in the heavens, for the mulberry tree is known to have been called the tree of day, of light, and of the sun, and is therefore a *Yang* symbol. It was described as standing in the East, its roots and trunk in the netherworld and its branches and crown reaching up into the sky.[9] Complementing the mulberry tree is the cassia, standing in the West, the tree of the moon, of night, and of darkness, mentioned in many stories; its flowers were described as luminous stars lighting the world before sunrise. The Manual includes several examples of the *wu t'ung* tree *(dryandra),* which is associated and often painted with the phoenix and therefore believed to possess magic powers. This belief was extended to many other kinds of trees, either through their use in early religious rituals or through the meaning later interpretation gave them. Additional meaning is given to trees by their characteristic form, which suggests not only the universal Tree of Life but its numerous analogies; one of the most familiar of these is the idea of self-cultivation, which was often explained in terms descriptive of the form and growth of a tree. In the opening verses of the *Ta Hsueh* (Great Learning, or Learning of Greatness), for instance, are sentences such as these: "Things have their root and branches. Affairs have their end and their beginning. To know what is first and what is last will lead near to what is taught in the *Great Learning.* . . . All must consider the cultivation of the person the root of everything. . . ."[10] The *Book of Trees* in the Manual opens with such an underlying meaning, by pointing out that the main structure of trees is their four main branches, which are analogous to the Four Directions and to the Four Limbs of Man, representing not only his physical entity but also the four potentialities[11] essential to wholeness of character and personality.

[9.] Bulling, *The Meaning of China's Most Ancient Art,* p. 99.
[10.] Tr. Legge.
[11.] *Jen* (Goodness), *i* (righteousness), *li* (propriety), *chih* (wisdom).

About rocks, too, there have been many traditional associations of ideas that contribute to the belief in their living qualities and powers, and stimulate interest in their appearance, grouping, and symbolism in painting. From earliest times rocks and stones were believed to be more than geological matter. Their mineral ingredients were used in medicines, and the variety of their natural forms —very often like marvelous transformations—gave them a place in magic. In painting, they have always been interpreted as the bone structure of the earth, combining with water, which in its many forms represents the lifeblood, to compose a picture as a living organism. The *Pen Ts'ao Kang Mu,* the encyclopedia of medicine, magic, and miscellaneous information, contains a section on minerals and stones that sums up a number of traditional ideas. Declaring that rocks and stones are the backbone of the earth, it speaks of the great variety of their forms, from the massive accumulation of hills and mountains to grains of dust, "gold and jade their essence, arsenic and its compounds their toxins." The encyclopedia explains the formations on the theory of degrees of concentration of the *Ch'i,* and refers to the many transformations "from the soft to the hard, as in the petrifaction of milk earth into solid rock, or from the animate to the inanimate, as in the fossilization of herbs and trees. . . . And in the petrifaction of animate beasts and birds, the transition is from the sensate to the insensate; in the formation of meteoric and other astral stones from thunder, lightning, and the heavenly bodies, the transition is from the invisible to the visible." An enumeration follows of the properties of the ingredients of rocks and their spiritual and physical effects, with the observation that they should therefore be studied by "good administrators and physicians." [12]

It may be observed that at each level of meaning given to subject matter and through each branching off into analogies, the idea of the *Yin* and *Yang* is constantly active, permeating and energizing each feature of a landscape. In this respect, the *Ch'i* of the First Canon—generally interpreted as the Vital Force of *Tao*— could be better translated as the Two *Ch'i,* the *Yin* and the *Yang* (for no indication is made of singular or plural and the term can be used in both ways). Using it in either sense in reference to landscape painting, the first principle can be said to express the belief

[12] Tr. in Mar, "The Use of Precious Stones in Ancient Medicine," pp. 220–32.

both that the Spirit of Heaven initiates life and that the balance and fusion of the spiritual *(Yang)* and material *(Yin)* result in the energy and movement of life. In expressing essentially the same idea, the two interpretations usefully corroborate each other. In respect to landscape painting, the idea was summed up by the painter Tsung Ping, at the beginning of the v century, as follows: "Landscape paintings have a material existence and also a spiritual influence."

The great achievement of the masters of landscape painting was their skilled representation of the details of nature together with their ability to transmit their conception *(i)* of the obscure and subtle operations of the spirit. Their surviving works, or copies that tell something of their styles and subjects, represent perhaps the most eloquent expressions of the Chinese genius. For, apart from technical proficiency, they succeeded in concentrating on *Tao* while adapting the elements of a landscape to their purpose. They managed to reconcile and combine the *yin* and *yang* aspects in the tradition and in themselves: the *yang* representing the Confucian training, the practical, rule-abiding, and keenly observant mind; the *yin,* the Taoist background, the imaginative, mystical, and searching soul attuned to the deeper and inner rhythm of nature. By this fusion in their approach to the subject, in rendering it through brush *(yang)* and ink *(yin),* and in transmitting it to paper with understanding and the use of their deepest resources, their work was in every sense an expression of the interaction of the *Yin* and the *Yang,* the harmony of Heaven and Earth. Furthermore, although in discussions of landscape painting much was made of the division, based on differences of style, into Northern and Southern Schools, it is known that a painter often worked in both the precise manner of the Northern School and the freer brushwork style of the Southern. Thus, the two main styles might also be described as *yang* or *yin,* representing respectively the Confucian and Taoist elements in the tradition. Experience in both styles actually provided an enlargement of outlook and of the means of expression.

In looking at Chinese landscape paintings on scrolls, one's first impression is likely to be of their shape. Long in their proportions and made even longer by their mounting, they are displayed vertically or horizontally. (Scenes painted on fans or for albums are not, to be sure, of this long shape, for they are done to fit particular frames or pages; they are a separate and minor branch of landscape or flower painting.) The characteristic shapes of landscapes on scrolls, however, contribute to the basic aim of the pictures. The vertical scroll, reaching straight up and down, emphasizes the relationship of Heaven and Earth; it might be likened to a direct ray of the sun, with the many implications, philosophical and psychological, linking Heaven, Earth, and Man. The horizontal scroll, intended to be looked at in sections gradually unrolled from right *(yang)* to left *(yin),* is an ideal way in which to present a painting, revealing a view of nature in a manner equivalent to the unfolding processes of nature itself. As the eye travels from one scene to the next, the sequence in space introduces the element of time, both man's time and the unceasing continuity of *Tao.* While it is impossible to depict *Tao,* the course of nature, it is possible by such means to suggest its presence and to reflect its vitality. The rendering in scroll form of its continuous operation is also deliberately heightened by technical means and by implied analogies among ideas. The fundamental idea of the *Yin* and *Yang* sets the pattern of the aims as well as of the manner of composition.

Chapter XLII of the *Tao Te Ching,* explaining the key position of the *Yin* and *Yang* in Chinese thought, may be applied to painting: *Tao* produced Oneness, Oneness produced duality (the Two *Ch'i, Yin* and *Yang);* One and Two making Three produced the ten thousand things (all things on earth); and the harmony of these ten thousand things depended on the balanced blending of the *Yin* and the *Yang.* The *I Ching,* in its Appendix III, also stresses that the *Yin* and *Yang* "constituted what is called *Tao."* Thus, *Tao* is manifested through the primary elements or forces, the *Yin* and the *Yang;* and in painting, *Tao* is expressed through understanding and transmitting by every means possible this balance and fusion of the *Yin* and the *Yang,* and so achieving harmony and coherence among the ideas expressed as well as in the elements of the painting itself. With this principle of the two major elements established, proportion becomes a basic consideration: not only the arrangement of the composition, but a sense of proportion, the most essential aspect of which is that sense of fitness embodied in the Confucian *li,* discussed in the first chapter. Painters summed up this aim of harmony in the saying "Heart (the inner, *yin* resources and guiding instinct) and hand (the outer, *yang,* and technical expression) must be in accord," and they further referred to oneness and harmony in hundreds of ways. The author of the *Chieh Tzu Yuan,* for instance, in his introductory remarks, quotes another dictum, "Keep in mind the Five Peaks," the totality represented by the five sacred mountains, or, one might say, the sacred geometry of *Tao.* And in the *Book of Rocks,* the instructions demonstrate the brushstroke encompassing and unifying a mountain range of few or numerous peaks.

The usual proportions of sky and earth in a Chinese landscape painting allow a conspicuous amount of space for sky, mist, and voids in relation to that given to mountains, trees, and other terrestrial features: an over-all statement of the dominance of sky (Heaven, *Yang,* spirit) over earth (Earth, *Yin,* matter). This concept is carried through and applied to every element of the composition. Moreover, the fluidity of the *Yin* and the *Yang,* in unceasing fluctuation, separating and merging, is also indicated by the many possible interpretations of factors in a composition. In the contrast between solids and voids, for instance, the solid, material, *yin* aspect complements the voids, the emptiness of which is interpreted as filled with spirit *(yang);* at the same time, the solidity of a mountain, a *yang* manifestation, complements the mystery and *yin* atmosphere connected with water, darkness, the hidden, and the invisible. Similarly, space is passive *(yin)* in contrast to movement *(yang)* of line produced by the brush *(yang);* but, at the same time, passivity of space, like *wu wei,* represents the kind of indescribable activity pertaining to Heaven, the Spirit, and *Yang,* in relation to which line, as the materialization of brush movement, is *yin.*

The double action of the *Yin* and the *Yang,* on the one hand in conflict as opposites, on the other hand complementary as two halves of the whole *(Tao),* is also translated into principles of tension and balance in composition: in the rendering of perspective, in placing, in drawing, and in tonality of ink and color.

Perspective is rendered by means of line and tones: linear perspective by drawing and placing and aerial perspective by light washes of color or ink. But both types of perspective, attained through technical means, are governed by symbolism, that is, by laws of nature and *Tao,* in contrast to laws of science, which provide the rules of perspective in traditional Western painting. When Wang Wei *(tzu* Mo-chieh), of the VIII century, described in his essay on landscape painting how layers of air, increasing with distance, obscured color, tone, and detail, he not only was observing changes in appearance but, by his description of air and atmosphere, was also noting the action of the *Ch'i* (Heaven's Breath). When he used light washes of aerial perspective, his concern to heighten those effects of distance and vastness of space was influenced by interpretations of distance and space associated with the concept of *Tao* and the *Yin* and *Yang.* Thus rooted, perspective in Chinese painting is primarily a question of idea. The idea of the constant and unceasing interaction of the *Yin* and the *Yang,* of *Tao* in operation, is equivalent to *Ch'i yun* (the circulation of the Vital Force). An expression of it in painting is the term *yuan chin* (far-near, perspective). The movement out of the void of far distance forward into the clarity of middle distance and foreground, and back again, is analogous to the cycle of coming out of *Tao* and returning. The tension and balance set up by far and near, obscure and clear, unseen and seen, are *yin* and *yang.* And the essential element of movement, illustrating the processes of transformation in nature, is further evident in the fact that both painter and spectator move through the painting: the painter draws and paints and the spectator views the results from many points, never from a single position or at one moment of time. Mountains are seen from heights and figures on a level, and the eye travels, ever conscious of depths of distance and vast expanses of sky and mists. The significance of space as the harmony of the Great Void will be examined a little later, since its technical and symbolic importance lay in its powerful, unifying function.

In rendering forms in the distance, Chinese painters traditionally place them on planes above those at close range, the farthest away the highest. This technique may have been derived from the handling of perspective on carved reliefs in early times. A further explanation might be the idea that what is far away is nearer the limitless horizon, the infinity of *Tao,* and therefore more elevated than forms on earth clearly visible to the spectator. As Wang Wei pointed out, what was far in the distance was wrapped in more layers of *Ch'i,* and therefore belonged above.

Painters also speak of sequence and rhythm in composition, using such terms as *k'ai ho* (open-together) and *ch'i fu* (rise-fall), which refer to skill in arrangement, placing, connecting, and balancing. The terms are also descriptive of movement, of the *Yin* and *Yang,* the exhalation and inhalation of the *Ch'i.* They imply whole cycles of change, of growth and decay, of the eternal rhythm of nature. Connective strokes or sections of the composition—including spaces, eloquent in their "emptiness"—used to relate two parts of a picture are called *lung mo* (dragon veins), suggesting immense power of integration.

The application of the *Yin* and *Yang* extends to the placing of details and to interpretations in terms of human relationships. To give only one or two instances: in the painting of bamboos, an important consideration is the placing of some leaves "withdrawing" and "conceding" to others in front or pushing forward; in the drawing of the two parts forming the knot of a bamboo stem, the lower "supports" the upper; in painting two trees, a large one and a small, they are described as old and young, standing together but observing their proper ceremonial positions and attitudes, and a similar analogy is used for a large rock surrounded by child rocks. The relationships of prince and ministers and of host and guests are often applied, for instance, to the main peak among a group of mountains. Thus, ritual attitudes representing reciprocal and co-operative relationships aimed at general harmony are an important basic element of a picture. Such associations are numerous; but the vitality of the single natural forms and their places in a composition are never lost sight of, for the aim in painting them is *chen* (trueness) and *tzu jan* (naturalness). Another term, *shih* (living quality), is closely related to these two qualities. It is used frequently in Parts II and III of the Manual, often in connection with another *shih* (structural integration); both are sometimes translated as "power." [13] *Shih* (living quality)

[13] See Appendix, Sec. VI, for the two *shih.*

describes substance, actuality, realness; while *shih* (structural integration) has the sense of authority and power and is used also to connote "form," "style," and "integration." In the sense of "integration" it is related to *ku fa* (bone-means, structure), a term often used for mountains as the backbone or bone structure of a landscape painting, and also for the unity of the composition as a whole and living organism.

Perhaps the most important factor in unifying and harmonizing all the elements of a picture is space. As that which contained everything in nature, the receptive, *yin* aspect of *Tao* is emphasized. As space is filled with *Ch'i,* the Spirit or Vital Force, it also has its *yang* aspect. It is this concept that makes the handling of space the most original contribution of Chinese painting and the most exhilarating aspect of the works themselves. While innumerable quotations could be cited from the Chinese literature of early periods, in particular the Taoist, to show how space was regarded as an equivalent of *Tao,* it was mainly the influence of Ch'an or Zen Buddhism that led to the supreme statements about *Tao* in the works of the Southern Sung painters, and in particular the landscapists. In the handling of vast space, their ink paintings are some of the greatest expressions of the human spirit. Where the Northern Sung painters excelled in height, in towering mountain peaks rich in detail, conveying an impression of the magnificence and multiplicity of nature, the Southern Sung painters merged the details in mists, obliterated them in space, and emphasized by depth of distances the silent majesty of nature and the mystery of *Tao.* Both styles of painting lifted the spectator from the earth into liberating space. Both were virtually maps of the cosmos, for underlying philosophical ideas inspired these sublime views of nature. The great oceans on these maps were space, the perfect symbol of which was merely the blank silk or paper, and in many instances space was so represented in paintings. By the directness and purity of this device, the awareness of space was made more acute and its effects more profound. It should be added, however, that the effectiveness of blank spaces was achieved only through contrast with the vitality of the brushwork that rendered the forms it surrounded. Brushwork devoid of expressive power fails to contribute meaning to space and spoils the painting as an integrated statement of the unity and harmony of nature. A striking example of the fluctuations of the *Yin* and *Yang* is presented in the contrast between the eternalness of space depicted by the "absence of brush and ink" and the temporal, passing quality of that which was drawn and painted: the permanence of space and the transience of the substantial. To carry the *Yin-Yang* interpretation still further, space as it was rendered in the best of Chinese painting might be described as a spiritual solid.

The ideas about pictorial space are taken from the sources of Chinese thought. In Chapter XII of the *Chuang Tzu,* for instance, it is stated: "At the Great Beginning there was Non-Being. . . ." This Non-Being was described as "emptiness *(hsu* and *k'ung)*"; and *"Tao* abides in emptiness." By analogy, "to a mind that is still the whole universe surrenders." [14] An amplification was given in the following passage: "Maintain the unity of your will. Do not listen with ears, but with the mind. Do not listen with the mind, but with the spirit *(ch'i).* The function of the ear ends with hearing; that of the mind with symbols or ideas. But the spirit is an emptiness ready to receive all things." [15] A Buddhist term, descriptive of movement and space, expresses this state of receptivity as *k'ai wu* (open-awareness), to apprehend in the deepest and widest sense. By "stilling his heart," that is, shedding the thoughts and emotions of his personal life, an individual can reflect in his heart-mind *(hsin),* or as in a pool or a mirror, as the Taoists described it, the power *(Ch'i)* of *Tao,* the harmony of Heaven and Earth. Hence the phrase "mirrorlike wisdom."

The stillness associated with emptiness of space and *Tao* also is silence, which adds to the mystery of *Tao* and stresses the reserve and meditative habits necessary for the painter to be receptive and able to express any aspect of *Tao.* Silence and emptiness of space possess vast powers of suggestion, stimulating the imagination and sharpening perception. And only through exercise of these highest faculties can *Tao* be apprehended and expressed. At about the time the Manual first appeared, a painter named Yun Shou-p'ing commented that "modern painters apply

---

[14] *Lieh Tzu,* as tr. in Waley, *The Way and Its Power,* p. 58. Also described in *Chuang Tzu,* Ch. XIII.

[15] *Chuang Tzu,* Ch. IV (tr. in Fung, *History,* I, p. 241).

their minds only to brush and ink, whereas the ancients paid attention to the absence of brush and ink (the empty spaces). If one is able to realize how the ancients applied their minds to the absence of brush and ink, one is not far from reaching the divine quality in painting." [16]

In the Great Void of *Tao,* the elements of a picture are represented under certain conditions of season, weather, and time of day. These circumstances set the mood of a painting in accordance with the moods of Heaven or the aspects of *Tao.* Thus there is concern to depict both the symbolic significance of the contents of a picture and their accurate representation. The term *ching* (seasonal aspect, atmosphere) describes this aim. To note and remember the great variety of effects of season and weather, constant observation is necessary: how things grow, their habitats, the stages of their growth; the forms of peaks and rocks, shaped by location and weather; the formation of clouds and mists; the natural groupings of rocks, water, trees, plants, and flowers. All the implications in the aims of *chen* (trueness) and *tzu jan* (naturalness) and *shih* (living quality), summed up in the phrase *sheng tung* (life-movement), must be kept in mind.

The mood of a painting is a natural and unifying factor of great importance. And the harmony achieved by skillful rendering of forms and details under specific conditions is reinforced by the harmony of *Ch'i,* the Breath of *Tao* that permeates space and forms. Rain, sunshine, heat, cold, and wind are still called the Five *Ch'i* or breaths. They represent different forms of *Ch'i,* whether explained in ancient expressions about the inhalation and exhalation of the *Ch'i* or in meteorological terms describing changes in air pressure owing to the action of heat and cold. The terms used in weather reports are, in fact, rather apt descriptions of the operation of the *Ch'i.*

Wind as a tangible and direct manifestation of the *Ch'i* is described in the *I Ching* as a force of Heaven visibly stirring life. One sees why bamboos in the wind are a favorite subject of painting. Landscapes and individual plants, trees, and flowers have, however, been painted under all sorts of conditions. These conditions, the result of changes in the seasons *(yang-*spring-summer

[16] Tr. in Sirén, *The Chinese on Painting,* p. 199.

and *yin*-autumn-winter), also contribute to the expression of seasonal change in paintings, although with characteristic flexibility. Rain, mist, dew, frost, and snow, being related to water, are *yin* conditions; yet rain from Heaven can also be *yang*—in the *Su Wen,* an ancient treatise on medicine, rain is "the perspiration of the *Yang.*" Heaven-sent rain brings to mind the symbol of the dragon, in turn associated with thunder, clouds, and lightning. Masterpieces of dragons were direct representations of the power of Heaven arousing life with rolls of thunder and flashes of lightning through thick clouds, dispensing its power by wind and nourishing rain. In landscape paintings, the dragon itself is invisible but the weather suggests its presence.

The awe and reverence with which the dragon was regarded were part of the general attitude toward nature. Acceptance of what seems natural and inevitable is evident in the observant, reflective, and respectful approach of the masters. It may also be seen in the representation of human beings in paintings, meditative and reverent as they move along a mountain path or stop to gaze at the scene around them, seeming to listen to the rhythm and harmony of life, stilling themselves in order to be in tune with it. In discussing the forms of such figures and of other objects in paintings, painters refer to *hsing* (form, shape) and *hsiang* (likeness, symbol), and extensions of these terms such as *hsiang hsing* (formal resemblance), *hsing ssu* (formal likeness), and *hsing chuang* (outline of form). In the oldest written sources, *hsing* and *hsiang* were used to denote "symbols," in connection with divination. When they came to mean the "forms" in paintings, they retained some of their earlier sense of "semblances" and "emblems," which nicely defined their function in a composition. As symbols, their outer appearance and their positions and attitudes are drawn in conformity with what is called "the directing idea" *(li i).* The term represents a stage in rationalizing the aim embodied in the First Canon, and it reveals the influence of the gentlemen-painters and the literary men who dominated Chinese painting. They were the leading painters and also the critics, for they set the standards and formed taste. They upheld very high standards, but they seem always to have had a strong tendency to intellectualize concepts. Maintaining the focus of the harmony of Heaven and Earth, "the directing idea" summarizes ideas expressed in the terms *li* (principle, essence), *i* (idea, conception), *ssu* (thought, the selective faculty), and the Confucian *li* (rituals and the sense of fitness).

Li (principle) has the meaning of "reason" and "law." The composition of the character, by its representation of the grain or markings on jade or the thread of a pattern, shows this to be "inner law and constant principle"; in use, it was in many ways similar to the *Ch'i*. For the *Ch'i* is constant while the *ch'i* is variable. The philosopher Chu Hsi raised the term *li* to a position of such prominence that painters declared it the most important thing in painting. One or two examples will show its application to painting. Su Tung-p'o, poet, painter, and critic, in praising the masterpieces of bamboo painting by his friend Wen T'ung, declared that he had genuinely succeeded in transmitting the soul *(li)* of the bamboo. In a colophon, Su remarked that craftsmen could represent form *(hsing)* but only painters of surpassing ability could fathom the Essence *(li)* and understand the law *(li)* behind the form.[17] Numerous other painters and critics in the Sung and later periods made similar statements. To them *li,* as inner law and Essence, was of deeper import than appearance and outer form. Yet the two aspects were mutually dependent. A recent essay on embryology offers a remarkably appropriate comment here: "Form is both deeply material and highly spiritual. It cannot exist without a material support; it cannot be properly expressed without invoking some supramaterial principle."[18] This was the essential point Chinese painters were trying to make when they seemed to be separating aspects that were not separable, for their concern was to guard against both the neglect of the idea, which gave life to the form, and the neglect of the form, which alone could convey the idea. The complementary nature of the two aspects may be clarified by applying the *Yin-Yang* interpretation. Moreover, the conception of thinking as the function of the heart-mind *(hsin)* explains how these terms denoting principle, thought, and idea stand for results of both reasoning and intuition. Painting, guided by the heart-mind through the means of

[17.] Clark, *The Prose-Poetry of Su Tung-p'o*, p. 10: a reproduction of a specimen of Su's calligraphy, with translation.

[18.] Dalcq, "Form and Modern Embryology," in *Aspects of Form*, p. 91.

skillful handling of brush and ink, should thus exhibit thought and reflection, sensibility and intuition. And it is the proper balance of these factors that can produce the harmonious results worthy of being described as expressions of the harmony of Heaven and Earth.

It is hardly necessary to add that harmony does not mean sameness. The goal of a state of general harmony is, as the *Chung Yung* puts it, "the great way for the Great Society," and when the equilibrium of Heaven and Earth is maintained, everything would then be in proper position; all creatures would be nourished. Harmony is creative, sameness is sterile. In painting, harmony of all the elements and ideas in a composition produces general harmony, and by "spiritual influence" it can inspire and sustain the desire and effort to achieve it. Thus painting may present the felicitous results of perfect rhythm and harmony, offering clues to the secret of life itself for those able to discern them. Sameness in painting, resulting from monotonous or imitative brushwork and mere copying of themes, produces only lifelessness. The difference between harmony and sameness is effectively illustrated by the following passage in the *Tso Chuan:* "Harmony is like soup. There being water, heat, sour flavoring and pickles, salt and peaches, with a bright fire of wood, the cook harmonizing all the ingredients in the cooking of the fish and flesh. . . , if water be used to help out water, who could eat it?" [19]

In discussing the terms and concepts of Chinese painting, the necessary (yet never quite adequate) explanations tend inevitably to emphasize the intellectual content. This aspect was, of course, only one part; the primary focus was on the realm of the spirit, which is well known to be elusive and almost impossible to put into words. Nevertheless, some notion of the spiritual direction of Chinese painting has perhaps emerged from the foregoing exploration. And a sense of the inner power in Chinese painting may perhaps also be gained by a closer look at brushwork, the direct means of expression. The basic strokes and methods *(fa)* of combining them are demonstrated in the *Chieh Tzu Yuan,* and its examples and instructions illustrate the close relationship between painting and calligraphy. The Manual, however, pro-

[19] Tr. in Fung, *The Spirit of Chinese Philosophy,* p. 107.

ceeds on the assumption that the attitudes and views about painting and calligraphy are well known. A closer look may therefore
be useful, particularly as the ties between painting, calligraphy,
and also poetry had a fundamental effect on brushwork. Indeed,
they made brushwork the characteristic feature of Chinese painting and one of the most important contributions of this *tao* of
painting to the language of painting in general.

From the days of their common origin, painting and writing
have been allied arts. When the brush and ink came into general
use, the relationship amounted to identification. The two arts
use the same equipment and share aims, technique, and standards. Painters speak of painting and writing as fundamentally
the same, and of styles of brushwork in terms of calligraphy,
and they often use the word *hsieh* (to write) in place of *hua* (to
paint). The handling of space, the simplification of brushstrokes
to the bare essential, and the symbolism of painting are equivalent to the aims and manner of expression in poetry, which, with
a few characters in short poems, imply a wealth of thought and
underlying meaning. It is often said that a well-written character is an artistic thought. The terms for the two main styles of
painting are directly related to styles of writing: *kung pi* (finished
brushwork), which might literally be transcribed "labored brushwork," describes the precise and detailed painting style that is
the equivalent of *k'ai shu* (formal or model writing); *hsieh i*
("write idea" or freehand style) is like *ts'ao shu* ("grass" writing).

From the method of learning to write the practice of copying
was borrowed. The accepted types of copying in painting illustrate the progressive stages of writing. For the three ways of
copying are tracing, faithful reproduction, and interpretation of
the model; the purpose is to learn brushstrokes, methods, and
certain recurrent designs in composition. This practice has preserved and transmitted many styles and designs that otherwise
might have been lost, and in this respect sustained the *tao* of
painting. Copying is a proved way of acquiring the necessary
technical means of expression and, for many, a helpful step-
pingstone to creative results. There were, however, obvious pit-
falls. Painters and critics were well aware of them, for again and
again their essays and comments warned against imitative brush-

work and the fatal habit of overreliance on copying. Su Tung-p'o, who scorned the practice, was said to have described it as groveling in the dust. Nevertheless, only the truly great painters were strong enough to break from traditional methods and styles to originate their own manner of expression and inaugurate new schools of style.

There is an aspect of copying that should be mentioned, for copies and reproductions of calligraphy became available at quite an early date, were widely popular, and led to some significant results. The meaning of the characters was often not understood and often they were not even read, but appreciation of brushwork was markedly increased by the dissemination of such examples. The consequent sharpening of sensibility must have been considerable. The spread of such examples of brushwork contributed to an awareness and esteem of painting and calligraphy on a popular scale far exceeding the limits of the relatively small scholarly and literary groups who created the works and formulated the standards. And this particular kind of appreciation, broad in extent with a finely developed core of cultivated discernment, accounts largely for the refined taste generally ascribed to Chinese civilization. It has, in fact, been remarked of Chinese painting that it has a long and vigorous tradition, a vague aesthetic, and a great deal of taste. The age and continuity of the tradition is well known, and the present inquiry into the ideas of Chinese painting serves to show that what seemed to be vagueness and a lack of an aesthetic system was due to the way painters and critics endlessly discussed a few basic concepts without attempting to arrange them formally. They recognized, however, that an understanding of them was essential; and out of the thought, discussion, and constant examination devoted to the principles emerged the ideals, high standards, and pattern of discipline that produced works with the quality known as taste.

Quality of brushwork has always been the basis of judging both painting and calligraphy. Discussions of it speak of the strokes as muscles, bones, flesh, and *ch'i*. Muscles refer to the short and sinewy strokes, bones to the longer and firm ones, flesh to the rise and fall of the rhythm of their forms and connecting strokes, and the *ch'i* is of course the essential quality of spirit productive of life-movement *(sheng tung)*. Attention is directed to the particular degree of pressure of the brush and the manner of applying the ink in strokes thick or thin, rugged or delicate, light or dark, dry or moist. The way strokes are joined is also noted, and their speed and direction. Such points explain why Shih T'ao remarked that painting and writing "are not small *tao*."

The brush is held in a vertical position, and no part of the hand touches the paper or silk. Controlled flexibility of the wrist is therefore of great importance, and can be attained only after constant and intensive practice. Experience in handling the brush usually comes in the course of learning to write and in its subsequent daily use. When the brush is applied in painting, the habit of practicing the strokes is still indispensable to attaining skill and ease. The emphasis on brushstrokes led to the preference for line and to the attention given to linear rhythm. Line is the primary means of expressing movement. Line in relation to space creates rhythm in the composition and also represents the inner rhythm and harmony of the *yang* line on the *yin* paper, of *yang* expression across *yin* space, of light *(yang)* and dark *(yin)* tones in the line itself. Full appreciation of Chinese painting thus depends a great deal on the spectator's sensibility to the tempo of the brush, following it with eye and imagination as it dots, flicks, or moves forward, sweeping, turning, lifting, plunging, thinning out, swelling, sometimes stopping abruptly, sometimes crouching to leap again. It has often been remarked that the brush dances and the ink sings. Calligraphy at its finest and most expressive is indeed the dance of the brush and ink at its highest point of achievement, when movement, vitality, rhythm, and harmony are uppermost and the intellectual content of the written characters purposely is abandoned in the swift rendering of them by the perfectly disciplined and therefore completely free brush. Absolutely natural and spontaneous *(tzu jan)* brushwork is like the flight of a bird. And works of calligraphy of this caliber might truly be described as the prime examples of abstract art.

The nature of the soft brush and ink does not permit correcting, changing, or retracing a stroke without marring the effect of the whole picture. The hand has to be sure, and co-ordination of "heart and hand" is essential. As expressed in the Manual, "each brushstroke should be a living idea." Brushwork is thus the direct expression of the mind in action. Its function is to make visible the invisible. The power to do this is often referred to as *pi li* (brush strength), a term embracing skill and dexterity and, of equal if not greater importance, the mental and spiritual motivation. It is noteworthy that, in explaining brushstrokes for modeling, the Manual opens that section with the statement: "He who is learning to paint must first learn to still his heart, thus to clarify his understanding and increase his wisdom." And painters pointed out that, when painting is guided by the heart *(hsin,* the heart-mind), the principle of the circulation of Heaven and Earth *(Tao)* is revealed and the *tao* of painting is made manifest.

"Stilling the heart" expresses beautifully the quietness necessary for creative results, an inner quietness related to the silence of *Tao* and its processes. Taoist writings describe it as similar to the stillness of deep waters reflecting *Tao* on their smooth, mirrorlike surface; they also equate stillness with the clarity of the heart-mind rid of *ssu yu* (egotism), a state analogous to the emptiness and purity of the space that was the Great Void of *Tao*. And just as the *Ch'i* of *Tao* permeates the whole universe, so the *ch'i* can fill the stillness of the undistracted heart-mind and hence the whole being. The practice of meditation and of exercises in deep and controlled breathing have as their end the stilling of the heart. In the *Chuang Tzu* may be found this pertinent passage: "The pure men of old slept without dreams, and waked without anxiety. They ate without discrimination, breathing deep breaths. For pure men draw breath from their uttermost depths; the vulgar only from their throats." [20]

In stilling the heart an individual can become one with the elements of nature, the great creative forces of *Tao*. This becoming one is the true meaning of wholeness. In painting, this goal is translated into the aim of the painter to identify himself with the object depicted, that is, to relate that in himself with that in

[20] Tr. Giles, *Chuang Tzu,* p. 69.

all things which shared the Oneness of *Tao.* "Becoming one with the universe" is the literal connotation of the character *ch'an* of Zen (i.e., Ch'an), which is shown in the Appendix: it is composed of *tan* (one, singleness) and *shih* (sun, moon, and stars hanging from Heaven, hence the universe). The same *tan* character is used in the term *tan se hua* (one-color painting), referring to ink monochrome and stressing the expression of one flash of comprehension of *Tao,* the Sudden Enlightenment of Taoism and Buddhism.[21] Identity with the object depicted might be explained in another way: the painter has to experience the rhythm of life to be able to express it in his work by means of the rhythm of the brush. And it may be deduced that "to clarify understanding and increase wisdom" means a contemplative attention to all things and to all of nature's changes in order gradually to gain a sense of the permanent and significant. The brush will then be swift and sure, setting down only the essential strokes, in some places expressing by "absence of brush and ink." Painters summed up this power in the phrase *i tao pi pu tao* (idea present, brush may be spared performance). In the style called freehand or free-sketch painting *(hsieh i,* write idea), this kind of brushwork is often carried out by sweeping strokes of a fairly dry brush that leaves the paper or silk showing within the strokes or by deliberate breaks in the stroke that yet do not interrupt the continuity of the idea. Such results are possible only after the painter has reached an advanced stage of cultivation and technical skill, the stage at which rules and methods are no longer consciously applied but are implicit in the results. It is the stage when the *ch'i* of the painter is effortlessly transmitted through the painting. In one respect, it might be described as the stage at which his whole personality is revealed in a painting, since the co-ordination of brushstrokes and of the composition is a direct expression of his character. Such an interpretation, however, misses the vital point: that all the steps of the painter's arduous training, all his accumulation of all the means

[21.] The aim of ink painting and its brevity and directness of expression, which has "color" and does not need colors, is well summed up by a statement in the *Li Chi:* "Acts of the greatest reverence admit of no ornament."—Bk. VIII, Sec. I, 14 (tr. Legge).

available, all his efforts in the long process of his development of the self, should be directed by the concept of *Tao* and so be ritual acts sanctifying the painting that he produces. Then the tactility of brushwork is evidence less of the personal touch than of the power of *Tao*. The anonymity of the ritual act is, in effect, oneness with *Tao*. And painting is not self-expression but an expression of the harmony of *Tao*.

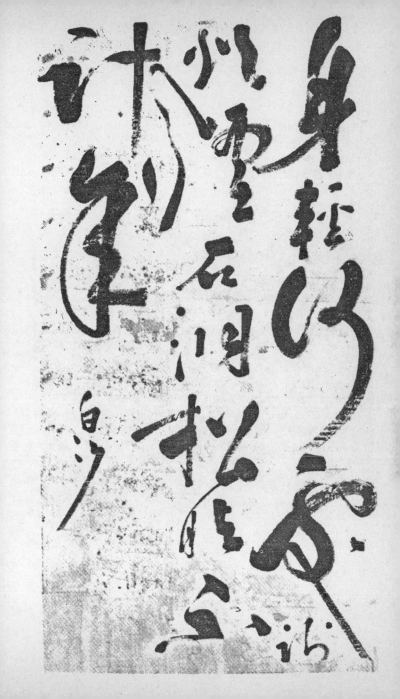

PART TWO

SELECTIONS FROM THE
CHIEH TZU YUAN HUA CHUAN
(MUSTARD SEED GARDEN
MANUAL OF PAINTING)

PREFACE TO THE FIRST (1679) EDITION[1]

PEOPLE nowadays enjoy looking at landscape paintings as much as at the scenery itself. Panels of screens offer countless vistas, scrolls and albums spread before us a variety of scenes—distant hills, plains, blue-green mountain peaks, and murmuring brooks. At one moment a landscape may appear overcast with mist and clouds, at another the view emerges clear and fair. Or one may find oneself by a spring of pure flowing water, ready to set out over hills and ravines, free to roam without having to wax one's sandals or take up a bamboo staff.

It is one thing, however, to look at pleasant pictures painted by other people and another matter entirely to paint such pictures. Appreciating the works of others, one is essentially a spectator receiving impressions; whereas, in painting pictures, the conception originates from the deepest recesses of the heart. There is this significant difference in the approach to landscape painting.

All my life I have loved landscape painting, but it has been the pleasure of looking at other people's work, for I myself can-

[1] Part I of the Manual. With Parts II and III, the complete work appeared in 1701. This is a foreword typical of such remarks by an intellectual of Ch'ing times, expressing conventional sentiments imitating the Ming critics. It is, nevertheless, an amiable promoting of the Manual. Of greater value today, the preface describes the circumstances that brought the work into existence, gave it its title, and its original format; Li Yu also confirms that Wang Kai, *tzu* An-chieh, was the author and illustrator of Part I, and not Li Yu himself as has often been stated. The work done by Wang's brothers and others on Parts II and III is explained in the preface to this study.

not paint. In the past, when I used to travel, I often met painters, men who had followed in the footsteps of Mo-chieh and Ch'ang-k'ang,[2] who kindly let me discuss with them the *Tao* in painting. When, however, I began to ask questions, they would knit their brows and declare: "It is easy to appreciate the idea of *Tao* but quite another matter to give it form."

I have been ill now for the past year and unable to travel, being confined to sitting or lying in my room, shut off from all activities. Fortunately I have paintings and so can unroll whole landscapes on my table. They are here before me even while I eat or sleep. I enjoy this kind of wandering while at rest. It has prompted me to write on one of these scrolls: "Many walled cities under my roof, many landscapes before my eyes." In my solitude I have regretted not having the knowledge and ability to write about this branch of the Seven Manifestations.

This thought was in my mind one day when I was talking with my son-in-law, Yin-po,[3] and I said to him: "Painting is an ancient art. How is it that there are excellent treatises on the painting of figures, birds, animals, flowers, and plants, yet the most important category, landscape, seems to have been neglected? Do you suppose that most of us can only enjoy looking at landscape paintings?—that, while we may understand the idea of *Tao* in painting, it is really impossible for us to be more definite about it? Is it true, do you suppose, that landscape painters through the centuries have purposely guarded this secret among themselves?"

Thereupon, Yin-po brought out an album. "This has been in our family for many generations," he said.

At the sight of the album my curiosity was aroused. On examining it carefully, I found that it contained copious examples of the methods of individual masters of various schools of (landscape) painting. I particularly noted the comments and their calligraphic style, for they seemed to bear the touch of Ch'ang-heng,[4] of our family. At the end of the album were two seals, inscribed "Li Family Collection" and "Liu-fang," which

---

[2] The two great masters, Wang Wei (c. 698–759) and Ku K'ai-chih (c. 344–406).
[3] Shen Hsin-yu, publisher of the Manual.
[4] Li Liu-fang (1575–1629).

confirmed my impression that the album was compiled by Ch'ang-heng.

Since the album was a record of a private collection, the material and its arrangement were not suitable for a manual of painting. Just then, however, Yin-po brought out another album and smilingly explained: "When I was living at the Mustard Seed Garden in Nanking, I commissioned Wang An-chieh to rearrange, enlarge, and edit the whole work, an arduous task. Finally, after three years, he completed the work."

Eagerly I took up the album and examined it. I could not help applauding the whole and each of its parts, stopping here and there to sigh with admiration. The plan of the book included the original forty-three pages, to which had been added detailed instructions on the painting of trees and branches, including methods of dotting leaves and of drawing mountain ranges, peaks, rivers, and waterfalls, as well as banks, slopes, rocks, bridges, paths, palaces, houses, boats, and carts. Wang An-chieh, in moments of leisure, had copied out the whole work, enlarging and rearranging it to a total of one hundred and thirty-three pages. He included examples of the styles of many of the masters and of every important school of painting. Furthermore, to aid the beginner, he added forty pages of text on brushwork and the handling of ink tones, composition and perspective. Following the instructions in this book, one might eventually paint a picture of what hitherto had been locked in one's imagination—could produce results, as it were, with a few twists of the wrist. Would it not be a pity to hide this wonderful book from the world? I have been most anxious to see it published so that generation after generation of those who love to look at landscapes may also learn to appreciate landscape painting and, moreover, may not only read the Manual but also try to paint. For, as the saying goes, thus may ten thousand miles be illustrated in a foot, and one may wander in a landscape while actually at rest and never have to go any distance.

Written on the third day after the summer solstice in the Chi Wei cycle, the eighteenth year of the reign of K'ang Hsi (1679), by Li-weng (Fisherman of the Lake) Li Yu at Ts'eng Yuan in Wu-shan.

DISCUSSION OF THE
FUNDAMENTALS OF PAINTING

Lu Ch'ai [1] says:

Among those who study painting some strive for an elaborate effect and others prefer the simple. Neither complexity in itself nor simplicity is enough. Some aim to be deft, others to be laboriously careful. Neither dexterity nor conscientiousness is enough. Some set great value on method; others pride themselves on dispensing with method. To be without method is deplorable, but to depend entirely on method is worse.

You must learn first to observe the rules faithfully; afterwards, modify them according to your intelligence and capacity. The end of all method is to seem to have no method.

Among the masters, it was a different matter. Ku K'ai-chih applied his colors sprinkling and splashing, and the grass and flowers seemed to grow at the movement of his hand. Han Kan, whose picture *The Yellow Horse* was unique, used to meditate before he painted, and his brush was inspired. At a later stage, therefore, one may choose either to proceed methodically or to paint seemingly without method.

First, however, you must work hard. Bury the brush again and again in the ink and grind the inkstone to dust. Take ten days to paint a stream and five to paint a rock. Eventually you

[1] Pseudonym used in the Manual by the author-compiler, Wang Kai. The names of the masters and critics mentioned in this opening "book," and throughout the Manual, represent the affirming and transmitting of the tradition; often, in the original, only a surname appears, or one of several names used by a painter, and at times only part of one of these names. In this translation, for clarity and ease in reading, the full name by which a master is now generally known is used. Other names adopted by the various painters are given in the Index, with dates or periods.

may try to paint the landscape at Chialing. Li Ssu-hsun took months to paint it; Wu Tao-tzu did it in one evening. Thus, at a later stage, one may proceed slowly and carefully or one may rely on dexterity.

Above all, learn to hold in your thoughts the Five Peaks. Do not concentrate on the whole ox.[2] Study ten thousand volumes and walk ten thousand miles. Clear the standards set by Tung Yuan and Chu-jan and pass straightway into the mansions of Ku K'ai-chih and Cheng Fa-shih. Follow Ni Yun-lin painting in the style of Wang Wei: when he painted, mountains soared and springs flowed, waters ran clear and forests spread vast and lonely. Be like Kuo Chung-shu, who with one stroke of the brush released a kite on a hundred-foot string, who painted with equal facility the large and the small—towers and many-storied buildings as easily as the hair of oxen and the thread of a silkworm. Thus, at a later stage, an elaborate effect is acceptable and a simple one is equally acceptable.

If you aim to dispense with method, learn method. If you aim at facility, work hard. If you aim for simplicity, master complexity.

Finally, there are the Six Canons, the Six Essentials, the Six Qualities, the Three Faults, and the Twelve Things To Avoid. How can one disregard them?

THE SIX CANONS

In the Southern Ch'i period (479–501) Hsieh Ho said:

Circulation of the *Ch'i* (Breath, Spirit, Vital Force of Heaven) produces life-movement.

Brush creates structure.

According to the object draw its form.

According to the nature of the object apply color.

Organize composition with the elements in their proper places.

In copying, seek to pass on the essence of the masters' methods.

---

[2] The focus of achievement is nothing less than what is symbolized by the Five Sacred Mountains, marking the harmony of the universe, and by analogy, microcosmically, the outer and inner harmony of man. The ox story from the Taoist work, *Chuang Tzu*, refers to Prince Hui's cook, whose skill as a butcher attained to an art; that is, the work of the mind rather than of the eye. To these two points, concerned primarily with the cultivation of inner resources, are added exhortations to acquire knowledge and technique, and to observe the ways of nature, toward enrichment of the spirit.

(Lu Ch'ai, citing one school of thought, adds:) All but the First Canon can be learned and practiced to the point of true accomplishment. As for the ability to make manifest aspects of the *Ch'i*, the Spirit, one has to be born with that gift.

THE SIX ESSENTIALS AND THE SIX QUALITIES

In the Sung period, Liu Tao-ch'un said:

First Essential: Action of the *Ch'i* and powerful brushwork go together.

Second Essential: Basic design should be according to tradition.

Third Essential: Originality should not disregard the *li* (the principles or essence) of things.

Fourth Essential: Color (if used) should enrich.

Fifth Essential: Brush should be handled with *tzu jan* (spontaneity).

Sixth Essential: Learn from the masters but avoid their faults.

First Quality: to display brushstroke power with good brushwork control.

Second Quality: To possess sturdy simplicity with refinement of true talent.

Third Quality: To possess delicacy of skill with vigor of execution.

Fourth Quality: To exhibit originality, even to the point of eccentricity, without violating the *li* of things.

Fifth Quality: In rendering space by leaving the silk or paper untouched, to be able nevertheless to convey nuances of tone.

Sixth Quality: On the flatness of the picture plane, to achieve depth and space.

THE THREE FAULTS

In the Sung period, Kuo Jo-hsu said:

The Three Faults all are connected with the handling of the brush.

The first is described as "boardlike", referring to the stiffness of a weak wrist and a sluggish brush. Shapes of objects become flat and thin, lacking in solidity.

The second is described as "carving," referring to the labored movement of the brush caused by hesitation. Heart and hand are not in accord. In drawing, the brush is awkward.

The third is described as "knotted," referring to the knotted effect when the brush seems to be tied, or in some way hindered from moving freely, and lacks pliancy.

THE TWELVE THINGS TO AVOID

In the Yuan period, Jao Tzu-jan said:

The first thing to avoid is a crowded, ill-arranged composition.

The second, far and near not clearly distinguished.

The third, mountains without *Ch'i,* the pulse of life.

The fourth, water with no indication of its source.

The fifth, scenes lacking any places made inaccessible by nature.

The sixth, paths with no indication of beginning or end.

The seventh, stones and rocks with one face.

The eighth, trees with less than four main branches.

The ninth, figures unnaturally distorted.

The tenth, buildings and pavilions inappropriately placed.

The eleventh, atmospheric effects of mist or clearness neglected.

The twelfth, color applied without method.

A GENERAL LIST OF THE BRUSHSTROKES USED FOR MODELING[3]

He who is learning to paint must first learn to still his heart, thus to clarify his understanding and increase his wisdom. He should then begin to study the basic brushstroke technique of one school.

[3] To offer intact as much as possible of the discussion on technique and the equipment of painting, five short sections of mainly historical notes preceding this on brushstrokes are omitted. The terms describing standards of merit, the division into Northern and Southern Schools, the names of Great Masters and several of the scholars and connoisseurs listed, in fact appear later in the Manual. The fifth section, Important Changes, is a condensation based on early records. Briefly, in figure painting, between the IV and VIII centuries, a greater plasticity was evident in the modeling and freer brushwork in drawing figures and objects. The changes in landscape painting are more difficult to trace through the mere listing of names: emphasis is placed in contrasting the Northern School's detailed manner with color with the Southern School's free brushstroke style in ink. Actually, greater innovations appeared with the rise of the gentlemen-painters and their impressionistic works in ink, when, for instance, Mi Fei produced his individual style of layers of dotting or daubing brushstrokes.

He should be sure that he is learning what he set out to learn, and that heart and hand are in accord. After this, he may try miscellaneous brushstrokes of other schools and use them as he pleases. He will then be at a stage when he himself may set up the matrix in the furnace and, as it were, cast in all kinds of brushstrokes, of whatever schools and in whatever proportion he chooses. He himself may become a master and the founder of a school. At this later stage, it is good to forget the classifications and to create one's own combinations of brushstrokes. At the beginning, however, the various brushstrokes should not be mixed.

Here, briefly, is a general list of brushstrokes used for modeling *(ts'un):*

P'i ma ts'un: brushstrokes like spread-out hemp fibers
Luan ma ts'un: brushstrokes like entangled hemp fibers
Chih ma ts'un: brushstrokes like sesame seeds
Ta fu p'i ts'un: brushstrokes like big ax cuts
Hsiao fu p'i ts'un: brushstrokes like small ax cuts
Yun t'ou ts'un: brushstrokes like cloud heads
Yu tien ts'un: brushstrokes like raindrops
T'an wo ts'un: brushstrokes like an eddy or whirlpool
Ho yeh ts'un: brushstrokes like the veins of a lotus leaf
Fan t'ou ts'un: brushstrokes like lumps of alum
K'u lou ts'un: brushstrokes like skull bones
Kuei p'i ts'un: brushstrokes like the wrinkles on a devil's face
Chieh so ts'un: brushstrokes like raveled rope
Luan ch'ai ts'un: brushstrokes like brushwood
Niu mao ts'un: brushstrokes like hair of cattle
Ma ya ts'un: brushstrokes like horses' teeth

There also are combinations: spread-out hemp fiber strokes with dotting strokes like raindrops, and veins-of-lotus strokes with the ax-cut strokes.

EXPLANATION OF TERMS

Applying the brush with light ink, around and around, stroke by stroke, is called *wua* (revolving); using the tip of the brush obliquely is called *ts'un* (brushstrokes for modeling or "wrinkles").

Applying three or four light ink washes is termed *hsuan* (wash). An ink wash soaking the whole painting is called *hua* (cleansing).

Holding the brush upright for horizontal or vertical strokes is called *tsu* (grasping); holding the brush upright and using the pointed tip is called *cho* (pulling up).

Applying the tip of the brush is called *tien* (dotting). This is used in painting *jen wu* (figures and things), and also for mosses and leaves. Outlining with the brush is called *hua* (drawing or outlining). This term, for instance, is used for the drawing of buildings and towers, also for the drawing of pine and fir needles.[4]

Applying light washes on the natural color of the silk of a picture, to indicate mists without traces of brushstrokes, is called *jan* (painting or applying a wash). Traces of the brush showing in the painting of clouds or rippling water is called *tzu* (saturating). In painting waterfalls, drawing on the natural color of the silk with dry brush and light ink is called *fen* (dividing or distinguishing).

Using light ink to indicate crevices and hollows on mountains and fissures of tree trunks in order to render their character and essence is called *ch'en* (lining or reinforcing).

USE OF THE BRUSH

The ancients used the expression *yu pi yu mo* (have brush, have ink). Many people do not grasp the significance of the meaning of the two terms *pi* (brush) and *mo* (ink). How can there be painting without brush and without ink?

To know how to outline peaks of a mountain range but not know the strokes for modeling *(ts'un)* is described as *wu pi* (not having brush). To know the strokes but not know how to handle ink tones or indicate the nuances distinguishing near from far, clouds from reflections, light from shadow, is *wu mo* (not having ink).

Wang Ssu-shan said: "He who has command of his brush should not allow the brush to control him."

---

[4] *Hua* originally meant scratching or incising on stone or wood. Later, it was applied to drawing and painting with the soft writing brush, and thus equivalent to *hsieh* (to write).

In general, the following brushes are used in painting:

Hsieh chao pi: crab-claw brush, large and small sizes

Hua jan pi: brush for painting flowers

Lan yu chu pi: brush for painting orchids and bamboo

Brushes used for writing:

T'u hao pi: rabbit's hair brush

Hu ying pi: Hunan sheep's hair brush

Yang hao pi: sheep's hair brush

Hsueh ngo pi: snow-goose brush, made of sheep's hair

Liu t'iao pi: willow-twig brush, made of sheep's hair

Some painters depend on the point of the brush, others on its fullness and flatness. It is a matter of habit. Each has his preference; everyone does not have to hold a brush the same way.

USE OF INK

Li Ch'eng used ink sparingly, as if it were gold. Wang Hsia splashed it liberally in the manner called *p'o mo* (splash ink). Those who study painting should keep in mind the four words *hsi mo p'o mo* (spare ink, splash ink).

Lu Ch'ai adds: In general, old ink is good only for painting on old paper and for copying old paintings, for when the gloss has gone the life is ended. On new silk, gold-leaf paper, or fans, old ink is not as good as new ink, which has brilliance and life. Not that old ink is no good: it simply does not go well with new paper or new silk. New paper and new silk will not easily absorb old ink. The combination is like putting the robes of the ancients on the newly promoted and the newly rich. Or it is like covering a gourd and trying to smell its contents; how could one possibly smell it? That is why I say: Reserve old ink for painting on old paper, new ink for new paper or gold-leaf paper. Above all, paint with confidence and ease, and do not spare the ink.

BRUSHWORK AND COLOR WASHES

In drawing rocks, begin with light ink, so that corrections can easily be made; step by step, more ink can be applied.

Tung Yuan drew many small rocks at the foot of slopes, gradually building up the structure of a lofty mountain. He began by indicating the outline and *ts'un* (brushstrokes for modeling); then, with light ink, he drew in the crevices and hollows. At that stage, color may be used; it should be applied dark and deep in painting rocks. Tung Yuan's brushstrokes in drawing small mountains and rocks were the kind called *fan t'ou ts'un* (brushstrokes like lumps of alum).

Where clouds and mists gather among mountains, washes should be soft and light. Where the ground is sandy, a light ink should be used in sweeping brushstrokes, and breaks in the ground and rocks should be indicated in the manner called *p'o mo* (broken ink).[5]

In painting mountains in summer, just before rain, the brush should be soaking wet and applied freely in a light wash. In modeling the mountains and rocks, use a touch of *lo ch'ing* (snail green) in *fan t'ou* brushstrokes; additional accenting with the same color will bring out an effect of moisture, and the picture will exude freshness. In painting rocks, either snail green or rattan yellow *(t'eng huang)* mixed with ink will also add a deliciously fresh quality.

In painting winter scenes, use the ground of the paper or silk as part of the snow and add light touches of white at the summit of mountains. Then, with heavier touches of white, dot in moss *(tien t'ai)*.

In painting trees, do not use dark or heavy ink. Draw the tree trunks, boughs, and branches without foliage, and the result will be a forest in winter. A light ink wash over the trees will create forests of spring.

In painting mountains, use both light and dark tones. Shadows of clouds will pass over the mountains: where there are shadows there are dark tones, where there are no shadows there will be light and color and brightness. The ink tones should accurately render these differences, and the picture will then express beautifully the rhythm and harmony of clouds and brightness, sun and shadows.

Snow scenes are very often done in a banal manner. But I have seen a snow scene by Li Ch'eng in which peaks, forests, and houses were all drawn with light ink and the surface of the silk

[5] Breaking through flatness to produce forms and depth, distinct from the *p'o mo* (splash ink) method, a wash style dispensing with outline.

138   FROM THE MUSTARD SEED GARDEN MANUAL

was used plain for the water, sky, and empty spaces, with only touches of white, and it was an extraordinary picture.

In beginning a picture of distant mountains, it is advisable to use a stick of charcoal to place them and establish their forms; then, using green mixed with ink, stroke by stroke, pick out the mountains. The first wash for the mountains should be laid with light ink, the next darker, the third ever darker. For the most distant mountains, wrapped in dense clouds, the color is further deepened (i.e. with more ink than color).

In drawing the beams and structure of bridges and houses, draw in lightly with ink and then strengthen the outline. With color or ink, if it is not applied moist and in repeated washes, the tones will be too light and thin.

Wang Meng used little color in his paintings, only umber lightly in a wash on pine trunks and in outlining some angles of rocks; the effect was wonderful.

PLACING THE SKY AND EARTH

When planning a picture, first, before picking up the brush, estimate the proportions of sky and earth. What is meant by the sky and the earth? The top half of a panel is the space for the sky, the lower is for the earth. In the middle space, the scenery of the landscape is organized.

I have seen beginners clutch a brush and scribble over the whole panel. To watch such a procedure hurts the eyes. Immediately one feels that the whole conception is blocked. How can work done in this manner be taken seriously?

AVOIDING THE BANAL

In painting, it is better to be inexperienced (young in *ch'i)* than stupid. It is better to be audacious than commonplace. If the brush is hesitant, it cannot be lively; if commonplace, it most likely will produce only banalities. If one aims to avoid the banal, there is no other way but to study more assiduously both books and scrolls and so to encourage the spirit *(ch'i)* to rise, for when the vulgar and the commonplace dominate, the *ch'i* subsides. The beginner should be hopeful and careful to encourage it to rise.

NOTES ON THE PREPARATION OF COLORS AND
OTHER MATERIALS OF PAINTING

Lu Ch'ai says:

The sky has tinted clouds, glistening like brocade; that is the key to the color of the sky. The earth brings forth grass and trees, all contributing ornamental touches; that is the key to the color of the earth. People have eyes and eyebrows, lips and teeth, clearly defined accents of black, red and white on specific parts of the face; that is the key to the color of human beings. The phoenix spreads its tail, the cock rears his crest, the tiger and leopard proudly display their stripes, and the pheasant preens its beautiful form; such is the key to the color of these creatures.

Ssu-ma Ch'ien, drawing on ancient records, took "color" from these sources and completed his own *Shih Chi* (Historical Records). This might be described as the "color" of scholars. Chang I, the politician, was a great talker and enjoyed argument; he was capable of declaring black white and white black. Itinerant and braggart, he had a mouth that encompassed oceans and seas, and his tongue wagged as he boasted of seeing the curved roofs of mythical cities. Everything he wished people to believe he exaggerated. This might be called the "color" of windbags. Finally, it should concern those who seek "color" in writing and speaking that words and sentences have not only form but also sound.

Ah! Considering the vastness of the heavens and the earth, looking around at people and things, reading polished essays, listening to brave utterances, all these go together and make a whole and colorful world. How can color be said to apply only to painting? Today so many people live in limited and colorless worlds. How may they be offered a fuller life and contentment? Pictures are one means, so let us speak of painting.

After grinding red to powder and softening white, one may produce fine figure paintings; using light green and light yellow, one may create beautiful landscapes. In them, clouds like bands of white silk, sky rose-tinted, peaks dotted blue and green, trees mantled in bright green, red flowers clustered at the mouths of valleys, convey the fact that it is late spring. When yellow leaves drop in front of the cart, one knows that it is late autumn. In one's heart one must be thoroughly acquainted with the *ch'i* of the four seasons[6]—and not only in the heart, for that knowledge must flow to the finger tips to guide the creation of the work. How the Five Colors can brighten men's eyes!

MINERAL BLUE *(shih ch'ing,* AZURITE)

The best kind is called "plum blossom" because of the resemblance in its shape. In figure painting this color may be used quite thick and dark; in landscape, it should be used light and clear.

Take the mineral blue and put it in a bowl; add a little water, drop by drop, and crush it into a fine mixture. Do not grind too hard and make only as much as is needed. Immediately after grinding, pour the mixture into a porcelain bowl; add a little more clear water and stir. Let this stand a while and powder of a very light blue tone will rise to the surface. Skim off this top layer. This blue is called *yu tzu* (oily residue) and is used for painting garments in pictures. The layer of color underneath, the middle layer in the bowl, is a good blue for painting blue-and-green landscapes. The layer of color at the bottom of the bowl is of a very dark tone. Use it for dotting between leaves and on the backs of paintings.

There are these three shades of mineral blue: first blue *(t'ou ch'ing),* second blue *(erh ch'ing),* and third blue *(san ch'ing).*[7]

The light clear blue of the first blue may be used in painting the faces of leaves, the second blue for blue flowers and for accents on the heads and backs of birds, and the dark tones of the third blue for touches among leaves. Generally, in using blue in painting birds and flowers, accenting is done with indigo *(tien hua).* When, however, mineral blue is used, touches of rouge red *(yen chih)* should be added.[8]

[6] The outer aspects of the seasons and their inner significance, involving innumerable analogies about time, change, rhythm and harmony in nature and in man.

[7] Approximately Peking, Watteau, and Beryl blues, according to examples in Maerz and Paul, *A Dictionary of Color* (2nd edn., 1950).

[8] In the original Manual, some notes on colors, pertaining to bird and flower

Mineral blue and mineral green are used for painting on the face of the picture. Sometimes, however, they are also used on the back, giving the painting a wonderful richness.

There is one kind of mineral blue that is difficult to grind. If a little earwax is flicked into the bowl, the color can then quite easily be ground to the consistency of mud. This trick can also be used with ink that has grains in it. The secret was revealed in the Ming work, the *Yen Hsi Yu Shih* (Writings on Secret Matters Collected at a Mountain Retreat).

MINERAL GREEN *(shih lu, MALACHITE)*

To prepare mineral green, proceed as with mineral blue. This green is, however, very hard and may need first to be broken up with a hammer. Then it can be put into a bowl and ground very fine.

There is a kind called *hsia mo pei* (toad's back), and it is the best. It should be ground and dissolved in water.

Mineral green also has three shades: first green *(t'ou lu)*, second green *(erh lu)*, and third green *(san lu)*.[9] All three are used in the same ways as the three blues.

Glue should be mixed with both the blue and the green, though not until just before the colors are to be used. Begin by putting some clear glue and water in a clear saucer or bowl. Add a little water and put over a low fire; slowly it will dissolve. Let it boil a little while, and then skim the glue from the surface. No glue should be left in the blue or the green, because it would ruin the colors. To skim off the glue, use a little boiling water with the glue and color. Place the saucer itself in some boiling water, which must be shallow so as not to overflow into the saucer. Let the water boil a little while. The glue will rise to the rim. In skimming off the top layer of water, the glue also will be removed. When glue has not been completely removed, the blue and green

painting, were added to Part III. In these selections, the instructions about the use of colors in bird and flower painting are incorporated, as in this paragraph, into this main section on colors. The notes on preparing colors, duplicating material here, are omitted.

9. Approximately emerald, serpentine, and a pale Chantilly green.

will lack brilliance. When the colors are to be used again, fresh glue should be added in the manner described.

In bird and flower painting, the dark green can be used only in touches in the background of leaves or grass. The medium green may also be used for this accenting, and with additional touches of grass green *(ts'ao lu)* may be used in painting the king-fisher and on the face of leaves. The light green is best for the backs of leaves. In general, when mineral green is used, grass green should be applied in outlining. When a dark tone of mineral green is used, the grass green should have more blue in it; with a light tone, grass green should have a touch of yellow in it.

VERMILION *(chu sha)*

The best vermilion is the kind called *chien t'ou* (arrowhead), the next best are the kinds called *fu yung k'uai* (hibiscus section) and *p'i sha* (cinnabar grains).

To prepare vermilion: Put a little in a bowl and grind it to fine powder. Mix in a little clear glue. Add a little boiling water and pour into another bowl. Stir. In a little while skim off the top layer, which will be an orange color called *chu piao* (red banner), used in the painting of men's garments. The layer of color underneath is very fine and is the best vermilion. Skim this off and put it aside for the painting of red leaves, terraces, pagodas, and temples. The bottom layer is very deep vermilion. It is used in figure painting but never in landscape.

The middle layer of this vermilion may be used in painting the camellia, pomegranate and most other red flowers, the petals of which should be accented with deep vermilion *(yin chu)*. The bottom layer of dark vermilion should be used only for the back of a painting.

DEEP VERMILION *(yin chu)* [10]

If you do not have any *chu sha* vermilion, a good substitute is *yin chu*. Use the kind called *chu piao* (red banner), which has a touch

[10] The first and lighter layer of vermilion, derived from cinnabar, is called *chu piao*, the red like Satsuma orange; the heavier and lower layer, *chu sha*. Deep vermilion is the equivalent of Goya red or currant.

of yellow in it. It should be dissolved in water before use. This color should never be used in painting the lotus. Painters today add a little white to this vermilion, but one should not do this.

CORAL RED *(san hu mo)*

In T'ang paintings a kind of red was used that has lasted without fading. The color is as bright today as when it was applied. It is called coral red. It was used at the Hsuan Ho Palace for the imperial seals. Although it is a color that is seldom used, one should know about it.

COCK YELLOW *(hsiung huang)* [11]

The best kind of this yellow is that called *chi kuan huang* (coxcomb yellow). It is prepared in the same way as *chu sha* vermilion. It is used in painting yellow leaves and people's clothing. It should never be used on gold-leaf paper. If used on gold-leaf, the paper will in a few months look burned and the color vile.

This yellow may be used in painting golden flowers, but it should be noted that the tones will later change. Rattan yellow *(t'eng huang)* serves equally well and, with touches of vermilion, will give the same effect of a golden yellow.

MINERAL YELLOW *(shih huang)* [12]

This color is not often used in landscape painting, although the ancients occasionally used a little of it. The *Ni Ku Lu* (Notes on Ancient Household Arts) states: "To prepare mineral yellow, put a little water in a bowl and cover with a piece of old matting. Place the bowl on a charcoal fire until the water simmers. Wait until the yellow is as red as the fire, then take it out and place it covered on the ground. When it has cooled, it is ready for grinding and preparing for use."

Mineral yellow is used in painting the bark of pine trees and in tinting autumn leaves.

[11] An orange, perhaps the "masculine yellow" of the alchemical works, derived from orpiment (arsenic sulphide), also taken for health and longevity.

[12] Sunflower yellow, from orpiment, in ancient times often classed as gold.

LIQUID GOLD *(ju chin)*

First, put a little glue and water in a saucer. Then take the gold-leaf between thumb and index finger. Cut your fingernails before doing this. Dip the gold in the glue, speck by speck, using the index finger to stir the mixture smooth and until the gold begins to dry. Transfer it to another saucer. Add a little clear water, drop by drop, and gently stir. When the gold begins to dry, add more water drop by drop. Repeat this procedure several times until the gold has been ground extremely fine. Do not use too much glue or the gold will rise to the surface, and then it is not possible to reduce it to extreme fineness. Tap it gently while it is still wet, and if it is sticky, wait a bit. Wash your finger and the saucer. Put the mixture in another saucer and place on a low fire. In a little while the gold will sink. Pour off the black water that covers the gold at the bottom. Dry the gold in the saucer in the sun.

Just before using the gold, add a little clear glue and water and stir well. Do not put in too much glue, or the gold will turn black. Another method is to use the pulp of the *fei tsao heh* (soap bean). Take out the white pulp from the pod and boil it to make glue. This glue is lighter and clearer than ordinary glue.

For the most brilliant effects, gold should be used with *chu sha* vermilion and mineral blue. It will heighten the plumage of the phoenix and pheasants. It may also be used in painting fruit and in drawing the veins of blue or green leaves.

PREPARING WHITE *(fu fen)*

The ancients used white made by pulverizing oyster or clam shells. Their method was to heat the shells over a fire and then grind them into fine powder, which, mixed with water, was used as white paint.

Nowadays, in the four prefectures of Min (Fukien), this white powder from crushed shells is still used as a substitute for lime in whitewash. The ideas of the ancients still have meaning.

Painters today use lead white *(ch'ien fen)*. Preparation of this kind of white begins with rubbing the lead powder with the finger, dipping it into clear glue in a saucer, and continuing to rub until the white is dry. It must then again be dipped in glue, and the process repeated ten times. When the glue and powder have been thoroughly blended, it is then pinched into a flat cake, which is put aside in a saucer to dry in the sun. Just before this white is used, it should be boiled in water and a few drops of glue added. Skim off and use the top layer; the lower layer is of no use. The powder should be ground with the finger because lead dissolves easily at the human touch.

There is an easy method to extract the lead from the white before the piece has been ground to powder. Make a hole in a piece of bean curd. Put in the piece of white lead and steam in a pan. The lead will be absorbed by the bean curd and the white is ready to be ground and used. For painting the white should be mixed with a little hot water. A light coat of it should also be applied on the back of the picture. If the colors in the painting are light and clear, pure white should be used; if the colors are dark or in a low key, the white on the back should be tinted with tones of those colors.

White should be applied lightly and never run into the black of outlines. With washes of white, each should be very light. All in all, white must be used with care for in time it will darken.

In painting white flowers, such as the lotus or water lily, the tips of the petals should be touched up with white. The veins of the water lily and the hibiscus may also be traced with white, then color applied over this. Likewise with the long vein in each petal of the chrysanthemum. Stamens of flowers may be drawn in white with accenting of the tips with a yellow.

PREPARING RED (t'iao chih)

There is a saying that rattan yellow should never touch the mouth. Neither should you touch rouge red (yen chih),[13] for it can stain indelibly; in fact, if you do not use vinegar to remove the stain, it will not come off at all.

The kind of this red to use for painting is Fukien red. Take a little of it and soak it in boiling water. Use two brushholders the

[13.] A red derived from several kinds of plants, among them the safflower, yielding a brilliant pink red, carthamin, used as a drug as well as in dyeing and in painting; the flowers and berries of the Sophora japonica; and the flowers and leaves of the vine Mirabilis jalapa.

way dyers use their two sticks to dip and wring the cloth. Any fine grains should be strained off. Place the red in lukewarm water and bring to a boil; boil until the water is absorbed; it is then ready for use.

RATTAN YELLOW *(t'eng huang,* GAMBOGE)

In explanatory notes on the *Pen Ts'ao (Materia Medica)* Kuo I-kung records that on the mountains of the State of Ngo (Hupeh), people used to gather the pollen of a rattan vine that dropped on the rocks. They called it *sha huang* (sand yellow). When it was picked from the plant, it was called *la huang* (wax yellow). Nowadays we confuse these colors with *t'ung miao* (copper) and *she shih* (snake-venom yellow); this is incorrect.

Chou Ta-kuan stated in the *La Chi* (Records of the Winter Sacrifice) that yellow was from the sap of trees and that there was a custom among foreigners of cutting into a tree so that the sap ran out and was gathered the following year. This statement differs from that of Kuo, who was also writing about grasses, trees, flowers, and their juices.

Although this yellow is not literally the venom of snakes, its taste is sour and it is poisonous. If it touches the teeth, they will drop out. If one licks it, the tongue will become numb. Therefore be careful not to let it touch the mouth.

The kind of rattan yellow to use is that which is the same tint as a brushholder, for which reason it is called *pi kuan huang* (brush-tube yellow). It is the best.

The ancients used rattan yellow mixed with a little ink in painting trees. A little of it in the painting of small branches adds a touch of freshness.

INDIGO *(tien hua)*

The kind from Fukien is the best. Today many people say that the kind from the district of T'ang (in Shantung) is also good; it has not, however, rotted in the earth, and so contains less lime and is completely different from the blues of other regions.

In selecting indigo, choose the quality that is very light in weight and in which red specks appear in the blue. It should be sifted through a piece of fine silk to separate the bits of grass from it. Then with a teaspoon add water drop by drop. Pour into a bowl, and with a pestle crush the mixture smooth. When the mixture is dry again, add more water. Then grind again. Ordinarily the refining of four ounces of indigo in order to bring out the full brilliance of the color is a whole day's work.

Before adding glue and water, wash a pestle and bowl. Put the contents into a large bowl. Drain off the top layer and put it aside. The color at the bottom of the bowl will be dull and black; this should be thrown out. Take the part that was skimmed off the top and put it in the hot sun. Drying it in one day's sun is exactly right; if it is allowed to stay till the next day, the glue will be too old. Generally, one may prepare colors in any of the four seasons, but with indigo it is better to wait for the hottest time of the summer.

In painting, indigo is used a great deal, for it is a beautiful color.

GRASS OR VEGETATION GREEN *(ts'ao lu)*

Six parts indigo mixed with four parts of rattan yellow produce old green *(lao lu)*. Three parts of indigo with seven parts of rattan yellow produce young or fresh green *(nun lu)*.

UMBER *(che shih,* LIMONITE)

Choose an umber that is hard and of a beautiful hue. These are the two points to keep in mind in picking the best. There are kinds that are hard as iron, others soft as mud; they are not all desirable.

Use a small earthen bowl in which to grind the color, with a little water, to the consistency of mud. Then add a lot of clear glue and water and stir well. Skim off the upper layer for use. Drain off the bottom layer, which is coarse and dull in color, and throw it out.

Umber is used in painting old branches, dried leaves, and magnolia buds. It may also be mixed with other colors. Mixed with ink, it turns to the color of iron and is used in painting trunks and roots. Mixed with rouge red and ink, it turns to a dark reddish brown and is used for the calyxes of the wild plum and apricot. Mixed with rattan yellow, it turns to the color of sandalwood and is used in the painting of the petals of the chrysanthemum. Mixed with green, it turns to a dark green, which is used for the calyxes of the winter plum and the hibiscus, also in the drawing of young branches of plants with wood stems and of old branches of herbaceous plants.

YELLOW OCHER (che huang)

Use rattan yellow mixed with umber for the painting of the greenish yellow leaves of autumn trees. These are, of course, different from the fresh leaves of spring, which are light yellow. This color should also be used on mountain slopes and for paths through the grass in autumn landscapes.

OLD RED (lao hung)

Chu sha vermilion should be used in painting the fresh and brilliant leaves of the maple or the coldly beautiful leaves of the tallow tree.

Old red should be used in painting the backs of the leaves of the persimmon and chestnut. To mix old red, use deep vermilion and umber.

GRAY-GREEN (ts'ang lu)

In the first frost, when the green of the leaves begins to turn yellow, they appear to be of a pale somber tone. To obtain this tone, mix grass green with umber. Use this also in the painting of mountain slopes and paths at the beginning of autumn.

BLENDING INK WITH COLORS

In painting forests in sunlight and shadow, the clefts and angles of rocks on mountains, and the tones of shadows in hollows, ink should be blended with the colors. Gradations of tone will then be clear, and there will be distinctions in depth and dimension. Ink should be added to colors, moreover, to enrich the venerable air of trees and rocks. There should be in the atmosphere of the painting an element of the mysterious, a dark and fertile dignity hovering over hillock and pool. The vermilions, however, should be applied lightly and pure, never mixed with ink.

Ink is, of course, indispensable in flower painting. In some works in color, the leaves are painted in ink. In others, ink is used to outline and to dot. Ink tones are brought out entirely by the light and dark shades of ink alone. Tones of ink for flowers should be distinct from those for leaves.

Soot black, which may be gathered from a small bowl placed for a little while over an oil lamp and then mixed with a little glue, is used only in bird and insect painting, to touch up the feathers of the thrush and the blackbird, the wings of the crane, and the wings of butterflies. Also in drawing the tail and wing feathers. These accents of soot black are distinctively mat in contrast to ink effects which are glossy.

SILKS

Up to the beginning of the T'ang dynasty, pictures were painted on unsized silk. And until the time of Chou Fang and Han Kan (VIII century), silk was prepared by immersion in boiling water. White powder was added, and the silk beaten until it was like a silver board. Figures and objects painted on it had a wonderful brilliance.

Nowadays, people in search of T'ang paintings try to date the pictures by the silk. When they see that the weave is coarse, they say that the picture is not a T'ang painting. This is not necessarily so. The pictures of Chang Seng-yu and Yen Li-pen that still exist are painted on rough silk. The paintings of the Southern T'ang period were all done on coarsely woven silk. The silk of the paintings of Hsu Hsi were sometimes like linen or cotton.

In the Sung period, there was a silk called *Yuan chuan* (Academy silk), woven for the painters of the Imperial Academy, which was of a clear fine texture. There also was the silk called *tu so chuan* (single-shuttle silk), with a texture as fine as paper, which was woven sometimes into pieces as long as seven or eight feet. Silk of the Yuan period was similar to that of the Sung period. The Yuan period also had a finely woven and clear silk called *Mi chi chuan,* which was woven by, and therefore named for, the Mi family in Wei-tang (in Chekiang), which also happens to be my home district. Chao Meng-fu and Sheng Mou used this silk a great deal.

The silk used in the inner courts of the Ming palaces was very fine; it was considered equal in quality to the Sung silks. The silks of ancient pictures are the color of light ink and have a fragrance of antiquity that is delicious. When there are rips, they make a form like the mouth of a carp. There are usually three or four broken threads, which are never broken in a straight line; if they are straight or split, the silk is faked.

APPLYING ALUM IN SIZING

The silk woven in Sungchiang (in Kiangsu) is the kind to use. It should be chosen not by weight but by texture, which should be extremely fine, like paper, and with no rough threads. It should be fixed on a frame at three sides, top, left and right. If the sides seem to be fastened too tightly, they should be moistened by beating with a wet stick, or else it will be impossible to remove the silk. On the back of the frame, behind the silk, insert little sticks of bamboo to hold it firm and tighten the frame by crisscrossing a fine cord on the bamboo pegs. Do not tie dead knots that cannot be untied. After applying the alum, stretch the silk flat and straight so that there are no hollows. Now tighten the knots. If the silk is seven or eight feet long, a stick across the middle of the frame will give further support. Wait until the silk is dry before applying the alum. If the edges are not thoroughly dry, the silk will come off. When applying the alum, do not touch the glued edges with the brush or the silk will become detached. Even when the edges are dry, do not touch with the brush. In the summer, when the humidity is high, the silk will sometimes come off. Alum should then be applied lightly along the edges.

If the silk should come off, take some small bamboo spikes, those called *ya ting* (mouse teeth), and nail the silk to the frame.

Preparation of alum and steps in applying it: In the summer months, use seven *ch'ien*[14] of glue to three of alum. In the winter months, to one *liang* of glue use three *ch'ien* of alum. The glue should be bright, clear and odorless. Nowadays, flour is added to Canton glue—a faked mixture that should not be used.

The alum should first be soaked in cold water until it dissolves. It should not be put into hot glue or the alum will cook. In applying the glue and alum to the silk, there are three steps. The first coat should be light. The second should consist of several layers of light coats. And the third should be very thin indeed. If the glue should be too heavy, the result will be disastrous; the color will become dull and the picture will crack. Neither should the alum be too heavy. If it is applied too thickly, it will raise a white streak on the silk that will be rough for the brush; moreover, colors on it will lose their brilliance. A solution of alum and water may be applied lightly for protection on the front and back of blue-and-green landscape paintings.

If the alum has been applied with care, it will be clean as snow, clear as the purest river; and even if the silk is not used for a picture, it in itself is a joy to behold. If, before painting, the silk is slightly rough, first moisten it with water, slap it flatly against a stone, then fix the silk on the frame and apply alum.

PAPERS

The Sung paper named after the Ch'eng Hsin T'ang, the bamboo-pulp papers, the kind called Old Treasure House roll, and the paper made in the ancient State of Ch'u (Hupeh) are all good and may be used as one pleases.

Others are the bamboo-pulp paper known as Mirror Smooth, several coarse yet thin papers from Kao-li (Korea), and a Yun-nan paper called Polished Gold. There is a paper made today that is gray and of a heavy quality but contains too much lime.

[14.] 1 *ch'ien* = 1/10th Chinese ounce or *liang*, which is a little more than an ounce avoirdupois.

It is not satisfactory for paintings of orchids or bamboos, in which brushstrokes are few and swift.

FIRING DISHES

All dishes used in preparing colors should be put in water that has been used in washing rice, and then placed over a slow fire until the water boils. After this, spread raw ginger juice and mashed soybeans over the bottom of the dishes. Again place them over a slow fire and bake them. Then they are guaranteed not to crack.

PURIFYING WHITE

In paintings, the areas where white is used often darken. Chew the heart of a bitter apricot seed, and with the juice wash these spots once or twice. The dark spots will then disappear.

WIPING GOLD LEAF

Gold-leaf paper and fans generally have oil on them so that it is difficult to paint on their surfaces. Take a piece of woolen cloth and wipe the surface; the paper should then take ink. Sometimes it is necessary to sprinkle a little powder over the surface before wiping, but when this is done, some of the powder is bound to remain on the gold paper. Some people use red-lead powder to remove the oil. In the long run, none of these ways is as good as just using a piece of woolen cloth.

The gold on gold-leaf paper will come off, and this makes painting on it difficult; the oil makes the surface slippery and the glue is likely to peel. It is really impossible to paint on this kind of surface. However, if a little alum water is brushed over it, the surface will take paint easily. Moreover, when one has finished painting on good gold-leaf paper, a light wash of alum water should be applied over the whole painting. Then there will be no need to worry about cracking or peeling when the picture is mounted.

At one time, I (Lu Ch'ai) was a pupil of Master Liang Hsia. While compiling a history of contemporary painters, he deigned to consult such an ignorant person as me. Together we discussed the subject. Now, much later, I have ventured to write a manual of painting. From the Chin (IV century) and T'ang periods up to now, there have been many biographies of individual painters and groups. Friends have described this work of mine as comprehensive, likening its extensiveness to an ocean. I now await its publication.

I have purposely written this book as simply as possible for the beginner. I have not, however, stinted brush or words to encourage him. The work is offered to those who are studying painting and also to those who may not know anything about painting. A friend has spoken of this book as a model manual, at which, however, I hasten to cover his mouth!

Written on the ninth day of the ninth month of the Chi Wei cycle, the eighteenth year of K'ang Hsi (1679), while a woodchopping guest at Hsin T'ing (by Wang Kai, tzu An-chieh).

Book of Trees

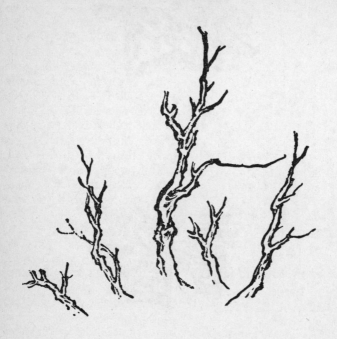

BASIC STRUCTURE OF THE FOUR MAIN BRANCHES [1]

TO paint landscapes, one should first know how to draw trees. To draw trees, one should be able first to draw the trunk and main branches, then to dot the foliage, eventually to depict a luxuriant forest.

After drawing the basic structure of trunk and main branches, add the smaller branches, establishing the form of the tree bare of foliage. The brushstrokes laying out the tree are the most difficult.

Mark well the way the branches dispose themselves, the *yin* and *yang* of them: those in front and those in the back, those on the left and those on the right; mark well the tensions created by some branches pushing forward while others seem to withdraw. In the places where, in nature, there are many branches, add more and elaborate; where few, simplify. That is how the ancients painted their landscapes of a thousand crags and ten thousand gullies; it actually is not difficult to do in one sitting. In looking at their works, observe in particular how the structure and setting of the trees have been rendered, and how they contribute to the expression of the whole composition. As in composing an essay, first make the outline of what is to be said. When that is done, what difficulty can there be in giving it color? It is essential, therefore, to know how to lay out the four main branches of a tree. After that, one may proceed to look into various methods and styles.

Painters call this fundamental step *shih fen san mien* (establishing the three faces of a rock), although here, in discussing trees, we speak of the four branches and, instead of faces, of paths and directions. To follow this rule one has to use imagination.

As branches fork out from the trunk, so a road branches off into other roads and paths. When one knows the way (the Four Directions), the main route is clear and its landmarks familiar, no matter how many byroads and paths. Put your whole mind into what you are doing and you will be on the right path. The thousand rules and ten thousand details all are based on this fundamental principle.

[1.] This opening example indicates the approach of the Manual and that of Chinese painting in general. On the one hand the instructions pertain to technique; on the other, a deeper significance and inner power, hence greater brushstroke vitality, may be gained through understanding the underlying meaning composed of traditional ideas that are based on the belief in and reverence for the order and harmony of nature, *Tao*. The four main branches are analogous to the four cardinal points, the universe, and microcosmically to the four limbs of man, his physical totality, and his four basic potentialities, the Confucian ideals of Goodness, Uprightness, Sense of Fitness, and Wisdom. Thus, when one is clear about the Four Directions, these ideal qualities can grow and one's course may be a steady development in the art of living, one expression of which is the art of painting.

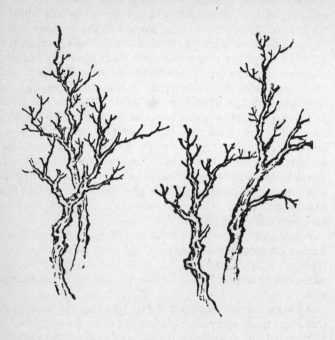

TRUNKS AND MAIN BRANCHES OF TWO TREES

There are two ways of painting two trees together. Draw a large tree and add a small one; this is called *fu lao* (carrying the old on the back). Draw a small tree and add a large one; this is called *hsieh yu* (leading the young by the hand). Old trees should show a grave dignity and an air of compassion. Young trees should appear modest and retiring. They should stand together gazing at each other.[1] The examples show two trees crossing and two trees together yet separate.

[1.] The trees are described in ritual terms; in the relationship of old and young, the old trees have an air grave and ceremonial, exhibiting the Buddha-quality of compassion; the young trees, appropriately unassuming and charming.

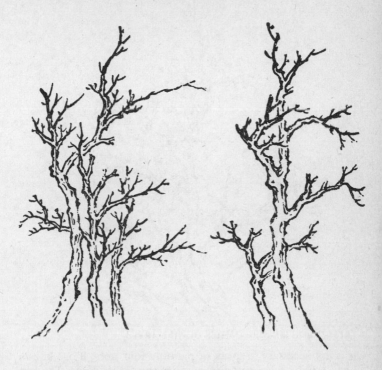

THREE TREES, AND A LARGE AND A SMALL TREE

Although trees may be in a row, like swallows in flight, avoid making them the same height, with tops and roots at the same levels. That would look like a bundle of firewood. They should be painted so as to seem to yield place to one another and to stand together naturally *(tzu jan)*.

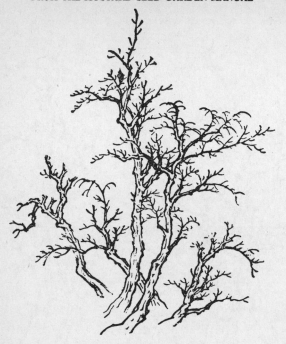

TRUNKS AND MAIN BRANCHES OF FIVE TREES

It is not necessary to speak of painting four trees; if one knows
how to paint five trees, any number can be rendered. The key
is skill in joining and crossing the branches. The ancients painted
trees mostly in groups of five. Ni Yun-lin painted a picture entitled *Five Trees in a Mist*.

In painting four trees, compose a group of three and add another, or draw two pairs. No need to go further into this.

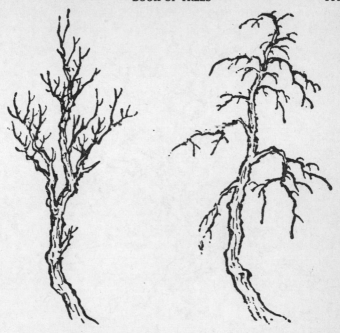

EXAMPLES OF THE STAG-HORN AND CRAB-CLAW BRUSHSTROKES

The *stag-horn* strokes are frequently used, offering much leeway. In painting autumn trees, do not place too many kinds of trees together. Use a thick dark ink at the top of a tree and it will stand out in the group like a crane among cocks. If it is a tree in early spring, add touches of a fresh green. If the trees are to be frostbitten, use small touches of vermilion and umber to dot the leaves (i.e. leaves literally burned or consumed by the frost).

The sharp points in the *crab-claw* strokes should be very clear. They are also called *dropping-needles* strokes. They may be combined with the *lotus-leaf-veins* strokes, which are also made with the sharp point of the brush. If dry ink and a light wash are used in painting the trees, the effect will be that of a forest in mist. Trees drawn in this manner, with the wash applied in circling strokes, can be used in paintings of mountains in winter.

EXPOSED ROOTS

When trees grow on mountains with thick undergrowth, their roots are usually hidden. When they grow among rocks, are washed by springs, or are clinging to steep cliffs, the roots of old trees are exposed. They are like hermits, the Immortals of legends, whose purity shows in their appearance, lean and gnarled with age, bones and tendons protruding. Such trees are marvelous.

In painting a group of trees, it is good to vary the pattern by drawing one or two with roots exposed, knotted and gnarled. All the roots should not be shown or they will look like the teeth of a saw, not a pleasant sight.

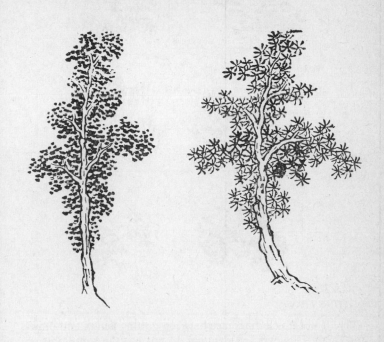

Foliage may be dotted in strokes called *mouse-tracks*. A favorite
method of Wu Chen was dotting in groups of five dots *in the
form of a plum blossom* (shown among the examples on the next
page). Another method (here on the right) is *dotting in the form
of a chrysanthemum.*

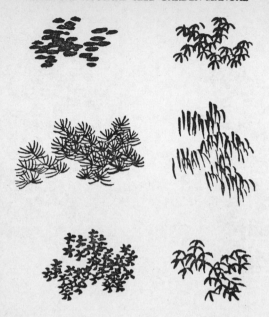

DOTTING LEAVES

There is not much difference between dotting leaves and drawing them. However, all painters do not use the same dotting methods. Here are examples of various dotting brushstrokes for leaves used by the ancients. The way in which each painter used them of course varied, but as one actually wields the brush making these strokes, many similarities among them become apparent. One should be familiar with the various brushstroke styles but be careful to avoid the deadening effects of merely copying the methods of the ancients.

(The examples at the top show) *dotting like small eddies* and in the form of the character *chieh.*[1] (Next,) *dotting like pine needles* and *like a hanging vine.* (Below,) *dotting in the form of a plum blossom* and in the form of the character *ko.*

[1] See Appendix, Sec. IX, for Chinese characters cited for their forms.

Dotting in three strokes coming together, and like a water grass.
Dotting like blades of drooping grass, and in sharp points.
Dotting in the form of split brush points, and like a sprig of red-
leaf leaves.

Examples of vines.

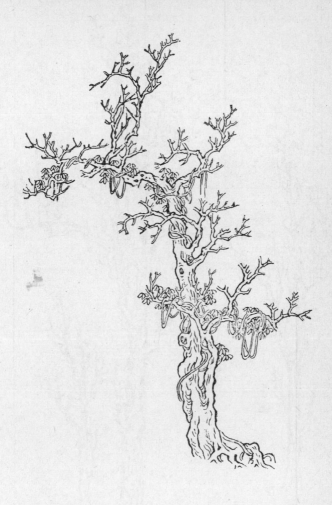

In painting trees, Wang Wei often used the method called *shuang kou* (double contour or outline). Even when drawing the ends of vines or the tips of branches, he did not neglect a single detail.

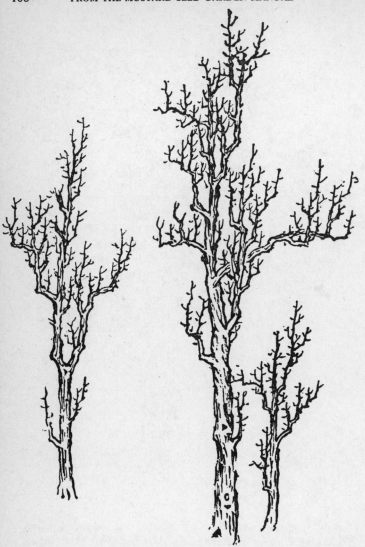

Hsiao Chao's style of painting dead trees.

Wu Chen's style of painting trees, which was copied by Shen Hao.

The examples show some of the established standards in painting trees. One should be familiar with the various styles and methods. While the manner of composition and the methods cannot be separated, the beginner has to examine them separately in order to learn the details of each method. They cannot be ignored. As with the Five Flavors, results depend on blending and proportions. An expert cook manages to produce dishes not too salty, yet not without flavor, in fact just right; moreover, he is able to create a great variety of flavors by different proportions of blending. Or it is as with soldiers, alert to the signals of drums and banners, who listen attentively for the Four Tones of Command. An able general gives orders, handling the situation with ease, however large the army. It is the same in painting trees; they should be paired or combined or separated with authority and style.

Ching Hao, Kuan T'ung, Tung Yuan and Chu-jan absorbed the methods of the ancients and added their own distinctive touches. Those who are studying painting should in turn study and absorb the methods of Ching, Kuan, Tung and Chu. Their brushes will then become fluent and expert.

This example shows Fan K'uan's manner of combining various kinds of trees, which he painted in the blue-and-green style.

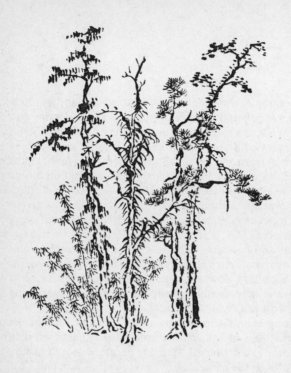

Ni Yun-lin usually used the side of his brush *(ts'e pi)*, whether applying it lightly or heavily, even for the round strokes known as *yuan pi*. The advantage of the oblique brushstroke is in the sharp and pointed tip.

STYLE OF MI FEI AND MI YU-JEN

The styles of Mi and his son are so similar that it is difficult to tell them apart. In their manner of painting, the brush had to be used dripping wet and ink tones handled with precision. In this method the strokes build the picture layer by layer. It is a good test of the saying *yu pi yu mo* (to have brush, to have ink; i.e. drawing and tones). When one has brush but not ink, the results are dry and brittle. When one has ink but not brush, the results are greasy and commonplace.

(On the left is an example of) the elder Mi's style; (next,) the Mi method of painting willows; (and on the right,) young Mi's style of painting trees.

TUNG YUAN'S STYLE OF PAINTING TREES IN THE DISTANCE

Tung Yuan often painted small trees on the summit of mountains. He did not indicate branches but simply dotted in the trees, using only one kind of brushstroke. This was a secret method. He painted trees that appeared to be of various kinds, but all were done with one kind of dotting. The Mi style of brushwork called *lo ch'ieh* (drops shaped like an eggplant) was derived from this. For this method one must apply the ink dripping wet, using few strokes where branches join and many among the shadow forms of the foliage.

Trees in the distance are painted by means of small flat dotting with light ink. They should be placed in the hollows on mountains or at the foot of mountains in the distance. If color is used, apply light green to heighten the effect of mist and clouds.

Trees in the far distance should be dotted in and placed in the same manner. A light ink wash applied on the back of the picture will produce an effect of distant trees in a landscape in snow.

Pine trees are like people of high principles whose manner reveals an inner power. They resemble young dragons coiled in deep gorges; they have an attractive and graceful air, yet one trembles to approach them, awed by the hidden power ready to spring forth. Those who paint pines should keep this meaning in mind. The brush will then effortlessly produce extraordinary results.[1]

Pines painted by Ma Yuan (such as in this example) were lean and strong as iron.

---

[1] The pine is a favorite subject, loved for its sinuosity, sturdiness and venerable age. The symbolism which developed around it added meaning to its decorative qualities. Its association with the dragon, a primary symbol of power, made the pine also a symbol of the *Yang* force and vitalizing spirit *(ch'i)* of Heaven. By analogy, it also represents the inner resources of man. The image of a young dragon coiled in the deep valley suggests the potential in man and the stillness before the manifestation of spiritual power.

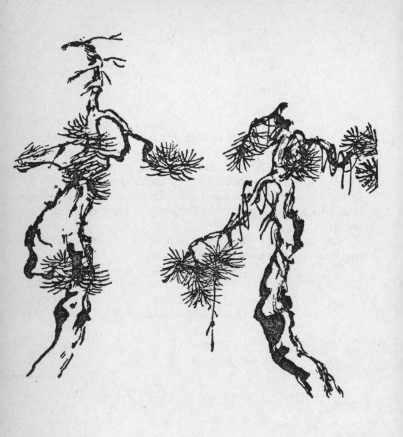

Ma Yuan also often used the style known as *p'o pi tien* (split brushstrokes). To paint in this style is very difficult.

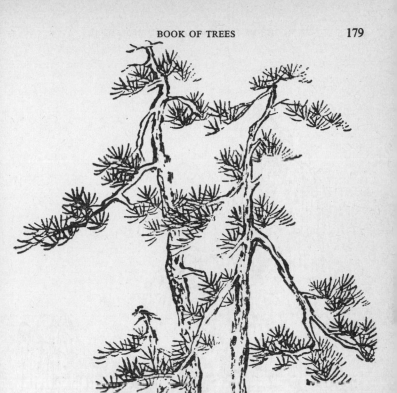

Wang Meng liked to paint great pines with straight branches.
Their needles were long compared with those painted by other
masters. Although at first glance they sometimes seemed in disorder, they were drawn with skill and great style.

There are, in general, four methods of painting willows. The first is to outline *(kou le)* and fill in with green. The second is to use a light fresh green to draw in new shoots, a fresh yellow for the tips of new leaves, and a dark green for shadow and accents. The third method is to add a dark green to the light green dotting first applied, and to touch up with ink some of the parts where the green has been applied. Lastly, some parts may be left with only a few fine ink strokes and a bit more dotting in dark green.

Painters of the T'ang period generally used the outline method, Sung painters usually dotted in the leaves, and many Yuan painters drew the foliage directly in color.

In dividing the branches to indicate their outlines, it is important to take into account how the wind stirs and spreads the willow leaves. In the second month, in the early spring, branches of willows do not bend over. In the ninth month, in the autumn, willows are past their full growth. The two aspects should not be confused.

Chao Meng-fu, in his picture *A Hamlet at the Edge of the Water,* painted willows in ink monochrome with a rare subtlety. Ink monochrome is one more way to paint willows.

Painters of the Sung period often painted willows tall with dripping foliage (as in this example).

Painters of the T'ang period often used this dotting method for
the foliage of willows.

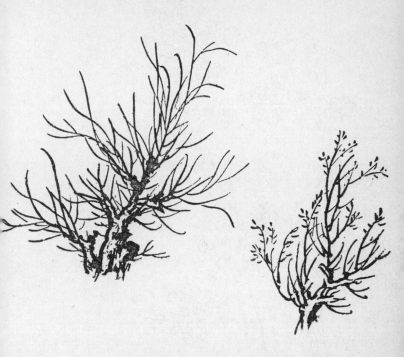

(For scenes) at the end of autumn and at the beginning of spring, willows that look as though they had been cropped should be painted against bamboo fences and near hamlets; they are like a young girl whose hair has been trimmed in a fringe on her brow.

Willows in scenes of early spring may also be placed with peach trees in blossom. For this use light ink with a free brush to draw the stems and to indicate dark and light tones. If color is used, paint the shoots green. If one is painting on thin silk, mineral green may be applied on the back of the painting. In painting willows in winter and late autumn scenes, for modeling use only umber mixed with a green. That will do it!

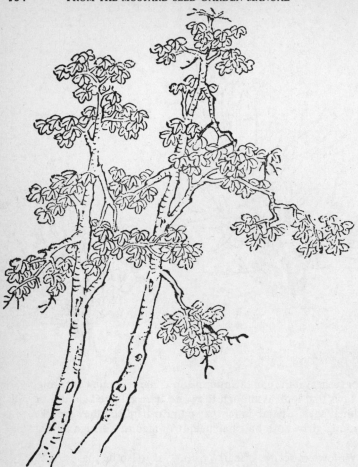

The *wu t'ung* (dryandra, *Sterculia platanifolia)* done in outline style *(kou le)* may be seen in the famous painting by Wang Wei of his home *Wang Ch'uan,* which was also the title of the picture.

Painters of the Yuan period (following the Sung style) often painted it freely in ink with dotting in ink and greens in the free-sketch manner called *hsieh i* (write idea or meaning).

The painters of the T'ang period often painted banana trees in fine outline *(hsi kou)*. If it is painted in the free-sketch manner in ink (as in the example on the right), the thin line of the central vein should be left untouched.

There are many kinds of trees that blossom. The peach should not be painted to resemble the plum or apricot; these, in turn, should not be painted so they may be mistaken for other trees. Generally, the branches of the plum are characterized by a strong angular and crosswise pattern. In painting the apricot, the ancients drew in the trunk and dotted in the leaves and flowers. The branches of the peach tree, though complicated, should be clearly defined.

(These examples show) dotting on the branches of the plum (left), the peach (upper right), and the apricot.

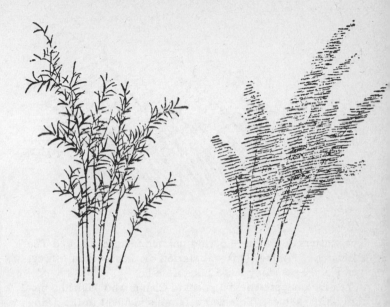

Ni Yun-lin often painted a dense grove of dwarf bamboos at the foot of rocks and trees, and also sunset scenes of a hamlet around which cluster a screen of young bamboos. In looking at these bamboos, one has the feeling that they are like the hermits who follow unswervingly the *Tao*. With the power of their spirit they could comb the wind and sweep clear the full moon. They should not be painted confused or crowded, for the air around them is clear and pure. There are three ways of rendering bamboos: (two are shown here, done in the dry brush manner called *fei pai* or "flying white," and the third is outlining and filling in with color). One should observe the trees and stones near bamboos and match their ruggedness or delicateness.

The masters of the Sung period painted pictures entitled *The Pleasures of Fishing*. This was started by that lover of fishing, Yen P'o, the pseudonym of Chang Chih-ho.

Yen Lu-kung presented a poem to Chang, who painted a picture on the subject. This was a famous incident in the T'ang period. People after his time often tried to copy Chang and to find pleasure in retreating to fish. In the Yuan period, there were still others. The Four Great Masters,[1] who all came from Chiangnan (Kiangsu and Anhui), where reeds are abundant, knew the joys of fishing in solitude. In most other paintings trees are the main interest. In pictures titled *The Pleasures of Fishing*, waves and mist are predominant; reeds and rushes, not trees, are the main focus of attention. That is why this is placed at the end of the *Book of Trees*.

---

[1] Chao Meng-fu, Wu Chen, Huang Kung-wang and Wang Meng. Some Ming critics named Ni Yun-lin in place of Chao.

Book of Rocks

Full title: *Shan Shih P'u*—Book of Mountains and Rocks

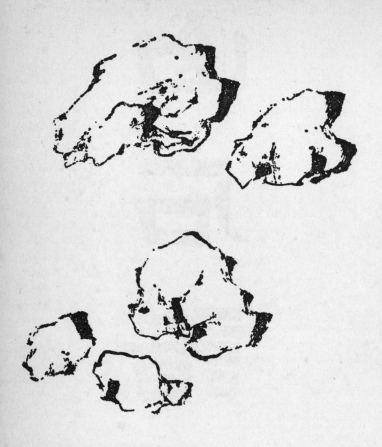

ESTABLISHING THE THREE FACES OF A ROCK [1]

IN estimating people, their quality of spirit *(ch'i)* is as basic as the way they are formed; and so it is with rocks, which are the framework of the heavens and of earth and also have *ch'i*. That is the reason rocks are sometimes spoken of as "roots of the clouds." Rocks without *ch'i* are dead rocks, as bones without the same vivifying spirit are dry bare bones. How could a cultivated person paint a lifeless rock?

One should certainly never paint rocks without *ch'i*. To depict rocks with *ch'i*, one must seek it beyond the material and in the intangible. Nothing is more difficult. If the form of the rock is not clear in one's heart (-mind) and from there to the finger tips, the picture can never be completely realized. I have, however, at long last learned that this is not so difficult to achieve.

The three faces or aspects of a rock are to be found in the depths of its hollows and the height of its projections, in the rendering of which attention must be given to light and shadow *(yin* and *yang),* placing, and height and depth and volume. There are the following different formations of rocks: *fan t'ou* (alum head), *ling mien* (water-chestnut top), *fu tu* (half-covered with earth), and *tai ch'uan* (source of a spring). While one must know the types of rocks, it is only through complete knowledge of their structure that the *ch'i* will emerge naturally as the forms are drawn.

There are not many secret methods in the painting of rocks. If I may sum it up in a phrase: rocks must be alive.

[1.] As with the four main branches of a tree, the principle of distinguishing the three faces of a rock contains the essence of the *tao* of painting. Rendering the solidity and volume of a rock, the sculptural aspect, is achieved by drawing or "writing the form" with the brush, an art essentially of line. Rock formations are keenly observed but the main concern is to transmit the living quality of *ch'i* in them. The technical and aesthetic aspects are given an extra dimension of meaning by the symbolism of the Three Faces of a Rock: the rock or mountain as the One, *Tao,* given expression through the Three according to the early cosmogonic theory that the One became Two, Two became Three, and out of Three the multiplicity of things issued *(Tao Te Ching* Ch. 42, and *I Ching,* Appendix III).

I (Lu Ch'ai) said that the main thing in painting rocks was that they should be alive. Even before one indicates the three faces of rocks, their first outlining should be alive with *ch'i*. Each brushstroke should move and turn, with abrupt stops *(tun)*,[1] sinuous as a dragon.

First, with light ink place and outline the rocks. Then use darker tones to accent the outline. If one side is already dark enough, the other should be slightly lighter in tone to make the distinction between light and shadow and front and back.

Whether one is painting a thousand or ten thousand rocks, this step in beginning to compose them is basic. There are, however, several ways of composing a small rock among large ones or a large one among small.

Once the outlining has been done, the brushstrokes for modeling *(ts'un)* should follow. Brushstroke methods vary among the different schools and the setting of the rocks determines their formations. Although there are many variations within the methods of even one school, and in the way in which rocks are painted on mountains or at the edge of water in one picture, there are in general only one or two basic ways of painting rocks.

Without going into the styles of various schools, one should mention the Mi style of painting mountains. (Mi Fei and his son) did not outline but used a method of dotting with ink in which the brushstrokes had the form of halos. This method created form not by outlining but by building it up in strokes, layer by layer. The results had a marvelous dignity.

Trees have one kind of intersecting lines, rocks another. In trees it is the ramification of branches, in rocks the markings of their veins. Large and small rocks mingle and are related like the pieces on a chessboard. Small rocks near water are like children gathered around with arms outstretched toward the mother rock. On a mountain it is the large rock, the elder, that seems to reach out and gather the children about him. There is kinship among rocks.[2]

[1.] *Tun* (weight; to stop, to stamp). Here describing movement of the brush as it pauses, presses, and turns, rendering the angularity and volume of rock forms.

[2.] The analogy of kinship implies the relatedness and an ideal of harmony in all of nature, illustrating also the underlying ritual and reverent attitude. The groupings of rocks near water and on a mountain suggest also the idea of *Yin* (Feminine and Water Principle) and *Yang* (Masculine and Mountain Principle).

Wang Ssu-shan (of the Yuan period) said: "In painting rocks it is best to begin by using light ink so that it will be possible to correct and make changes, then step by step to apply darker tones." He added: "In painting rocks, use rattan yellow skillfully blended with ink. The color will have a natural freshness. However, do not use too much or the brush will be overloaded. It is also good occasionally to use a touch of snail blue mixed with ink."

In painting rocks Huang Kung-wang and Ni Yun-lin often placed them by slopes of earth. The scenes looked like places where one could sit or sleep. There should be such spots in landscapes, at the edge of water and under bamboos where hermits would like to linger. A painting should not depict exclusively mountain peaks and rocky wilderness that might arouse only fear in people's hearts.

In painting rocks, Yun-lin copied the style of Kuan T'ung, although T'ung used the brush upright in the manner called *cheng feng* (upright and pointed), while Ni more often used the brush obliquely in the manner called *ts'e pi* (side of brush). The results were fresher and offered greater variety. As the saying goes: "Learn from the teacher but avoid his limitations."

The brushstrokes for modeling in this example are called *p'i ma ts'un* (spread-out hemp fibers). Tung Yuan, Chu-jan, Chao Meng-fu, Huang Kung-wang, and Wu Chen all painted in this style.

In the center (of this example) is an upright rock like the beak of a hawk. This is called *shih chun* (rock nose). Huang Kung-wang in particular liked to paint this form.

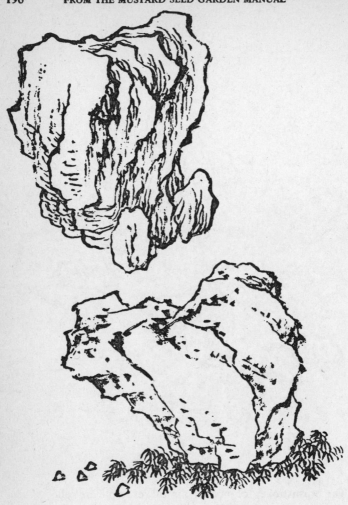

(At the top,) an example of *chieh so ts'un* (brushstrokes like raveled rope), often used by Fan K'uan. (Below,) *ta fu p'i ts'un* (brushstrokes like big ax cuts) such as Ma Yuan and Hsia Kuei often used.

(At the top,) an example of brushstrokes called *luan ch'ai ts'un* (like brushwood in disorder) and *luan ma ts'un* (like hemp fibers in disorder), a combination often used by painters of the Yuan period. (Below,) an example of *hsiao fu pi ts'un* brushstrokes like small ax cuts).

(This is) an example of *ho yeh ts'un* (brushstrokes like veins of a lotus leaf), a modification of Wang Wei's style of painting rocks. Here the principle of basic structure *(ku fa)* is supreme. If color is used, apply blue and green.

Example of *che tai ts'un* (brushstrokes like iron bands), often used by Ni Yun-lin.

METHOD OF BEGINNING TO PAINT MOUNTAINS

First, establish the outline called *lun k'uo* (wagon-wheel rims); after this come the brushstrokes used in modeling *(ts'un)*. Painters today are inclined to start here and there on a picture and, in building up a mountain, add a little bit first in one place and then in another. This is the wrong way to begin. The ancients worked on large scrolls and divided the space into three or four main parts. This is how they managed to accomplish what they did. Although their pictures contained many details and often several kinds of brushstrokes, the important fact was their knowledge of the structure and integration *(shih)* of the whole composition.

Yuan painters declare the three masters closest to their hearts were the two Mi's and Kao K'o-kung.

The ancients spoke of the principle *yu pi yu mo* (to have brush, to have ink). People do not know much about the two terms "brush" and "ink." But how can there be painting without brush and ink? When there is outline but no brushstrokes in modeling, that is *wu pi* (not having brush); when there is knowledge of brushstrokes for modeling but no indication of light and dark tones or of volume and depth, that is *wu mo* (not having ink). The tones indicating volume and depth are not to be found only in the brushstrokes for modeling; they should be present in the sketching in of the outline. As in building a house, the beams must be in place before the rafters are put up; and when the beams are in place, even (the god of carpenters) Kung Shu cannot change the basic structure by the way he puts in the rafters.

This example shows the method called *chang kai* (encompassing the mountain range), in which the outline envelops all the peaks in one composite and crowning peak. Adding the *mo le* (veins and arteries) strokes connects and balances the peaks to left and to right. Whether one draws one thousand or ten thousand more peaks, all are based on this method.

ESTABLISHING THE OUTLINE AND INTERLOCKING BRUSHSTROKES

In human beings, before the hundred bones of the body are formed, the nose begins to take shape. In the drawing of mountains, the first brushstrokes outline the central peak *(pi chun,* hawk's beak form) on the face of the mountain.

In estimating the body of the mountain and placing its head, the brushstroke encompassing the mountain range *(chang kai)* marks the top of the skull of the mountain. This is the dominating form, but its *ch'i* is in the brushstrokes like veins *(mo le).* Other features of the picture, whether tree or rock, pay homage to the summit. The relationship is like that between emperor and ministers. Thus when Kuo Hsi painted mountains, he made the main one lofty, sturdy, heroic, and with an air of spiritual purity. This all-encompassing outline is essential and, moreover, with support below, in front and in back.

(The example shows) the face of a mountain with the outlining of peaks in brushstrokes like veins.

RENDERING THE CEREMONIAL ASPECT OF MOUNTAINS

Wang Wei said: "To paint mountains one must first know their spiritual forms [1] and so be able to distinguish between the pure and impure elements. One may then determine the various attitudes of the peaks and select the position of the host and the guests. When there are too many peaks the effect will be confused; too few, the effect will be dull."

Among mountains there are peaks which are high and others which are low. On a high peak the veins are at the base and the limbs are spread out; the base is thick and strong, encircled by numerous peaks with rounded summits. This is the appearance of a high peak, and certainly it must be so, otherwise it would be isolated and abandoned. On a low peak the veins are at the top and the summit is flat, giving an impression that the top and

brow are touching; the base is wide, firmly implanted in the earth, so that it is impossible to measure. This is the appearance of a low peak, and certainly it must be so, otherwise it would be thin and feeble.

In order to make clear the use of the *lun k'uo* (wagon-wheel rims) and the *mo le* (veins) outlines, the brushstrokes for modeling *(ts'un)* are not indicated here. There are many kinds of such brushstrokes.

[1] *Ch'i hsiang,* "the forms or symbols of their *ch'i,*" distinct from *ch'i ku (ch'i* of bone, the structural *ch'i),* and distinct also from *ch'i shih* (style based on *ch'i),* the air of true culture, the result of possession and cultivation of one's own *ch'i.*

The preceding pair of examples showed the grouping of guest peaks to create the atmosphere of a mountain range. Here is an example of a main peak that constitutes the whole mountain, showing also another aspect of the host-guest relationship among peaks. As the main peak raises its head and spreads its arms, all the forms are included and united within it. There is no need of superfluous scenery. As for the picture, the effect will be mas-

sive. The main intention has been to render clearly and without embellishment.

Compare this example with the preceding one in which the mountain is like a great emperor presiding in his audience hall, the ministers prone around him. In this picture, the mountain is like an emperor alone for a moment in his palace and deep in silent thought. Wang Wei often painted a mountain like this.

REMARKS ABOUT THE THREE TYPES OF MOUNTAIN PERSPECTIVE

Mountains have three kinds of perspective: looking at a peak from base to top is called *kao yuan* (high distance or perspective in height); looking across from a mountain in the foreground to mountains in the back of a painting is called *shen yuan* (deep distance or perspective in depth); and looking from a place in the foreground into the far distance across a flat landscape is called *p'ing yuan* (level distance or perspective on the level).

A painting of a mountain with perspective in height presents a precipitous view; with perspective in depth gives an effect of a repetition of planes; and with perspective on the level the effect is of a flat landscape extending into a vast distance. These principles control the whole composition of a picture. If the mountain is massive (deep) but is drawn without perspective, it will appear flat; if it extends horizontally but is drawn without perspective, it will appear to be too close; if it is high but is drawn without perspective, it will appear low. When these faults are made in a landscape painting, they are like vulgar and shallow characters, or like runners and menials (who are crude and insensitive). When the hermits in these pictures see such things, it is enough to make them abandon their families, flee their huts, and, holding their noses, run away as fast as they can!

This is an example of *kao yuan* (perspective in height).

When mountains are drawn with perspective and one wishes to accentuate their loftiness, they may be made to appear higher and grander by drawing in springs and waterfalls; wild geese may be drawn flying around the base of mountains of a thousand *hsin*,[1] and huts may be placed at three different levels on the mountain. If this doesn't convey perspective in height, what does? When mountains are drawn with perspective and one wishes to emphasize their depth, clouds will help the effect, also Yu Nu (Jade Lady, the moon) veiled by mists and bright stars imprisoned at the summit of the mountains. If this doesn't convey perspective in depth, what does? When mountains are drawn with perspective and one wishes to emphasize their range and extension, they can be made to spread out even more expansively by the suggestion of mists; flowers and their companions, cranes, may be drawn on knolls, or ridges, and Yu Kung[2] resting in the valley. If this doesn't convey perspective on the level, what does?

This is an example of *shen yuan* (perspective in depth).

---

[1] A *hsin* is about 9½ feet.
[2] A legendary giant of the valley of Mount Pei.

An example of *p'ing yuan* (perspective on the level).

This is an example of the brushstrokes for modeling called *chieh so ts'un* (raveled-rope strokes). Wang Meng used this type of brushstroke. He also combined it with *p'i ma ts'un* (brushstrokes like spread-out hemp fibers) and *fan t'ou ts'un* (brushstrokes shaped like alum lumps). Many painters have tried to copy this style but they did not really grasp the method and produced brushstrokes which were stiff and angular.

Brushstrokes like entangled hemp fibers *(luan ma ts'un)*. Improperly used, this method can create confusion, like a child trying to disentangle a bundle of hemp fibers. Can one call this a brushstroke method? Definitely not! As in fishing, one must not let the cord around the net get entangled; so, in learning the brushstroke methods of the ancients, one must know not only how to put them together but also how to separate them. Even if the brushstrokes get mixed, one should be able to bring some order out of the muddle.

The style of *ho yeh ts'un* (lotus-leaf strokes) gets its name from the similarity of its form to the veins of a lotus leaf. Tung Yuan often used this brushstroke.

When one has learned to draw the *mo le* (veins) of a main peak, the next step is usually the rendering of the *lun k'uo* (wagon-wheel rims) outline. After that, it is a question of which school to follow in brushwork. Tung Yuan is a good example of one who mastered all the various kinds of brushstrokes; his brushwork is well worth serious study.

When one has some experience in handling the brush, the variety of styles will not seem so difficult. While learning, however, one should be careful not to acquire bad habits of the hand and wrist. The brushwork methods shown here cannot develop bad habits in brushstrokes. How could I lead you astray (when I have selected examples from established masters)?

Tung Yuan's rounded mountain peaks (such as shown here) have a purity and profundity of conception as great as that found in the works of the ancients. The critics consider his ink paintings to be like the work of Wang Wei, and those in color like Li Ssu-hsun's. He often used brushstrokes like spread-out hemp fibers, using actually few strokes and color quite thickly

The Four Great Masters of the Sung period[1] and Huang Kung-wang and Ni Yun-lin all worked in this manner. Huang in his later years changed his style and himself founded a school; but he did not go beyond this point.

[1] Ching Hao, Kuan T'ung, Tung Yuan and Chü-jan are often so mentioned in the records and in this Manual, in line with Ming and Ch'ing critics. However, the Sung masters were so numerous it would be difficult to pick the four outstanding.

Example of Chu-jan's style in rendering mountain peaks.

Example of Ching Hao's style in rendering mountain peaks.

Example of Wang Wei's style in rendering mountain peaks.

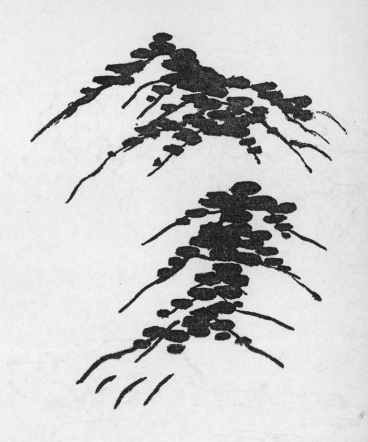

Example of Mi Fei's style in rendering mountain peaks.

PAINTING SLOPES AND PLATEAUS

There are slopes and plateaus of rocks, of earth, and of both rock and earth. Their particular formations depend on where they are placed in a picture. They should be flat when located near the summit of mountains and expansive at the base. They should be firm like an upturned bowl. The upper part of some of these forms is wide, joined in a straight line to a lower slope, and like a mushroom in shape; there are others, lost in the clouds, the shape of which is like an elephant's trunk. Their forms have great variety, but the platform parts are always flat and solid.

The brushstrokes indicating the sides of plateaus should be strong and firmly joined, for they depict forms of earth and rock that have stood long against wind and snow. And these forms should have an air of complete naturalness, born of Heaven. *P'i ma ts'un* (brushstrokes like spread-out hemp fibers) should be used, combined with a few ax-cut strokes *(fu pi ts'un)*. If color is used, mineral green with a little light red and touches of grass green should be used for the platform parts and umber for the sides. If umber is used on the face of slopes, it should be mixed with a little rattan yellow, the result being a yellow ocher. On the sides, one should apply umber or use it just to accent the outlines.

PAINTING WATERFALLS

Rocks form the bone structure of mountains and waterfalls form the structure of rocks. Some say that water is by nature weak, so how can it be described as forming structure? I say: see how water strikes the mountain and pierces the rocks; it has supernatural strength, nothing is stronger. It was for this reason that Master Chiao Kung said that water is structural. Moreover, is not water, whether trickling, flowing, spraying, foaming, splashing, or in rivers or oceans, the very blood and marrow of Heaven and Earth? Blood nourishes the embryo and the marrow nourishes the bones. Bones without marrow are dead bones. Such bones are like dry soil and can no longer be called bones. Mountains are bones, since water has formed them, and for this reason the ancients paid careful attention to painting waterfalls. The example is taken from a work of Huang Kung-wang in which the whole waterfall is shown cutting through a steep mountain gorge. Once again one must ask, how can water not be called the bone of mountains?

Wang Wei said: "When one is painting a waterfall, it should be so painted that there are interruptions but no breaks." In this matter of "interruptions but no breaks," the brush stops but the spirit *(ch'i)* continues; the appearance of the flow of water has a break but the idea *(i)* of it is uninterrupted. It is like the divine dragon, whose body is partly hidden among the clouds but whose head and tail are naturally connected.

In painting waterfalls, the ancients often used the device called *yun suo* (cloud lock), by which a cloud partly submerges the waterfall. In painting the cloud, one must be careful not to show any trace of brush or ink. It is indicated only by a light wash of color. This is the sign of a skilled hand.

PAINTING BILLOWS

Mountains have strangely shaped peaks and water also has strangely shaped peaks. Rocks are like great billows that roll and smash against mountains. When the moon is reflected on such waters, the waves are like galloping white horses, and at that moment one sees lofty mountains and peaks in their full grandeur.

PAINTING RIPPLING SHALLOW WATERS

As in painting mountains *p'ing yuan* (perspective on the level) should be observed, so also in painting shallow waters. When the wind subsides, waves and ripples calm down. When the clouds part, the moon emerges. The moonlit mists are vast and boundless, and the eye cannot see their limits. Rivers, seas, brooks and ponds all in one moment may suddenly become cold, calm and silent. In such a way the nature of still waters should be revealed.

PAINTING CLOUDS IN HSI KOU (SMALL HOOK) OUTLINE STYLE

Clouds are the ornaments of sky and earth, the embroidery of mountains and streams. They may move as swiftly as horses. They may seem to strike a mountain with such force that one almost hears the sound of the impact. Such is the nature *(ch'i shih,* spirit and structural integration) of clouds.

Among the ancients, there were two key methods in painting clouds. First, in vast landscapes of numerous cliffs and valleys, clouds were used to divide (and to hide) parts of the scene. Richly verdant peaks soared into the sky and white scarves of clouds stretching horizontally separated and imprisoned them. Where the clouds parted, green summits rose. As the literati say: "In the midst of hustling activity steal moments of quietness." Let the Five Colors cast such a spell on the spectator. Second, in a landscape where mountains and valleys extend into the distance, clouds were used as a means of uniting them. The clouds sometimes filled space where there were no mountains or water, billowing like great waves of the ocean and soaring like mountain peaks. As the literati say: "Invite guests, recite poems, improve style." [1]

I have placed this section on clouds here at the end because the ancients included clouds in their discussions of the main principles of painting mountains. In the emptiness of clouds there are no traces of brushwork, an ultimate feature of landscape (mountain-water) composition. Thus, paintings of mountains are often called cloud-landscapes and also cloud-water pictures.

[1] *Wen shih* (cultural foundation), style in the sense of "improve your air of culture," representing character as well as artistic accomplishment.

PAINTING CLOUDS IN TA KOU (LARGE HOOK) OUTLINE STYLE

In using color to paint clouds, washes of pure color should be applied. The clouds should appear to have volume but should show
no traces of ink. In the style called *ch'ing lu shan shui* (blue and
green landscape), however, when the method requires fine modeling brushwork, the drawing of the clouds should harmonize with
the rest of the picture: a light ink should be used for outlining
and a light wash of pale blue for tinting.

The painters of the T'ang period had two ways of painting
clouds. One, known as *ch'ui yun fa* (blow-cloud method), consisted of applying white powder lightly on the silk to simulate
clouds floating on the wind—light, clear, and graceful, a most
pleasing effect.[1] The other method, known as *kou fen fa* (white
outline method), is similar to touching up with gold the outlines
of clouds in *chin pi shan shui* (gold and blue and green landscape),
which Little General Li[2] used with great liveliness *(ch'i)* and style.

[1] The T'ang art historian, Chang Yen-yuan, commented on this method: ". . .
the ancients did not obtain wonderful results in their painting of clouds. Moisten-
ing the silk and sprinkling white powder over it in the blow-cloud method produces
a natural effect that may seem wonderful; but, since there is no brushwork in it, it
can hardly be called painting."

[2] Li Chao-tao, son of Li Ssu-hsun, called Big General Li and credited as the
founder of the Northern School style.

Book of People and Things

Full title: Book of People (*jen*), Things (*wu*), Dwellings and Structures (*wu yu*)

PEOPLE AND THINGS IN LANDSCAPES

In landscape paintings, in addition to scenery there should be figures *(jen)* and other things *(wu)*, animate and inanimate. They should be drawn well and with style, though not in too great detail. And they should, of course, fit the particular scene. For instance, a figure should seem to be contemplating the mountain; the mountain, in turn, should seem to be bending over and watching the figure. A lute player plucking his instrument should appear also to be listening to the moon, while the moon, calm and still, appears to be listening to the notes of the lute. Figures should in fact be depicted in such a way that people looking at a painting wish they could change places with them. Otherwise the mountain is just a mountain, the figures mere figures, placed by chance near each other and with no apparent connection; and the whole painting lacks vitality.

Jen-wu in a landscape should be pure as the crane, like hermits of the mountains, and should never bring into a picture the air of the city and market place to mar the spirit of the painting. In the pages which follow are examples of figures strolling, standing, sitting, reclining, contemplating, and listening. In some cases, the accompanying text is quoted from T'ang and Sung poems, showing how *jen-wu* in a landscape are equivalent to an inscription or title for a painting. The subject of a scroll is often indicated by the *jen-wu* in it. The ancients liked to write inscriptions on their paintings. The excerpts chosen here are not, however, necessarily the only ones for the poses shown. Certain kinds of inscriptions should go with certain pictures. Here, only a few examples are offered. Once a beginner understands the various kinds of pictures done by the ancients and the substance of the accompanying inscriptions, he will be able to find appropriate ones for himself.

"With hands clasped behind, walking on a mountain in autumn." [1]

"Standing alone in the open, reciting a poem."

"Returning home by moonlight, hoe on shoulder."

[1] Quotations accompanying the figures, from left to right.

"Sitting on a rock flat as a mat, head bent, watching the long flowing stream."

"The sounds of the chessboard dispel all sense of time."

"Meditating on a poem while crossing a bridge on a donkey."

"The traveler's horse eyes the spring grass. People on foot watch the sunset clouds."

(A selection here and on the next three pages, showing figures in action, is made from fifteen pages in the original Manual. Since the drawings seem self-explanatory, the short lines of text describing what each figure is doing are omitted to allow space for as many examples as possible, while preserving the scale of the figures as they appear in the original.)

FIGURES IN FREE-SKETCH STYLE

Here are examples of the style called *hsieh i* (write idea), giving
the swiftly drawn impression of an idea. In this style it is important that the brush move with speed and vitality.[1] Such was
the calligraphy of Chang the Madman,[2] who was expert in *ts'ao
shu* (grass writing), which is more difficult than *chen shu* (regular writing). That is the reason the ancients said: "If you paint
hurriedly, you will not have the necessary relaxed approach to
grass writing." Painting in the grass style *(hsieh i)* is more diffi-

[1] Literally "fly-dance-life-splash."
[2] Chang Hsu, VIII-century poet, one of the Eight Immortals of the Wine Cup.

cult than the copying-stroke-by-stroke style *(k'ai hua)*. That is
the reason for the saying: "Drawing must be linked with the idea
(i), for without meaning *(i)* the brush cannot function properly."
Figures, even though painted without eyes, must seem to look;
without ears, must seem to listen. This should be indicated in one
or two touches of the brush. Eliminate details to achieve the
simplest expression and the effect will be the most natural.
Actually there are things which ten hundred brushstrokes cannot
depict but which can be captured by a few simple strokes if they
are right. That is truly giving expression to the invisible.

ANIMALS AND BIRDS IN LANDSCAPES

Various kinds of animals and birds exist as parts of a landscape. While they may seem a small matter, they actually are of great importance. If one is painting a landscape in the spring, the season should be properly indicated: pigeons coo, swallow their feed. If these are not signs of spring, what is? If one wishes to paint an autumn scene, the season should be properly indicated: a wild swan in flight, a wild goose on its nest. If these are not signs of autumn, what is? Such details and the changing aspects of mountains and trees indicate the different seasons.

When one is painting the dawn, that time of day should be properly indicated: birds fly out of their nests in the woods, a watchdog barks. If these are not signs of the dawn, what is? If one wishes to paint the time of sunset, those hours should be properly indicated: chickens perch in their roosts, birds rest among the trees. If these are not signs of early evening, what is? Before the first drops of rain, the crane cries; before snow falls, the crows fly away in flocks; and when the wind begins to gather force, oxen and horses grow restless. The rhythm of life *(sheng tung)* is expressed in a painting by such details.[1]

[1.] The seasons, weather, and time of day or evening represent aspects of the order and mutations of nature *(Tao).*

METHODS OF DRAWING BUILDINGS

Most landscapes contain dwellings of one kind or another, the doors and windows of which are like eyes and eyebrows. When people have no eyes or eyebrows, they are blind or diseased. While eyes and eyebrows may be beautiful in themselves, their effect is due to their placing on the face. Of either feature there should not be too much. If a man had eyes all over his body, he would be a monstrosity. What is the difference when houses are drawn without thought of location and arrangement, of back and front views, with story piled on story? I therefore speak now of different ways of drawing buildings.

The face of a landscape, too, should be studied in all its aspects so that its eyes may be placed in a natural way. Whether in large pictures, several feet long, or in small ones, only inches long, people and dwellings should be placed in but one or two places. A landscape with people and dwellings in it has life, but too many figures and houses give the effect of a market place. Few painters today know how to place houses in a landscape. Although some may be skillful in landscape painting, there are very few who draw houses properly. The houses often look like snail shells or the mud houses children build. They lack construction altogether.

Recently Yao Chien-shu painted some pictures in which houses were as small as grains of rice, yet his command of the brush was such that the fronts could be easily distinguished from the backs, and the way the houses connected was clearly visible; their arrangement, moreover, was perfect. Looking at the groups of houses, one could feel their relation to the mountains. One may certainly say he learned from the ancients.

Doors and windows are like eyes and eyebrows; halls and inner rooms are also like eyes. Eyebrows should be graceful; so likewise walls should curve, encircle, and join. Eyes should not be too prominent; therefore the inner rooms should be spacious and quiet, their emptiness filled with *ch'i* (the atmosphere of the spirit). Two examples are shown here: at the top, the houses are those suitable for flat areas; below are buildings rising on the levels of a slope of a mountain. These are two basic patterns.

(At the top,) a pavilion in the middle of a lake with a small connecting bridge.
(Below,) a structure that may be placed among dense trees or on
a rocky cliff.

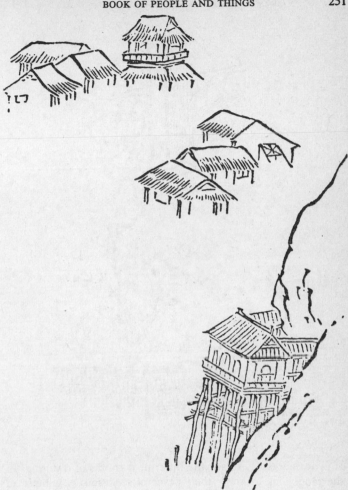

(At the top,) thatched dwellings suitable for villages in summer landscapes; the windows can be shaded or open to the sun. (Below,) the kind of structure suitable for paintings of Shu (Ssuchuan), where the mountains are rugged and precipitous, to be placed against steep cliffs at the bend of the river.

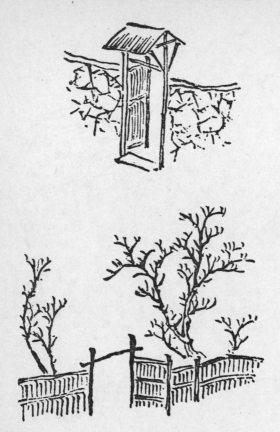

GATEWAYS

It is not necessary to see the innermost rooms of dwellings in the mountains to know their peaceful seclusion. A glimpse of the gate is enough to recognize the abode of a follower of *Tao* and to make one wish to linger. To be able to evoke such a feeling is evidence of true skill.

(At the top is an) example of a gate and a wall. The pattern of the stones of the wall resembles the skin of a tiger. (Below) is an example of a thatched gate.

A hut and its gate. A rambling vine grows across the top of the gateway, the stone steps are buried in grass, the tiles are like broken fish scales, and the cracks in the walls resemble the markings on the shell of a tortoise. The scene is completely natural, filled with the vitality *(sheng tung)* of the spirit *(ch'i).* Wang Meng painted such scenes. This kind of hut and gateway may be used in landscapes in rain or snow.

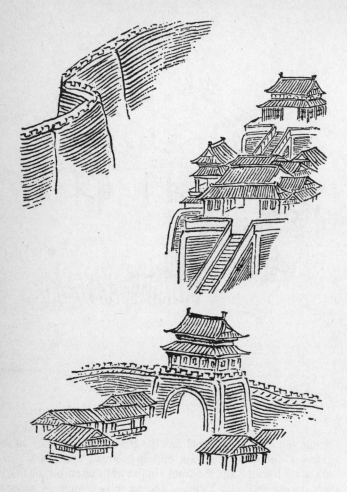

(Top left,) an example of a wall following the natural course of a river, or the foot of a mountain. (Right,) an example of terraces raised high above the houses, drawn in fine detail. (Below,) an example of houses around a city gate.

These examples, on a very small scale but well constructed, are for scenes in the distance. (At the top,) a village in the distance, seemingly composed of layer on layer of roofs. (Next,) a view of a temple and a palace rising among roof tops, drawn in fine detail. (Below,) a temple and pagoda, with the entrance to the main temple among other terraced buildings.

BRIDGES

In paintings in which there are steep precipices and water flowing endlessly, bridges may be drawn to sustain the continuity of
the *ch'i*. They should seldom be missing from pictures. Usually
where there is a bridge there will be signs of people; the mountain is not deserted. There is always good reason why a bridge
is located in a particular place. Bridges built of small rocks and
rising in the form of a mound are usually found in Wu (Kiangsu)
and Che (Chekiang). Bridges supported by heavy pillars of stone
to withstand erosion by floods and bearing a structure like a small
house are usually found in the provinces of Min (Fukien) and
Yueh (Kuangtung and Kuangsi). Furthermore, there are bridges
built high and steep, suitable for spanning a dangerous, narrow
divide; and there are bridges made of thin layers of stone, suitable for level ground. Between these two extremes are all other
kinds of bridges.

(The examples show) a type of bridge suitable for placing
among the Wu Mountains or across the Yueh River; the type of
bridge over the Ou River in Min (Fukien), which has a small covered structure on it; and a type of bridge suitable for parks.

(An example of) a wooden footbridge, built in a zigzag form, that may be drawn over churning waters since it is built on rocks in the water. And a wooden bridge with gaps, as though it had lost some of its teeth, suitable for a scene of an old village in the middle of bare fields, or in a painting of such a village in snow.

PAGODAS AND TOWERS

If one is painting landscapes with scenes in the far distance, towers and pagodas should be included. Painting mountains with great precipices and numberless hills and ravines cannot be done in an ordinary fashion. Such views should include pagodas to increase the effect of distance. People looking at these pictures feel that, reaching out, they could touch the stars, whose *ch'i* governs rivers and mountains. This accounts for the observation that mountains in painting are not completely right without some arranging by men.

(The examples show) two Buddhist stone pagodas; and an eight-sided glazed tile pagoda.

AN EXAMPLE OF A BUILDING OF SEVERAL STORIES AND TERRACES

In painting, the drawing of many-storied buildings is to other methods of brushwork what, in calligraphy, the styles named after the Chiu Ch'eng Palace and Ma Ku Altar[1] are to the regular style *(k'ai shu)*.

Some who believe themselves independent claim that they follow no rules. Actually, the stage at which one is most free in brushwork is the time when, in attempting to surpass the ancients, one is most keenly aware of their presence and methods. Often those without method will find in taking up the brush that all ten fingers suddenly freeze into a knot and for a whole day not a dot of ink is dropped. Among the ancients, Kuo Chung-shu should be mentioned, for his brushwork was bold. A scroll of more than ten feet received just a sprinkle of ink from his brush; then here and there he drew angles of buildings and some trees. This might seem to be working without rule or method. However, he sometimes used a square and rule, dotting in towers and buildings. Then suddenly there would be ridgepoles and rafters, pillars and posts, finished with doors and wooden screens in front of them, colorful and stretching out like clouds in the wind. The brushstrokes were as distinct as bristles. One could have walked along the verandas and ascended the many stories of the buildings. No painter today equals him in skill.

It may be observed that the ancients worked without rules only because they first paid careful attention to the steps in technique. One cannot work daringly without taking great pains. Drawing by square and rule *(chieh hua)* cannot be put down as work only of artisans. The method should be examined and studied. Its practice is similar to the disciplines of *Ch'an* (Zen) Buddhism. Those who study Buddhism must begin first with its disciplines, so that for the rest of their lives they will not stray or be involved with evil influences. Drawing with square and rule is a similar discipline of purification in the art of painting, among the first steps for a beginner.

---

[1] Characters on two famous stone engravings of the VII and VIII centuries, the styles of which were copied and regarded as being most elegant.

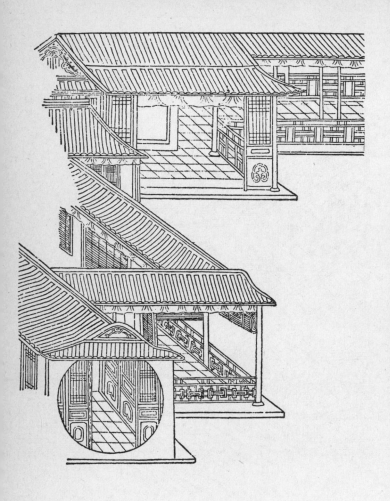

A winding veranda and porches of a palace.

A bridge of intricate construction and a flight of imperial steps.

Examples of boats.

FURNITURE

When palaces, pavilions, and terraces have been drawn, how can they be left empty? There should be tables and seats, something to lean on and something to sit on. They should not be drawn with too much detail; that would be banal. But they should not be drawn too sketchily, nor without method or arrangement; that would be untidy. When the landscape is beautiful, and the few furnishings are expensive but unbecoming, it is like a flaw in an otherwise perfect piece of jade.

In general, when the house is drawn facing left, tables and couches should follow the same arrangement. When turned right, the furniture should likewise be arranged. Furniture should balance, face to face and side to side, whether the pieces are large or small. That is the basis of arranging furniture.

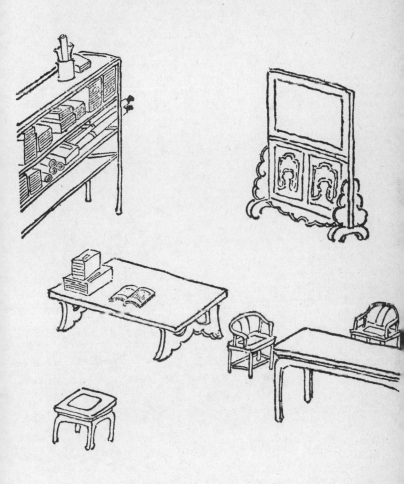

Book of the Orchid

DISCUSSION OF THE FUNDAMENTALS OF ORCHID[1] PAINTING

Mi-ts'ao[2] says:

Before attempting to paint finished pictures of the orchid, one should study the works of the ancients. Later one may inject one's own ideas. First, however, one should know the various methods; the rules phrased for memorizing by chanting *(ko chueh)*[3] should be learned; and one may then start with the basic strokes contained in the character *ch'iu.*[4]

In learning to write, one begins with simple characters made up of a few strokes and proceeds to complicated characters with several strokes. In the same way, in learning to paint flowers one begins with those with few petals and proceeds to those with many petals, from small leaves to large, and from single stems to bunches. All divisions of subject matter are classified here so that beginners may learn them thoroughly, not only beholding them

[1] *Lan,* general term for orchidaceous plants, used for orchids and irises, also sometimes for the artemisia and cassia.
[2] Wang Shih, elder brother of Wang Kai (Lu Ch'ai of the Manual). With their younger brother, Wang Nieh, he composed this book and the rest of the Manual.
[3] *Ko* (sing, chant) *chueh* (secret), an expression used here about learning the rules of painting. Chanting by phrases was a common practice in the process of memorizing, starting with the classics in childhood. *Chueh,* used in terms describing the mysterious and occult, suggests a relationship with mantras (the chanting of religious texts), the sounds of which were believed to set up vibrations in a manner that might be described as "tuning in" with the Infinite. In the *Shu Ching* (Book of History) is the statement: "Poetry is the expression of earnest thought; singing is the prolonged utterance of that expression" (tr. Legge, Pt. II, Bk. I, v.).
[4] See Appendix, Sec. IX, for Chinese form of *ch'iu.*

with their eyes but retaining the impressions in their minds. In calligraphy, one first learns to write *ch'iu*, which contains the eight basic strokes; though there are hundreds and thousands of characters, the fundamental strokes are all found in *ch'iu*. Likewise in painting flowers: when the beginner has learned the basic steps, he will have started on the way to acquiring experience and skill.

ORDER OF BRUSHSTROKES IN PAINTING ORCHID LEAVES[5]

The art of painting orchids depends entirely on the drawing of the leaves, and therefore the drawing of the leaves should be the first consideration.

The first brushstrokes one should learn are those known as *ting t'ou* (nail ends), *shu wei* (rat's tail), and *t'ang tu* or *t'ang lang tu* (belly of a mantis); next, the stroke called *chiao feng yen* (cross stroke forming the eye of a phoenix); then the stroke called *p'o hsiang yen* (breaking the eye of an elephant). Finally, one should learn the strokes for the leaves wrapping the base, the sheath at the roots that resemble the form of a fish's head *(chi yu t'ou,* usually described as that of a carp). Thus one draws leaves bending one way and raised in another, conveying the life-movement *(sheng tung)* of the plant. Leaves should cross and overlap but never repeat in a monotonous manner. Distinction should be made between the leaves of the grass or ordinary orchid *(ts'ao lan)* and those of the marsh orchid *(hui lan):* the latter are slim and supple, the former wide and strong. The above brushstrokes are the first steps in painting orchids.

PAINTING LEAVES TO THE RIGHT AND LEFT

In painting leaves, there are methods of drawing them to the right and to the left. The drawing of a leaf is described as "writing" it in the stroke called *p'ieh*. This is the stroke and the term

[5] Notes on the historical background of orchid painting, preceding this section, are omitted. They consist largely of names of painters associated with orchid painting, and of who followed whose style. The points of main interest are that orchids as a special subject in ink monochrome is said to have begun in the XIII century, that it was a favorite among the literati and also of some women painters, among them Lady Kuan, wife of the Yuan master, Chao Meng-fu.

used in calligraphy. When the hand moves from left to right the brushstroke is called *shun* (positive), and from right to left *ni* (negative). Beginners should first practice the *shun* stroke until they are able to handle the brush with ease. The counterstroke *ni* should be practiced until brush movement in both directions is mastered. This will give some experience with the brush. Skill in manipulating the brush only in one direction is limited experience and incomplete knowledge of method.

PAINTING LEAVES GROUPED SPARSELY OR DENSELY

Leaves are painted in a few strokes, and they should have a floating grace in rhythm with the wind, (moving like a goddess) in rainbow-hued skirt with a moon-shaped jade ornament swinging from her belt. No breath of ordinary air touches them. Leaves should half veil the orchids, and some should certainly be painted behind the flowers, supporting them; they should be drawn growing from the roots, though not in such a way as to appear bunched up. When one is able to convey the whole idea *(i)* without painting every leaf, then one indeed wields an experienced brush. One should study attentively the works of the ancients and practice drawing three leaves, then proceed to five leaves and then to scores of leaves. When there are only a few leaves, they should not have the appearance of being sparse; when there are many leaves, they should not appear entangled and in confusion—a matter of fine discrimination.

PAINTING THE FLOWER OF THE ORCHID

In painting the flowers, one should know how to draw them bending over as well as standing erect, how to draw their faces as well as backs, how to draw them in bud and in full bloom. The stems should appear wrapped by the leaves; the flowers should emerge from them. They should be seen face up, from the back, high and low; thus they will not be repeated in a monotonous fashion, all in a row. There should be leaves behind some of the flowers as though half hiding them. Some flowers should, however, stand free of the leaves, for they should not seem to be bound. The marsh orchid, although it resembles the ordinary grass orchid, is not as beautiful or as graceful. On a straight stem, the flowers face different directions and open at different times. The stem is straight and erect but the flowers are heavy, as though they hung from the stem. Each stem and flower has its particular position and angle. In drawing the flowers of both the grass and marsh orchids, one should be careful to avoid the effect of the five petals spread out like fingers of an open hand. They should partly cover each other, some curving toward their stem and others stretching out. They should be delicate, joined among themselves, and reflecting each other. After long practice and thorough familiarity with the methods, heart and hand will be in accord. At first, however, it is advisable to follow closely the prescribed methods; thus, eventually, one may reach perfection.

DOTTING THE HEART

Dotting the heart of the orchid is like drawing in the eyes of a beautiful woman. As the rippling fields of orchids of the River Hsiang give life to the whole countryside, so dotting the heart of the flower adds the finishing touch. The whole essence of the flower is contained in that small touch. How, therefore, can one possibly neglect it?

USE OF BRUSH AND INK

Chueh Yin, Buddhist monk of the Yuan period, said: "When the emotions are strong and one feels pent up, one should paint (write) bamboo; in a light mood one should paint the orchid, for the leaves of the orchid grow as though they were flying and fluttering, the buds open joyfully, and the mood is indeed a happy one."

The beginner should concentrate at first on practicing with his brush. The strokes should be made with elbow raised. They will then be natural and light, appropriate to the form to be drawn, firm without being tense, full and lively. As for ink, they should be a happy combination of light and dark tones. Leaves should be dark and the flowers light; the dotting of the heart should be dark and the sheath of the stem light. This is a fixed rule. If color is used, dark tones should be used on the face of the leaves and light on the back, dark tones for leaves in front and light for those in the back. This rule should be thoroughly absorbed.

OUTLINE METHOD

The ancients used the outline method in painting orchids. It was the method called *shuang kou* (double contour or outline), one of several ways of painting orchids. In using it, if one copies only the shape, filling in with color, blue and green, the essence of the flower will be lost and it will be devoid of grace. But this particular method should not be omitted in discussing the various methods, and that is the reason it is mentioned here.

RULES OF PAINTING THE ORCHID IN FOUR-WORD PHRASES FOR MEMORIZING[6]

The secret of painting the orchid rests basically in the circulation of the spirit *(ch'i yun)*. Ink should be of best quality. Water clear and fresh. Inkstone clean of old ink. Brush of quality and flexibility.

First draw four leaves. They should vary in length. A fifth leaf crosses them. In this there is grace and beauty. At the crossing of each leaf add another; place three in the center, four on the sides, and complete with two more leaves.

Ink tones should be varied. Old and young leaves should mingle. Petals should be light, stamens and calyx dark. The hand should move like lightning; it should never be slow or hesitant. Everything depends on structure and style *(shih)* by means of the brush.

Flowers should have a variety of positions: front, back, and side views. If they are to make an agreeable composition, they

---

[6.] In translation, the phrases cannot be rendered with the uniform brevity of the original; even there, however, many of the rules are phrased in two sets of four words. It was, of course, the conciseness and rhythm that helped in memorizing.

should be placed naturally *(tzu jan)*. Three buds and five blooms compose a picture. Flowers in wind or sunlight are elegant. In frost or snow, leaves begin to droop.

Stems and leaves should have movement like the tail of a soaring phoenix; the calyx should be light as a dragonfly. At the base of the plant there is a sheath of leaves that should be drawn in roughly with the brush; stones should be added, drawn in the *fei pai* (flying white) method. Place one or two orchid plants by a plantain tree as though they were ordinary grass, or on a secluded bank; add them to one or two stalks of green bamboo, or draw them beside thorny brambles. These improve the composition. Follow Chao Meng-fu, for that is the true tradition.

RULES OF PAINTING THE ORCHID IN FIVE-WORD PHRASES FOR MEMORIZING

In painting the orchid the first stroke is (the arc-shaped stroke) called *p'ieh*. The brush should be handled through the wrist with agility. Brushstrokes should not be equal in length. When the leaves grow in bunches, crisscrossing, bending, and drooping, they should have *shih* (style and structural integration). Bending over or facing up, each has a special aspect; distinction, moreover, should be made between the forms in the foreground and those in the background. There should be variety of ink tones. Flowers and more leaves should be added, also the sheath that covers the base. The flowers should first be drawn in light ink; soft and pliant, they are supported by their stems. Differences between the inside and outside of petals should be shown, each form being very delicate. The stem should be wrapped in a fine young leaf. Flowers gain distinction when their stamens are dotted with dark ink. In full bloom a flower stands erect with face upwards. The mood is that of a fair and happy day. When flowers are painted in a breeze, they should seem to be weighted with dew. Buds are closed as though they were firmly holding their fragrance. The five petals of the flower should not be arranged like fingers of an outstretched hand. They should be like fingers, though with one or two curled and one or two straight. The stem of the marsh orchid should be strong and upright, its leaf strong and vibrant, the leaves spread out on all sides more than with the ordinary orchid. Flowers hang from the tips of the stems; their subtle fragrances can be conveyed by the movement of the wrist. Through brush and ink it is possible to transmit their essence.

a. The first stroke like an arc.
b. The second stroke crossing to form "the eye of a phoenix."
c. The third stroke.
d. Stroke in the form of "the belly of a mantis."
e. "Idea present, brush absent" (hiatus in the first stroke).
f. Stroke in the form of "a rat's tail."
g. Three strokes at the base, formed by "carp's head" strokes.

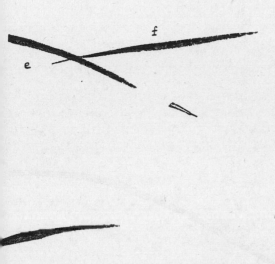

In painting orchids, the leaves should not all be of the same length. As the brush moves at a slant, there may occasionally be a break in the stroke. This does not matter. (Done properly,) it illustrates the principle that the idea has continuity even though there is a break in the brushstroke: *i tao pi pu tao* (idea present, brush absent). The pressure of the brush should conform with the concept in the heart; the hand will then achieve perfection in skill.

ORCHID LEAVES IN BRUSHSTROKES DRAWN FROM RIGHT TO LEFT

In painting orchids, the base of the plant should be indicated. While there may be scores of leaves, they should not be drawn the same length or without some order. They may be painted in light or dark tones, depending on the circumstances. This should be thought out and carried through with intelligence and discrimination.

Two orchid plants drawn in the host-guest relationship.

Leaves drawn in *shuang kou* (outline) style.

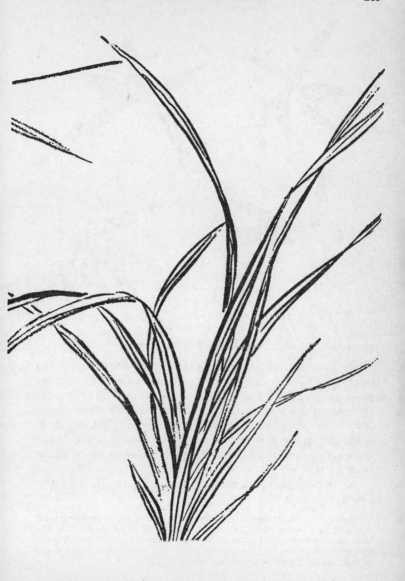

EXAMPLES OF PAINTING [1] FLOWERS

In the drawing of flowers, each should have five petals. The larger petals are straight and broad, the smaller and narrower petals curl. Use dark tones of ink to dot the stamens. When the stamens are in the center among the petals, the flower is facing front. When shown on either side of the middle petal, as though in its armpits, the flower is being viewed from the back. When the stamens are dotted in on the side, the flower is being seen from the side.

(At the top are) two flowers back to back; (below,) two flowers face to face.

[1] *Hsieh* (write). Gradations of tones were unfortunately lost in the lithographic reproduction of the first Shanghai edition and the later editions based on it. The tones should give the petals form and delicacy, and finishing touches such as the dark accents of the stamens. The tip of the petal, where a brushstroke begins, should be dark, and the rest of the form much lighter.

EXAMPLES OF DOTTING THE HEART

The form of the three dots (of the stamens) in the heart of the orchid is like the character *shan*.[1] Whether the flower is straight, turned over, leaning to one side, or facing upward, the dotting of the stamens in these various positions depends on the position of the petals. This is a fixed principle. In addition to the three dots of stamens, a fourth is sometimes added, because petals are often mingled and, in a group of flowers, one should avoid being repetitious. This does not violate the rules.

(The right column of examples shows) correct forms of the three dots; (the rest are) forms of the three with a fourth added.

[1] See Appendix, Sec. VIII, for the form of *shan*.

Examples of buds and flowers in outline style.

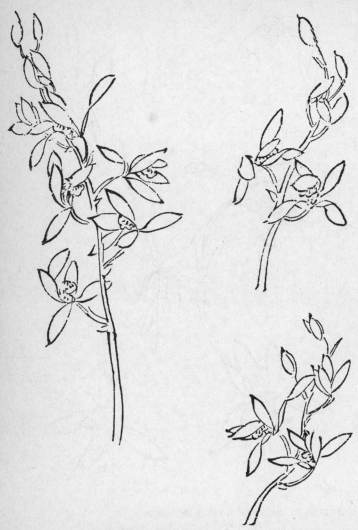

Flowers on their stems, in outline style.

Book of the Bamboo

DISCUSSION OF THE FUNDAMENTALS OF BAMBOO PAINTING

PRINCIPLES OF INK PAINTING OF BAMBOO[1]

In bamboo painting, the first step is concerned with the stems: space should be left between the sections of the stem for the knots; the sections between knots near the ends of the stems should be short, those forming the middle of the stem should be long, while at the base of the plant they again are short. Avoid painting bamboo stalks that appear swollen, withered, or too dark in tone. And they should not all be of the same height. The edges of the stem should be distinct. The knots should firmly join the sections above and below them, their forms being like a half circle or like the character *hsin* without the dots.[2]

At about the fifth knot above the soil, the branches and foliage begin to grow. In painting leaves, the brush should be saturated with ink; brushstrokes should move smoothly and without hesitation. The leaves will then be naturally *(tzu jan)* pointed, tapering, and sharp, unlike the leaves of the peach and the willow. The hand should be in turn light and heavy. Leaves ar-

---

[1] For reasons of space, and because many of the names mentioned have little meaning today, the notes on the historical background of bamboo painting, opening this discussion, are omitted. The outstanding painters are mentioned later in the Summary of Rules; such as Li K'an, who wrote the fundamental *Treatise on the Bamboo,* published at the beginning of the XIV century; and the famous two of bamboo painting and poetry, Wen T'ung and Su Tung-p'o, of the X century. Su's poems and colophons on Wen's paintings contributed to the traditional view of Wen as the greatest master of the subject in ink monochrome and as an ideal "gentleman-painter" in character, scholarship, and skill.

[2] See Appendix, Sec. IX, for *hsin* and other Chinese characters cited for their forms.

ranged in a form resembling the character *ko* have the dividing third leaf. Leaves drawn in the form of the character *jen* should be clearly separated. Leaves at the top of the plant should be arranged in the style called *tsuan feng wei* (gathered in the form of a phoenix's tail). The branches to the left and to the right should be clearly defined in their relationship, each branch issuing joint by joint, each leaf issuing from the stem.

In wind, fair weather, rain or dew, bamboos behave in a characteristic manner. Whether they are bending over or standing upright, hidden or exposed, each aspect has a particular form and integration.[3] Each movement of turning, bending, drooping, or rising holds a specific idea *(i)* and principle *(li)*,[4] that must be observed and felt through the heart for full understanding of the expressiveness of bamboo. If one stem is not firmly placed or one leaf not properly added, the whole composition may be spoiled, as one slight flaw mars a piece of jade.

FIRST PRINCIPLES OF COMPOSITION

In ink compositions of bamboo, the four parts of the plant to be considered are stem, knot, branches, and leaves. If the rules[5] are not followed, time and effort will be wasted and the picture never completed.

Ink should have dark and light tones. Brush should be deft and vigorous. In learning the brushstrokes from right to left and from left to right, one gradually learns also to discern variety of ink tones, coarseness or fineness of brushwork, and what has splendor and what lacks vitality.

[3] *Hsing shih* (form and structural integration, power and style).
[4] Neo-Confucianist *li* (principle, law, essence) in the sense of "soul of things"; it has been translated "inherent reason of things," "universal principle," and "fitness of things," in other words, that which is a reflection of *Tao.* The rest of the sentence, showing the influence of Taoist-Zen theories, refers to the idea of the painter identifying himself with the object, which, as Su Tung-p'o pointed out, was Wen T'ung's supreme achievement. Su wrote that craftsmen could depict form, but only those of surpassing ability and perception (the gentlemen-painters) could comprehend and transmit to paper the *li* of forms.
[5] *Kuei chu,* the pattern of custom, also referring to the compass and square, symbols traditionally associated with moral character and effort; by extension, also an analogy to the Circle and Square of Heaven and Earth, *Tao.* Hence, rules with deep significance.

The way in which a leaf grows from a branch should be clearly defined. Huang T'ing-chien said: "If the branches do not issue from the knots correctly, the leaves will be in disorder and have no proper support."

Each brushstroke should be a living idea *(sheng i)*, each aspect natural *(tzu jan)*. All four sides of the plant should be properly related and each branch and leaf alive. Only thus can bamboo be painted. But, while many from ancient times to the present have painted bamboo, there have been only a few who truly excelled. The tendency has been to make bamboo compositions either too simple or too complicated. In some instances, the stem has been beautifully placed, bending with grace, but the branches and leaves have been exaggerated and poorly composed: while the bamboo has been well placed, the direction of the leaves and the front and back of the cluster have not been properly related; or the leaves have the appearance of having been cut out by a knife; or the composition of the whole group of bamboos resembles a flat board with thorns sticking out. The grossness and banality of poor compositions of bamboo! One should not mention them.

In general, even those painters who were considered exceptional managed only to achieve the stage of making a pleasing or an exact composition. They did not reach perfection. Wen T'ung of Hu-chou alone was outstanding. Heaven gave him great powers, releasing his talent and inner resources; his brush had divine assistance, and he seemed one with nature. He may seem to have galloped through all rules and methods, to have gone beyond worldliness and the commonplace. Yet, following his heart, he was able to realize his whole conception without transgressing the rules. Those who come after him should not fall into grossness or banality. They should attend to what they ought to learn.

FIRST PRINCIPLES OF PAINTING THE STEMS

If only one or two stems of bamboo are being painted, the ink tones may be rendered as one pleases. If there are more than three stems, those in the foreground should be painted in dark tones and those in the back in light. If the same tone is used for all, it would be impossible to distinguish their relative positions.

From tip to root, although the stems are painted section by section, the continuity of the idea *(i)* expressed through the brush remains intact.[6] In drawing the stem, one should leave spaces for the knots. At the base and the tips of the stems, the sections of the stem should be short; in the middle of the stem they should be long. Each stem should have its proper tone. Each stroke of the brush should be even and firm. The edges of the stems should be slightly concave.

Above all, be careful to avoid swollen or distorted stems, uneven ink tones, coarseness of texture, a dryness that looks like decay, a density of ink that may look like rot, and equal spacing between knots. It is imperative to avoid these faults. I have seen painters, whom one can only call gross, use rattan cane, a piece of acacia bark, or a roll of paper soaked in ink to paint bamboo stems in ink, which then were of the same thickness, flat as a board, lacking any suggestion of roundness. One can only laugh at such tricks and not imitate them.

FIRST PRINCIPLES OF PAINTING THE KNOTS

When the stems are drawn, the knots, which come next, are very difficult. The upper part of a knot should cover the lower; the lower part should support the upper. Although there is a space between the two parts, the continuity of the idea *(i)* is intact. The two ends of the upper part turn up, the middle part curves down in the shape of the crescent moon. Thus one may see that the stem is rounded. With each brushstroke the idea advances rapidly, without hesitation. Naturalness *(tzu jan)* is necessary to the continuity of the idea.[7] The knots should not be too large or too small, nor should they be of equal size. When they are equally large, they will look like rings; when equally small, like

---

[6] Literally, and more vividly, "like the thread of a string of coins."

[7] This deceptively simple statement has several layers of meaning, discussed in Part One, Ch. IV, in reference to the qualities of *tzu jan* and *chen* in painting and in the painter himself.

sticks of ink. They should not be too curved nor the space between too large. If they are too curved, they will look like the
joints of a human skeleton, and if there is too much space between the two parts of the knot, the life and continuity of the
idea will be lost.

FIRST PRINCIPLES OF PAINTING THE BRANCHES

In the painting of bamboo branches, terms have been given to
the various parts and aspects. The places where the leaves sprout
are called *ting hsiang t'ou* (fragrant spots). The form of three
leaves forking out at the tips of the branches is called *ch'ueh
chao* (bird's claw). Upright forked branches are called *ch'ai ku*
(hairpin shapes). A branch shown with stems in the back and
leaves in the front is termed *to tieh* (heaped cluster). A branch
painted showing the backs of the leaves and inside the cluster is
termed *peng t'iao* (scattered around).

Brushstrokes should be strong and full, sustained by the idea
of life. The brush should move briskly, in no way dilatory. Old
branches are rigid and straight, their joints large and knotted.
Young branches are supple and pleasing to look at, their joints
small and smooth. When there are many leaves, the branches
bend; when there are few, the branches straighten up. Branches
in the wind or in the rain vary in form accordingly. They should
be depicted fittingly—this is something that can not be fixed by
rules.

Yin-po and Yun-wang[8] drew branches and knots in one sweep
of the brush. Since this is not a traditional method, there is no
need to discuss it here.

FIRST PRINCIPLES OF PAINTING THE LEAVES

Brushstrokes should be powerful and distinct, setting down the

---

[8] Without the surnames it is difficult to identify these painters. However, Su
Tung-p'o was said to have painted bamboo stems in one stroke, explaining that
they grew that way, thereby invoking the idea *(i)* and the soul or essence *(li)* of the
bamboo.

living quality *(shih)*[9] of the leaves yet at the same time evoking "emptiness." Each stroke should be extraordinarily expressive. If there is the slightest hesitation, the leaves will look thick and will lack the essential sharpness of form. This is an exceedingly difficult step in painting bamboo, and if talent is lacking, one might as well forget there is such a thing as painting bamboo in ink.

There are certain things to be avoided that the beginner should know. When leaves are large, they should not be painted to resemble those of the peach tree; when small and slender, they should not resemble those of the willow. Leaves should not be placed separate and alone. They should not be placed side by side in a row or in the form of the character *i,* though not crossed like *hsing,* or spread out stiffly like the five fingers of an outstretched hand or like the wings of a dragonfly. When leaves are laden with dew, or when they are in rain, snow, or wind, each of the various positions, back and front, bending or straight, has its own aspect. They should never be rendered incorrectly. That would be like staining the silk with black ink strokes.

METHOD OF OUTLINING *(kou le)*

First take a stick of willow charcoal, to place the stem of the bamboo. Then draw in the branches to left and to right. Next, use brush with ink to outline the leaves. When the leaves are drawn, the stem, branches, and knots should follow. The leaves at the top of the stems are drawn one by one, in the form called *ch'ueh chao* (bird's claw). Leaves should be arranged some together, forked, and some facing away from each other. The whole composition should be clear. Variation in ink tones (in the outlining) should distinguish the plants in front from those

---

[9.] *Shih* (living quality, that of being substantial and actual), different from *shih* (structural integration), though both have been translated "power." See Appendix, Sec. VI, for Chinese forms of the two *shih.* Here the substantial quality is stressed by contrast with the space around the forms, *hsu* (emptiness, receptivity to *Tao*); together they are capable of expressing an aspect of *Tao* and thus have power to lift the spectator "beyond the ordinary, out of the world." *Shih* (state of being actual) has been described in the *Lankavatara Sutra* (tr. Suzuki, p. 43) as "the ocean dancing in a state of waveness."

in the back, the former being painted in dark tones, the latter in light. Thus may bamboo be rendered in outline (and filled in with color). In its way of handling the parts in light or shadow, foreground and background, and of placing the stems and drawing in the leaves, this method is similar to that of painting bamboo in ink. Each method complements the other.

SUMMARY OF INK PAINTING OF BAMBOO PHRASED FOR MEMORIZING BY CHANTING[10]

Huang T'ing-chien was the first to teach the outline method. Su Tung-p'o and Wen T'ung started the painting of bamboo in ink. Lady Li traced the shadows of bamboo on a window. Li K'an, Hsia Ch'ang, and Lu Chi all painted bamboos in the same style, the main stem being drawn in the *chuan wen* (seal style) of calligraphy, the knots in the square and plain *li shu* (official style), the branches in the *ts'ao shu* (grass style), and the leaves in the *k'ai shu* (regular style).[11] There are not so many brushstroke styles and methods. There are, however, four factors essential to full experience in bamboo painting. Silk or paper should be of good quality. Ink should be fresh. Brush should be swift and sure. And do not start until the conception *(i)* is clear: the idea of each leaf and branch should be complete in one's mind before being drawn.

Begin with leaves composed in the form of the character *fen* and continue with leaves in the form of *ko*. Where in nature the leaves are sparse, in the painting they should be the same. And where there are many leaves, thus it should also be in the picture. But it should be borne in mind that where many leaves are drawn, they should not be tangled; and where leaves are few, branches should be drawn filling blank spaces.

Where bamboos are painted in the wind, their stems are

[10] *Ko chueh.* As in *Orchid,* these rules phrased for memorizing cannot be translated with uniform brevity.

[11] Not literally in these writing styles, though with similarities in form and brushwork. Briefly, the *chuan* and *li* styles were stylized and generally squared forms; the *ts'ao* a rapid shorthand style; and the *k'ai* a clearer version of *ts'ao,* though less stiff than the other two styles. The mention of them here, along with the use of certain characters as patterns of forms, illustrates the intimate relationship between painting and calligraphy and the lengths to which the literati tried to identify the two arts.

stretched taut and the leaves give an impression of disorder, their joints bend, and startled rooks fly out from the foliage. Bamboos in rain bend. How could it be otherwise? In fair weather, bamboo leaves compose themselves in pairs like the form of the character *jen.* A cluster of young bamboos should be composed on a foundation of a strong forked branch with small leaves at the tips of the branches, joined by groups of larger leaves in the body of the plant. Bamboos laden with dew resemble those in rain. In fair weather they do not bend; in rain they do not stand erect; heavy with dew, their tops bend and almost touch the lower branches. In blank spaces draw leaves in the form of *ko,* with the heads of the branches bending over. To paint bamboo in snow, apply a piece of oiled cloth[12] to the back of the silk and draw branches like those in rain; the forms of the leaves not covered by snow are jagged like saw teeth. When the oiled cloth is removed, an effect will be presented of the cold brilliance of snow on the leaves.

There are certain general faults in the painting of bamboo that one should remember to avoid. First of all and basically, *shih* (structural integration) should always be the main concern, but unless heart (-mind, *hsin*) and idea *(i)* are attuned, there can indeed be no good results. It is essential to have serenity, something that can arise only from a tranquil soul. Avoid making stems like drumsticks. Avoid making joints of equal length. Avoid lining up the bamboos like a fence. Avoid placing the leaves all to one side. Avoid making them like the form of the character *hsing,* or like dragonfly wings, or like the fingers of an outstretched hand, or like the crisscrossing of a net, or like the leaves of the peach or willow. At the moment of putting brush to paper or silk, do not hesitate. From the deepest recesses of the heart should come the power that propels the brush to action. How can one be apprehensive of committing faults that are all too human and not feel even more concerned that *Tao* might be obstructed?

Old stems of bamboo, their long branches warding off the cold and snow, have the appearance of protecting the treasures

[12] *T'ieh yu fu* (stick oiled cloth), a technical trick used in painting bamboo in snow.

they hold. In wind, fair weather, rain, snow, moonlight, mists, or clouds, and in all seasons, what is precious in bamboo is safely locked in by its fine knots. Paintings inspired by the River Hsiang, by the beauties of the gardens by the River Ch'i, by the famous poem about Ngo-huang, by the Seven Virtuous Sayings, by the Thousand Acres of Ten Thousand Stems of Bamboo, should all delight and move the beholder. [13]

[13.] Rules for painting stems, knots, branches and leaves are repeated in four sections following this summary and are omitted.

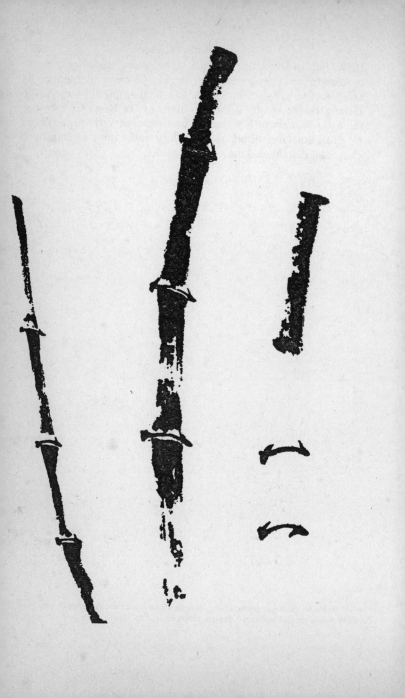

EXAMPLES OF DRAWING STEMS AND KNOTS [1]

(Downward, starting at right:)
The first brushstroke.
Knot in the form of the character *i*,[2] at the top of the joint.
Knot in the form of the character *pa,* at the lower part of the joint.
The first few strokes of a stem.
A thin stem.

---

[1] As in the *Orchid* examples, gradations of ink tones were lost in the printing of the lithographed Shanghai edition; stems should be lighter in the middle of the sections between knots; a variety of ink tones should show in branches and leaves. The examples therefore illustrate the drawing rather than the ink painting of bamboo; as the painters themselves expressed it, "have brush but not ink." The dry brushstroke (*fei pai,* flying white), however, appears in some instances, in which the hairs of the brush separate, the paper shows through, but the continuity of stroke and concept is uninterrupted.

[2] See Appendix, Sec. IX, for Chinese characters cited for their forms.

(At the top, an example of) the base of four stems. (Left,) a base of a ragged bamboo shoot.

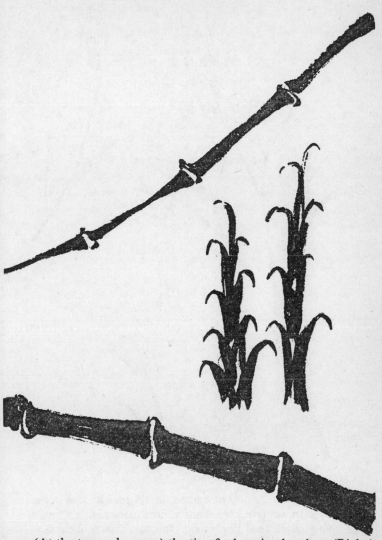

(At the top and across,) the tip of a hanging bamboo. (Right,) bamboo shoots at the base of a plant. (Below and across,) a horizontal stem.

EXAMPLES OF BRANCHES OF BAMBOO

(Left,) branches at the top of a plant, in a form like stag horns
(lu chueh). (Upper right,) branches in brushstrokes like a bird's
claw *(ch'ueh chao);* (and lower right,) in brushstrokes like a fish-
bone *(yu ko).*

Branches growing from a pair of stems; and a branch of a dwarf
bamboo.

EXAMPLES OF BAMBOO LEAVES

(Downward, starting at right:) Brushstroke like a side view of a boat *(heng chou);* brushstroke like a crescent moon *(yen yueh);* brushstrokes like a fish's tail *(yu wei);* brushstrokes like a wild goose in flight *(fei yen);* and brushstrokes like a goldfish's tail *(chin yu wei).*

(At the top,) four brushstrokes in (two) "fish's tail" forms.
(Lower right,) five brushstrokes, combining strokes called "fish's
tail" with those called "wild goose in flight." (And at the left,)
six brushstrokes doubling the three strokes of the "wild goose in
flight" form.

EXAMPLES OF LEAVES PENDANT

(At the top, right,) a brushstroke like a feather; (lower right,) brushstrokes like a swallow's tail *(yen wei)*. (Top, left) three brushstrokes in the form of the character *ko;* (and lower left,) four brushstrokes like a startled rook *(ching ya)*.

(At the top,) four brushstrokes like a wild goose alighting *(lo yen)*. (Lower right,) five brushstrokes like a swallow in flight *(fei yen)*. (Left,) seven brushstrokes based on doubling the form of the character *ko*.

Examples of the tops of bamboo plants.

Horizontal branch of a young bamboo.

Example of bamboo plants, with moss, grass, water and rocks around the base of the stems.

Book of the Plum

DISCUSSION OF THE FUNDAMENTALS OF PLUM¹ PAINTING

SINCE the T'ang and Sung periods, it may be said there were four schools of plum painting. There were those who used outline *(kou le)* method and filling in with color. This was begun by Yu Hsi (IX century), developed by T'eng Ch'ang-yu (IX century), and perfected by Hsu Hsi (X century). There was the method of painting the plum directly in color in the style called *mo ku* (no bones), which was invented by Hsu Ts'ung-ssu (XI century), many worked in this manner up to the time of Ch'en Ch'ang (XII century?), who modified it. Ink painting of the plum was started by Ts'ui Po (XI century) and was perfected by the monk Chung-jen, Mi Fei, and Chao Pu-chih. The *ch'uan* (ring) method of outlining the flowers without adding color was invented by Yang Wu-chiu (XII century). Wu Chen (early XIV century) and Wang Mien (late XIV century) developed this method and influenced the whole (Ming) period.²

---

¹· *Mei* is a general term for various trees of the genus *Prunus* and is used also in speaking of the blossoms or fruit.
²· The opening discussion on the historical background of plum painting is not given in full here. Its contents is summed up in this paragraph with which it closes. Mention should be made of Tsou Fu-lei of the XIV century, who is not included in lists of masters of plum painting but who certainly ranks among them; his superb ink painting on a scroll (13.43 in. x 88 in.) of a plum tree, entitled *A Breath of Spring*, in the Freer Gallery of Art, Washington, D.C., which is reproduced in *The Tao of Painting*, Vol. 1, is one of the masterpieces of Chinese painting that has survived.

SUMMARY OF YANG PU-CHIH'S[3] RULES OF PAINTING THE PLUM

When trunk and branches are slender, blossoms are small; when the tips of the branches are fresh, flowers are luxuriant. At the points where the branches connect and fork, flowers are numerous and mingle together. Where the tips of branches are few, flowers and buds also are few.

The trunk is drawn sinuous, like a dragon, giving an impression of iron power. Tips of long branches are like arrows, of short ones like spears. Where there is space at the top of the picture, the top of the tree is indicated; where there is too little space, no attempt is made to show the top.

When the plum tree is painted on a cliff or at the edge of water, its branches are curiously twisted and bear few blossoms; in fact, only buds and half-opened buds. When the plum tree is painted "combed by the wind" or "washed by the rain," there are many spaces on the branches, blossoms are wide open, and some of them crushed. When the plum tree is painted in mist, branches are delicately drawn and the blossoms depicted with tenderness as though they held smiles and gentle laughter on the boughs. When the plum tree is painted in a rising wind or after a light fall of snow, branches bend, the trunk seems old, and flowers are few. When the plum tree is painted in sunlight, the trunk stands proudly erect and the blossoms seem to give forth rich fragrance. Beginners should examine these various aspects and study them well.

There are many examples available for study of works of the schools of plum painting: in some, the blossoms are few, nevertheless fragrant and lovely; in others, the many flowers are alive; in a few, past their prime but still beautiful, the flowers are pure and clear almost to transparency and yet robust. How can words adequately describe all this?

---

[3]. Yang Wu-chiu, *tzu* Pu-chih, of the Sung period, was said to have learned plum painting from Chung-jen (see n. 5) and to have written the last chapter of the latter's *Mei P'u* (Treatise on the Plum Tree), which has served since Southern Sung times as the basis of all other works on plum painting, including this book of the Manual.

T'ANG SHU-YA'S[4] RULES OF PAINTING THE PLUM

The plum tree has branches, roots, joints, and knots, and on it is moss. It may be in a garden, on a cliff, at the water's edge, or by a bamboo fence. The places where it may be found growing are as various as its many forms.

Its blossoms have four, five, or six petals; generally five. The four- and six-petaled blossoms grow on the thorny plum *(chi mei)* but are unusual on other varieties. The roots may be old or young, crooked or straight, outspread or knotted, sometimes ordinary in shape but sometimes creating wonderfully strange forms. As for the tips of the branches, there are some like the handles of acorn cups and others straight, like the ends of iron rods; there are some like the claws of cranes, some like dragon's horns, some like stag's antlers, some like the tips of an archer's bow, some like fishhooks.

The forms of the plum tree may be large or small, seen from the back or the front, leaning or upright, crooked or straight. The blossoms have many forms, like grains of pepper, like the eyes of a crab, and sometimes like a smile. They may be wide open or closed or about to drop. Their forms are never the same; there is no limit to their variety. To catch their very essence in the fewest brushstrokes and with the least amount of ink, one must take Nature as teacher, be conscious of her law *(li)* and practice constantly with the brush. Thus the divine spirit will grow and gradually pervade one's whole heart and intelligence. Thought *(ssu)* may then grasp the form *(hsing)* and structural integration *(shih)* of the blossoms. Attention should be given to the structure of the whole tree in all its strange and wonderful shapes. Brush and ink should be free from restraint and tension.

The roots and the base of the tree are tortuous in some parts and outspread in others, the ends of the branches like flying plumes, the blossoms with their heads grouped like the character *p'in*. Old branches are distinct from young ones; blossoms are well arranged and their stamens drawn accordingly; and there are long and short branches.

Each flower is attached to a calyx, each calyx to the stem and

[4] A relative of Yang Pu-chih, and dated also in the Sung era.

branch, and the branch in turn to the trunk. The trunk seems
to have the scales of a dragon, the scales being like old scars. No
two branches are of the same length. Groups of three blossoms
are arranged like the feet of a bronze tripod. The calyx is long,
the sepals short. On the highest branches, the blossoms are small
with long calyx and stems. There are points at which blossoms
are luxuriant, but they should not be entangled. Branches and
their tips are rendered in dark ink tones, the stalks of the blossoms in even darker tones. Old and dried branches give an impression of being at leisure; crooked branches appear to have a
certain calmness. If one is able to represent the blossoms as
though wrought in jade, and the trunk as a dragon or a whirling
phoenix, it is evident that one's heart dwells on the hills of Ku or
among the mountains of the Yu range; one's brush will bring
forth branches like lithe young dragons. In such circumstances,
how can one be disconcerted by the infinite number of shapes or
fear the many possible variations?

HUA-KUANG CH'ANG-LAO'S[5] PRECEPTS ON PLUM PAINTING

In composing the flower and its calyx, the stamens should be
drawn correctly and with precision, the filaments long, the anthers
short. The stamens are strong and the calyx tapering and pointed.
When the stamens are upright, the flower also is upright; when
they lean to one side, the flower likewise is inclined.

Branches do not grow in opposite directions (from the same
point on bough or trunk). Nor do blossoms grow side by side
symmetrically. When there are a number of blossoms growing
close together, they should not appear to be entangled; when
blossoms are few, they should not give an impression of sparse-
ness. Old branches, though dry and decaying, should nevertheless convey an idea *(i)* of compactness. Sinuous branches should
give an impression *(i)* of growing and stretching out. Blossoms

[5] The monk Chung-jen lived at a monastery called Hua Kuang Shan, from which
he acquired his other name. There apparently was another and younger Chung-jen at
the same place, and the designation of Ch'ang-lao (aged and venerable) might refer
to the older monk. At any rate, the Chung-jen mentioned here was the author of the
famous *Treatise on the Plum* and was renowned for his ink paintings of the plum tree.

should seem to join each other by mutual consent, and branches likewise should seem to depend on each other.

The heart should be at ease and the hand swift. Ink should be light and brush almost dry. Blossoms should be round, not to be mistaken for those of the apricot. Branches should be thin and fine but not like those of the willow. The purity of the bamboo and the strength of the pine are manifest in the plum.

EXPLANATION OF THE SYMBOLISM OF PLUM PAINTING[6]

The symbolism *(hsiang)* of the plum tree is determined by its *ch'i*. The blossoms are of the *Yang* principle, that of Heaven. The wood of its trunk and branches is of the *Yin* principle, that of Earth. Its basic number is five, and its various parts and aspects are based on the odd and even numbers. The peduncle, from which the flower issues, is a symbol of the *T'ai Chi* (the Ridgepole of the Universe, the Supreme Ultimate, the Absolute), and hence it is the upright form of the calyx. The part supporting the blossom is a symbol of the *San Ts'ai* (Three Powers of Heaven, Earth, and Man) and consequently is drawn with three sepals. The flower issuing from the calyx is a symbol of the *Wu Hsing* (Five Elements) and is drawn with five petals. The stamens growing in the center of the flower are symbols of the *Ch'i Cheng* (Seven Planets: the five planets with the sun and the moon) and so are drawn numbering seven. When the flowers fade, they return to the number of the *T'ai Chi,* and that is why the cycles of growth and decline of the plum tree are nine.[7] All these aspects of the plum tree are based on the *Yang* and therefore are associated with the odd numbers.

The roots from which the plum tree grows are a symbol of the

[6.] This section and those that follow, through the "Ten Kinds of Plum Tree," are the most direct expressions in the Manual of number symbolism based on the *I Ching,* although at certain points the analogies seem somewhat labored.

[7.] The Taoist work, the *Lieh Tzu,* of about 400 B.C., explained this symbolism of the One to Nine as follows: "The changes of one produce seven, the changes of seven produce nine. Nine is the climax. It changes again and becomes One"—i.e., 1 (Monad), 7 *(Yin* and *Yung* and the Five Elements), 9 (the 7 and Heaven and Earth), symbolizing the process of evolution and constituting the universe as a whole (1 and 10). (Tr. Forke, *The World Conception of the Chinese,* p. 35 and n.)

Erh I (Two Forms: *Yin* and *Yang),* and this is the reason the trunk is divided into two parts. The main branches symbolize the four seasons and so are composed facing the four directions. The branches symbolize the *Lu Hsiao* (Six Crosswise Lines of the *I Ching* hexagrams) and so have six main "crossings" (for a complete tree). The tips of the branches symbolize the *Pa Kua* (Eight Trigrams of the *I Ching)* and so have their eight knots or forks. The whole tree with its trunk, branches, and blossoms symbolizes the complete and perfect number (Ten), and therefore ten kinds of plum trees have been designated. All these aspects concerned with the wood parts pertain to the *Yin* and are even numbers. But this is not all.

The front view of a blossom shows the form *(hsing)* of a circle and thus is a symbol *(hsiang)* of Heaven. A flower in back view has angles forming a square and thus is a symbol of the Earth.[8] Branches bending over have an aspect of Heaven, covering the Earth; upright, they appear like the pillars of Earth supporting Heaven.

The stamens also are symbolic. When the blossom is in full flower, it symbolizes the stage called *lao* (ripe) *Yang,* the full development of the flower just before the first step of fading, and the stamens number seven. When the blossom is faded, it symbolizes *lao Yin,* and the stamens number six. The half-opened flower symbolizes *shao* (diminishing) *Yang,* and the stamens number three. When the blossom has partly faded, it symbolizes *shao Yin,* and the stamens number four.

The bud symbolizes the entity of Heaven and Earth. Its stamens are not yet visible, although their essence *(li)* is already contained within the bud. Therefore one calyx and two sepals are indicated; Heaven and Earth are still an undivided entity, and Man (represented by the third sepal) has not yet appeared. The flower with its stem and calyx symbolizes the beginning of the interaction of the powers of Heaven and Earth; when the *Yin* and *Yang* begin to

---

[8.] An interesting parallel is presented on a Ptolemaic relief in the Boston Museum of Fine Arts, a limestone slab with the head of a ram god (deity of Day, Light, Heaven, and *Yang)* on the face, and on the back, the head of a cat goddess (deity of Night, Darkness, Earth, and *Yin).*

separate, the cycles of growth and decay and endless mutation are started, symbolizing the materialization and natural development of all things. There are, therefore, eight knots (comings together, connections of branches), nine stages or changes, and ten species of the plum. As may be seen, all these symbols come from Nature itself.

ONE CALYX

In form, the numerous calyxes are similar to cloves. They are attached to the branch and issue from it, successively one to the left and one to the right, but never side by side. The calyx should be drawn with precision and in strong brushstrokes. It should not bulge on one side, or the flower also would be out of shape.

TWO TRUNKS

The plum tree is spoken of as having two trunks, since its trunk should be drawn divided into two main parts, one large and one smaller, representing the *Yang* and the *Yin,* one to the right and one to the left, which also govern the placing of the branches in front and in the back. The *Yin* branches should not dominate the *Yang* ones; the smaller should in no way dominate the larger. The body of the tree is thus naturally established.

THREE SEPALS

In drawing the sepals, they should be formed like the character *ting,* broad at the top and narrow at the base. They are attached to the calyx. The point where two sepals meet is the base of the corolla. With peduncle, stem, and calyx, the sepals constitute one form and should at no point be disconnected.

FOUR DIRECTIONS (OF THE MAIN BRANCHES)

There should be method in arranging the position of the main branches from top to base and base to top, from right to left and left to right. Every aspect should be taken into consideration.

FIVE PETALS

The petals should be drawn with the brush held obliquely; they should be neither too pointed nor too rounded. When the flower is wide open, showing its seven stamens, it is as though it could be filled with dew. When the flower is half opened, only part of it may be seen. In full flower, the whole blossom is seen. The different stages should be properly indicated.

SIX BRANCHES

There are branches that bend and others that are upright; some that repeat these positions, some that are forked, some that are snapped off. They should be properly spaced, attention being given to their positions in the background and foreground, at the top and below, together and separate; then the tree will be a living idea *(sheng i)*.

SEVEN STAMENS

The stamens should be drawn with strong brushstrokes. The pistil in the center of the flower is long and without a head. The six stamens around the pistil are shorter and should be of different lengths. The pistil is the "fruit" stamen and is drawn without a head. Taste it, the flavor is sour. The stamens are drawn with heads (anthers). Taste them, they are bitter.

EIGHT TYPES OF CROSSINGS OF BRANCHES

There are branches with long tips and branches with short tips; some are young; some are in a cluster. Some are intertwined and some are solitary. Sometimes they are forked, and sometimes they have strange and wonderful shapes.

The structure and integration *(shih)* of each branch and each fork must be rendered correctly for perfect results. If each is in its proper position, the idea or conception *(i)* will be complete and the pattern of the tree will not be marred.

NINE TRANSFORMATIONS

First there is the calyx. Then, the bud. From the bud emerges the form, with petals closed. The petals issuing from the calyx gradually open. There is then the half-opened flower. Next, the full blossom. The process continues in the decline of the flower. The flower is half dead. The stage of fading is also a beginning, that is, of the transformations of the blossom into the green fruit.

TEN KINDS OF PLUM TREE (APART FROM DIFFERENT SPECIES)

Consider the different kinds of plum trees that may be painted. There are old and withering plum trees, young ones, those with abundant blossoms, the mountain plum, those whose blossoms are few and scattered, the wild plum, the ordinary plum, the kind that grows by a river, the garden plum, and those that are grown in pots. The forms vary and the distinction should be clearly indicated.

SUMMARY OF PLUM PAINTING PHRASED FOR MEMORIZING BY CHANTING

There are certain secrets in painting the plum tree. First, establish the idea *(i)*. Brush should be nimble, inspired with a certain madness.[9] The hand should move like lightning, without hesitation. Branches should spread, some straight, some crooked. Ink tones should be varied, light and dark, and never retraced. Roots should never be gross or broken. Do not put too many blossoms near the tips of branches. Young branches should resemble those of the willow, an old one should look like a kind of whip. Tips of branches should be drawn in *lu chueh* (stag horn) brushstrokes. Some branches are straight as the strings of a lute, some pointing upward like the arc of a bow, some curved like a fishing pole. Twigs bear no blossoms. The base is straight, pointing to Heaven. Trunk

[9] The expression *k'uang tien*, literally "mad at the top of the head," may be explained by the character *tien*, used by Taoists to describe true inspiration, i.e., the achievement of the state in which the heart-mind is emptied, the spirit is freed from the body, and inspiration is received from Heaven through the fontanel.

and branches of a withering tree are knotted. Minor branches and twigs should not be too numerous and should never cross in the form of the character *shih*. Blossoms should not all be whole and perfect. Branches to the left are easy to render; to the right, difficult. To draw them perfectly depends on the control of the hand even to the little finger. Space should be left on branches for adding the blossoms. When they are added, the soul of the flower should seem to be intact. On young branches, blossoms are single and separate. On old branches, blossoms are few. On branches that are neither young nor old, the idea *(i)* transmitted through the blossoms should be one of luxuriant abundance. The various aspects of old and young plum trees should be clearly indicated. The knots and bends on some branches are like the joints of a crane's legs, while some old trees are marked as with dragon's scales. Branches should surround the trunk, their tips gathering to complete the pattern.

In profile, the calyx shows three sepals. It should be properly joined to the stem. In full view (from below), the calyx shows five sepals. In a full view of the heart, the calyx is a circle.

The trunk of an old plum tree should be knotted, though not with too many "eyes"; its twisted limbs should not be too rounded.

The flowers of the plum tree have eight "faces": straight, side-view, facing upward, inclined, open, dropping, half-opened, and about to shed its petals. When the petals are awry and the flowers are bending over, the wind is blowing through the branches. When there are many blossoms, they should not seem crowded; few, they should not appear sparse. Plum blossoms are subtly fragrant, their complexion pure as jade. Two solitary blossoms growing at the top of a tree, high and tranquil, the tip of the branch like a thorn between them, resemble a branch of the pear tree.

Begin to draw a blossom at its heart, which has the form of the hole in the center of a coin. Stamens number seven and are strong as the whiskers of a tiger. The pistil is long and the stamens around it short. The anthers should be dotted in like grains of pepper or the eyes of crabs, adorning the elegance of the blossoms.

By means of the brush, light and dark ink tones are indicated. The calyx should be dark. The bark of the tree also should have a pleasing depth of tone. Young branches and tips should be rendered in light tones. The points at which the branches join should also be light. Trunks of old trees should be drawn partly with a half-dry brush. Thorns should be added in blank spaces. Around joints and knots, the brushstrokes should be like overlapping scales. There are as many ways of drawing the bark of the plum tree as there are of drawing the blossoms. The tortuous and crooked form of the trunk and limbs should suggest the form of the character *nu*.

With these basic rules and principles in mind, one should be able to produce strange and wonderful forms. Invention does not stop with the idea, although one should always keep in mind the dignity of the plum tree and what is appropriate to it. The foregoing covers the approach to plum painting and should not be treated lightly.[10]

[10.] Four sections following this summary are omitted since they are yet another summarizing of the essentials and the faults in plum painting already noted more than once in the discussion. As in the other books, Chinese characters cited for their forms are shown in the Appendix, Sec. IX.

FIRST STEPS IN PAINTING THE PLUM TREE

(Downward, starting at right:) Twig pointing upward in two brushstrokes; twig hanging down, in two brushstrokes. Twig hanging down in three brushstrokes; and twig pointing upward, in three brushstrokes.

(At the top,) a horizontal twig, growing from the right, in four brushstrokes. (Next,) a horizontal twig, growing from the left, in four brushstrokes. And a twig pointing upward, in five brushstrokes.

Two ways of drawing twigs growing from branches pointing upward.

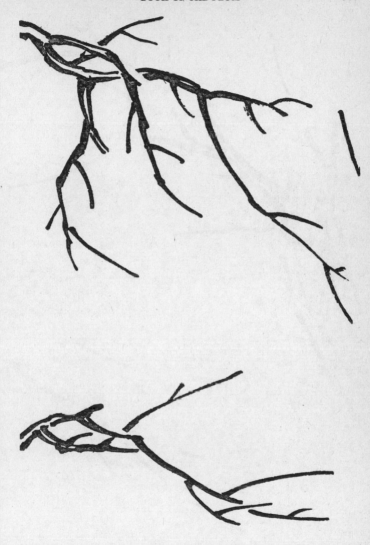

Two ways of drawing twigs growing from hanging branches.

Examples of intersecting branches and twigs from the left and
from the right, with spaces for filling in the blossoms.

Examples of blossoms at various angles.

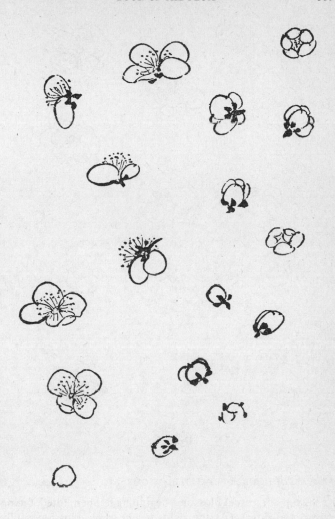

Buds and blossoms about to open, tilted, facing upward and down. (And at the lower left,) fading blossoms and a fallen petal.

EXAMPLES OF DOUBLE-PETALED BLOSSOMS

(At the top left, three) blossoms beginning to open, tilted, facing upward and down. (At the right, seven) whole blossoms, fully opened, tilted, facing down and up. (Lower left:) the calyx of double-petaled blossoms may be tinted pink, and for this reason it is outlined and not dotted in with ink.

(At the top left,) calyx and sepals in outline: front, back and side views. (Top right,) blossoms in ink, which also may be done in red, the method being the "no bones" style. (Mid-right, an example of) drawing the heart of a blossom. (Lower left,) dotting of the calyx and sepals: front, back and side views. (Lower right,) dotting of stamens, front and side views of blossoms; and an example of drawing the filaments.

(In the upper half, three examples of) two blossoms, back to back on an upright branch, on a nearly horizontal branch, and separate on a horizontal branch. (At the bottom,) three blossoms, fully opened and beginning to open.

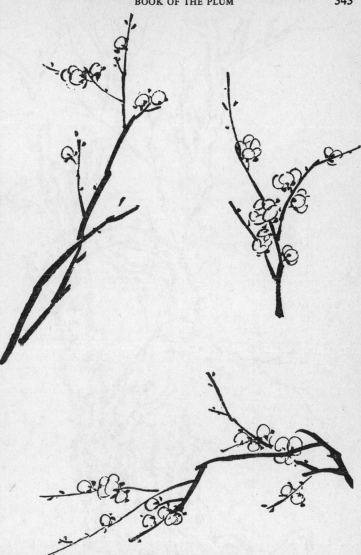

Examples of drawing buds and blossoms on branches, with the dotting of the calyxes.

EXAMPLE OF A WHOLE TREE

From the wrinkled bark of the trunk of an old plum tree branches
grow. In composing the tree from top to roots, space should be
left in which blossoms may be added. Starting with this basic
structure, more branches and blossoms may be added, depending on the space available in the picture.

Book of the Chrysanthemum

DISCUSSION OF THE FUNDAMENTALS OF CHRYSANTHEMUM PAINTING

THERE are many different kinds of chrysanthemums and great variety in their colors and forms. Without knowledge of the methods of *kou le* (outline) and *hsuan jan* (wash and tint), it is impossible to paint them *(hsieh hsiao,* write their likeness).

Up to the Southern Sung, Yuan, and Ming periods, only the literati and retired scholars treated the subtle fragrance of the chrysanthemum as a special subject of painting.[1] They expressed it in ink, not using any color. They excelled in expressing its purity. Others after them were renowned for ink painting of the chrysanthemum. In their works it may be perceived that the chrysanthemum is "defiant of frost and triumphant in autumn," a saying that expresses the essence *(ch'i)* of its character. In painting the chrysanthemum, this idea must be clearly understood so that the transmittal of it originates in the heart and passes through the wrist to the brush. Color can not convey the idea.

I (Wang Shih) have been commissioned to arrange these four books of the *Chieh Tzu Yuan* concerning the "subtle fragrance of the River Hsiang" (the orchid) and the "knotted stems of the gardens of the River Ch'i" (the bamboo), (the two plants praised as

---

[1] As with orchid, bamboo, and plum painting, the chrysanthemum as an independent subject was a fairly late development (about the x century), inaugurated and influenced by the literati. The associations and analogies of the chrysanthemum as the flower of late autumn, announcing the coming of winter and able to blossom in the cold, were developed through the XIII century. From this opening section, two short sentences in the next paragraph, consisting of about a dozen names, are omitted.

symbols of) virtue in the poem *Li Sao* (Falling into Trouble), in the *Ch'u Tz'u* (Elegies of the State of Ch'u), and in the *Wei Feng* (Airs of the State of Wei, in the *Book of Odes);* the "branch that, in the south, flowers in the winter" (the plum); and the "flower whose fragrance lingers along the bamboo fence to the east" (the chrysanthemum). These, like the solitary mountain in its dignity and calm, share a bond with people of noble character. These plants are unique. They represent the *ch'i* of the Four Seasons.[2] Is it not fitting that, to make this work on painting complete, each of these plants should be discussed?

GENERAL PRINCIPLES OF COMPOSING THE PLANT

The chrysanthemum is a flower of proud disposition; its color is beautiful, its fragrance lingers. To paint it, one must hold in his heart a conception of the flower whole and complete. Only in this way can that mysterious essence be transmitted in a painting. Some of its flowers should bend and some face upward; they should never be too numerous. Some of its leaves should be covered and some face upward, never in disorder. In brief, each branch, each leaf, each flower, each bud, must be rendered in its own full character.[3]

Although the chrysanthemum is usually placed in the category of herbaceous plants, its proud blossoms brave the frost and it is classed with the pine (i.e., with trees and ligneous plants). Its stem is solitary and strong, yet as supple as the stems of spring flowers. Its leaves are rich and sleek, yet they have aspects as varied as those that quickly fade. Its blossoms and buds should be shown in different stages of development, each in relation to another. The essence *(li)* of the plant should be kept in mind, whether the stem is bent or straight: when the flowers are fully opened, the

---

[2] Orchid, spring; bamboo, summer; plum, winter; chrysanthemum, autumn.

[3] An inadequate rendering of *te* (inner power), a term in Chinese thought implying moral strength and character, which is in accord with *Tao.* It may be seen, however, that the demand is for not only technical skill but the results of observation, experience, practice and perseverance; above all, an inner discipline. Rendering trueness *(chen)* and naturalness *(tzu jan)* in each detail of the plant reflects the stage of development of these qualities in the painter.

stem is weighted and therefore bends, while a stem bearing only buds is naturally lighter and stands straighter. A straight stem should not, however, be drawn as though it were rigid, nor should an inclined stem bend too far. These are the general rules of painting the plant. Specific methods apply to the painting of each part, the flower, calyx, stem, leaf, and base.

PRINCIPLES OF PAINTING THE FLOWERS

Each flower is different, the petals being variously formed: oval, rounded, long, short, broad, narrow, thick, or delicate, in a loose or a dense cluster. There are some that are split into two- or three-pronged petals, some with broken petals, some with petals that stick out like thorns, some with petals that curl or are rolled up. The forms are numerous. Long- and single-petaled flowers are generally flat and circular like a mirror, and the heart of the flower can be seen like a honeycomb or a sprinkling of golden grain. Flowers with small, short petals have a rounded form almost like a ball, and the heart of the flower is hidden. Although petals have a great variety of forms, all grow from the same kind of base or peduncle. However loose or few or however numerous, they must be drawn issuing from that base. The form of the flower will then be integrated, as it should be.

Flowers are of various shades of yellow, purple, pink, and pale green. The heart of the flower is dark in tone, while the outside petals are lighter; and between these dark and light tones there is a wide range of other tones. In painting white flowers, use white even in outlining and to indicate the veins of the petals.

All the above points depend on the painter's conception *(i)* of the flower and his ability to transmit it.

PRINCIPLES OF PAINTING THE BUDS AND PEDUNCLE

To paint flowers, one must know how to paint buds, half open, just about to open, and not yet opened. Each form is different. A half-open bud seen in profile shows its peduncle. In young buds, the petals are clustered together at the heart of the flower; the structural integration *(shih)* of the whole flower is already contained in that form. In buds that are just opening, the green leaves of the husk are beginning to break, a first petal is emerging like a small bird's tongue licking the nectar of a flower or like a fist with one of the fingers extended. In buds about to open, the petals hold close their fragrance but begin to show a hint of their color. Buds that are not yet open resemble pearls or jade buttons. Like stars on stems, they should be rendered individually, each flower for its own subtle charm.

To paint buds it is necessary to know how to paint the peduncle of the flower. Although the head of each flower may vary in form (according to the stage of its development), the structure of the peduncle is the same. Unlike that of other plants, it seems to be composed of layers of young leaves. When the bud is round, although the flower may be of any color, the husk and the whole form is green. At the moment the bud opens, a touch of the color of the petals is suggested. The characteristic beauty of the chrysanthemum is in its flower, but its spirit *(ch'i)* is concentrated in the bud. The petals that emerge from the bud come from the peduncle. This principle *(li)* can never be ignored. Thus, to the section on painting the flowers is added this part on painting the buds and peduncles.

PRINCIPLES OF PAINTING THE LEAVES

There are also a great variety of leaf forms in chrysanthemum painting: pointed, rounded, long, short, broad, narrow, luxuriant, and sparse. The Five Paths and the Four Spaces[4] are very difficult to draw. The leaves should not appear identical, with the effect of being stamped out flat and stiff. The positions of the leaves should be carefully considered: whether they are facing upward, turned back, curled, or folded. The face of a leaf is called *cheng* (upright, face); the back, *fan* (turned over); facing up but partly folded, *che*

[4.] As in *Trees* and *Rocks,* an analogy to the Five Points and the Four Directions: the fifth point, the Center, points upward; the four spaces refer to the spaces between the four indications of direction.

(diminished, folded); turned upward and over, *chuan* (curled).[5] After one knows how to render these four aspects, one must still know how to arrange them and also how to draw the veins of the leaves. Then the leaves will not all be alike, and the results will have variety.

The leaves immediately beneath the heads of the flowers should be rich and large, their color deep and luxuriant, for the strength of the whole plant is concentrated there. Young leaves on a stem should be pliant and delicate, their color light and clear. The leaves that are fading at the base of the plant should be yellow, their color indicating that they are beginning to wither. The color of the face of the leaves should be dark; of the back, light. So, we end the discussion.

PRINCIPLES OF PAINTING THE MAIN STEM

Flowers should cover the leaves and the leaves, in turn, should cover the stem. The main stem and base should first be sketched in with charcoal, then the flowers and leaves are placed, after which the painting begins. Only after the main stem has been finished can the flowers and leaves be added. This is done so that the flowers and leaves facing in various directions may be made to hide the main stem (at certain points). If the sketching in with charcoal is omitted, it will not be possible to establish the directions of the stalks and leaves. If, after establishing the position of the main stem, flowers and leaves are not properly added, they will incline this way and that, but all on one plane instead of around the stem. The main stem should be strong, the auxiliary

[5] These terms, significantly numbering four (cf. the Four Directions and the number of materialization of the One), have associated ideas: *cheng*, describing the face of the leaf, also has the connotation "upright" and, by analogy, the center of a target —hence it is a way of speaking of *Tao; fan* is used in Taoist works to describe the characteristic action of "returning" to *Tao; che* describes another aspect of returning, specifically "diminishing" or putting to rest (folding) worldly desires and ambitions. An important meaning of *chuan* (scroll, to roll) is indicated by the part of the character that depicts a hand picking or selecting, thus choosing with discrimination. These are minimum deductions, based on the characters themselves, to give an idea of the layer of deeper meaning apart from the technique of representing positions of leaves

stalks young and tender. The base of the stem should be old. The main stem should be supple yet should not look like a climbing plant, strong yet not like a lance; it should curve but not hang over. The chrysanthemum, as the flower "in the wind" and "with its face to the sun," holds its stem upright though not rigidly straight; sometimes it is "laden with dew" or it "braves the frost." The structural integration *(shih)* of flower, bud, stalks, base, and stem must be properly rendered; the charm of the flower will then be completely realized. The chrysanthemum may belong to a minor category of subject matter but the painting of it is not easily explained.[6]

[6.] Six short sections following this part are omitted. The rules summarizing the painting of the different parts of the plant, and the faults to be avoided, repeat points made earlier in the discussion.

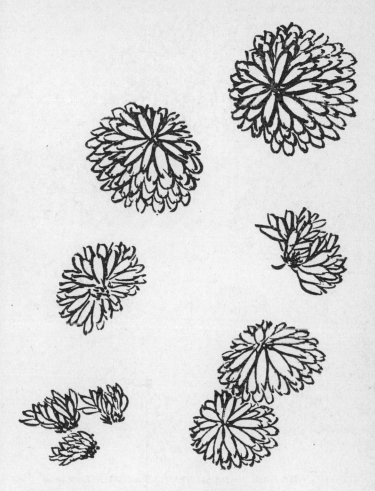

FLOWERS WITH FLAT HEADS AND LONG PETALS

(At the top,) two flowers, one bending, one looking up. (Mid-right,) side view; (mid-left,) back view. (Lower right,) two flowers, screening each other from the light. (Lower left,) buds opening.

FLOWERS WITH HIGH ROUNDED HEADS OF CLUSTERED PETALS

(At the top,) face of a fully opened flower; (immediately below, examples of) back and side views of a newly opened flower. (In the lower half,) cxamples of buds opening, one about to open, and the side view of a fully opened flower.

FLOWERS WITH POINTED PETALS ENVELOPING THE HEART

(At the top,) face of a newly opened flower; and buds opening. (In the middle,) side view of a newly opened flower; and face of a fully opened flower. (At the bottom,) a bud opening; and side view of a fully opened flower.

FLOWERS WITH HEADS FORMED BY LAYERS OF SMALL PETALS

(At the top,) face of a flower in full bloom. (Next, examples of) back view of a flower in full bloom, and side view of a newly opened flower. (And an example of the) face of a newly opened flower.

EXAMPLES OF LEAVES IN INK[1]

(Downward, starting at right, examples showing) face of hanging leaves, of leaves pointing upward, of a folded leaf. (In the left column, examples of) the backs of leaves facing upward, and of curling leaves; and the face of curling leaves.

[1]. As with the leaves of the orchid and bamboo, variations in ink tones were unfortunately lost in the lithographic reproduction of the Shanghai edition and the reprints based on that edition. As emphasized in the instructions, in the text preceding the examples, the face of leaves should be dark in tone, the backs, light, whether in color or in ink.

(At the top left,) face and back of five leaves near the top of a plant; (right,) two leaves, one bending and one facing upward. (Lower left,) group of three leaves; (and lower right,) four intersecting leaves near the base of a plant.

EXAMPLES OF LEAVES IN OUTLINE (KOU LE)

(Downward, starting at right, examples showing) face of leaf pointing upward, of a half-concealed leaf, of a hanging leaf, and of a curled leaf. (In the left column, examples of) back of a leaf pointing to one side, and of a curled leaf; a folded leaf facing upward, and one hanging down.

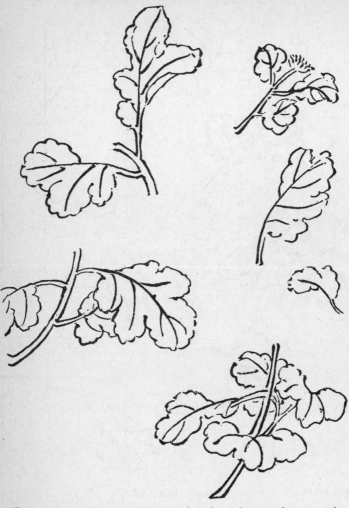

(Downward, starting at right,) peduncle and young leaves at the top of a stem; face of a leaf pointing to one side; back of a young leaf; and four leaves shielding each other. (On the left,) two leaves on either side of a stem, and a group of three leaves.

Examples of flowers on a cut stem.

(Right,) delicate petals clustered around the heart of the flower.
(Left,) flower with short petals and a rounded form.

草卉蟲譜

Book of Grasses, Insects,
and Flowering Plants

DISCUSSION OF THE FUNDAMENTALS OF PAINTING FLOWERING PLANTS, GRASSES AND INSECTS[1]

ALL the plants in the world rival one another in their beauty and give pleasure to the hearts and eyes of men. They offer great variety. Generally speaking, the wood-stemmed plants may be described as having a noble elegance, the grasses a soft grace. Grasses please the heart and eye mightily. They are a subject of this book. Among them are the many varieties of the orchid and the chrysanthemum, with their subtle fragrance, which have already been discussed in separate books.

Looking through the records of painting, one may see that each period had its masters. However, it was not until after the T'ang and Sung periods that noted painters of flowers differen-

[1] The title-page reads "Grasses, Insects and Flowering Plants"; the text heading puts the last first, perhaps because that is the order in which they are discussed. The classification is usually called *Grasses and Insects*. The subjects of these last two "books" on *Grasses and Insects, Birds and Flowers,* may be taken together; in the selection of material from the books for this work, they have been viewed in this light. In the original, the background notes and lists of masters in both books are much longer than in the preceding books, and therefore more has been omitted here, particularly as there is considerable repetition in the two books. Sections on essential points in technique and underlying concepts are of course fully presented. Sections of rules phrased for memorizing, which duplicate instructions already given, are omitted, but those on individual insects, with additional information, are given intact, though they are not rendered with the brevity and rhythm of the original.

tiated between grasses and wood-stemmed plants.[2] Those who were expert in painting flowers and plants were also, on the whole, skilled in painting birds. How can one pick them out from the vast history of painting? If one wishes to follow in their footsteps, the focus of attention should be on Hsu Hsi and Huang Ch'uan (both of the x century), who were outstanding. Their styles were different, and a section is added here on the essential difference.

Huang Ch'uan's and Hsu Hsi's wonderful works offer a great deal to students of painting. As in calligraphy, their styles have been handed down from generation to generation. Kuo Ssu wrote about the difference between Huang and Hsu. Huang Ch'uan's works were rich and elegant, Hsu Hsi's natural and unconventional. Both expressed their thoughts, what their ears and eyes observed, and what hand and heart had learned. But how can one really comprehend what was completely natural to each of them?

Huang Ch'uan and his son, Chu-ts'ai, were officials. At first (the elder Huang) was a Painter in Attendance; later, he was promoted to be an Assistant Commissioner; and finally, toward the end of his life, under the Sung dynasty, Ch'uan was elevated to the rank of a Palace Aide. His son, Chu-ts'ai, also was a Painter in Attendance. Both served at the Court. Consequently they painted what they saw in the Imperial Gardens, the rare flowers and strangely shaped rocks. Hsu Hsi, on the other hand, was a scholar who lived in seclusion in Chiang-nan. His aims were lofty. Free and intelligent, he usually took his subjects from river and lake, excelling in painting flowers on a bank and wild flowers and grasses. The two painters were like the spring orchid and the autumn chrysanthemum. Each dared to be himself and both were renowned. The brush of each produced rare works; their brushwork may be taken as models. Though their styles were extraordinarily different, both were masters. Following Huang Ch'uan were his sons, Chu-ts'ai and Chu-pao. Following Hsu Hsi were his grandsons, Ch'ung-ssu and Ch'ung-chu. They carried on the family styles and gained places in the front rank of painters past and present; not an easy achievement.

[2.] The distinction was a fairly late development, probably of the Ming period.

FOUR METHODS OF PAINTING FLOWERING PLANTS

In painting flowering plants, there are four methods. The first is outlining and filling in with color,[3] a method carried to perfection by Hsu Hsi. The majority of flower painters used to draw forms after placing them with touches of color, but Hsu Hsi was exceptional in that he first drew in ink the stem, leaves, stamens and calyx, then added color. In the second method, a style attributed to T'eng Ch'ang-yu (of the IX century), no outline is drawn and color defines form. The idea *(i)* is transmitted through the laying out in color and, moreover, represents a living idea. T'eng added cicadas and butterflies as adornment. After him, Hsu Ch'ung-ssu also did not draw an outline but painted directly in color, in the method called *mo ku hua* (no bones painting). In the third method, no color is used at all, the brush with ink being used to dot and to make washes. This method is attributed to Yin Chung-yung (of the T'ang period); he caught the true character and inner power *(te)* of flowering plants. In the fourth method, ink is used not as a wash but only in outlining, without color or shading, in the manner called *pai miao*. This method is attributed to Ch'en Ch'ang (of the Sung period), who drew the stems and stalks in the *fei pai* (flying white) style.[4]

ESTABLISHING THE *shih*[5] OF FLOWERING PLANTS

In painting flowering plants, the main thing is to establish their form and structural integration *(shih)*. Although the stems and

[3.] Style of landscape painting of Li Ssu-hsun (VIII century) and the Northern School. According to tradition, Hsu Hsi, in the X century, established it as a method in flower painting, an innovation, since the general method was to place the flower with a blob of color and then with ink draw the details.

[4.] Dry brush in a sweeping stroke, so that the paper or silk shows in the brushstroke.

[5.] See Appendix, Sec. VI, for this *shih* (structural integration) and *shih* (living quality). In Chinese thought, *shih* (to maintain strength; by extension, structural integration) was used, for instance, by the Legalists in a political and social sense: a ruler through his *shih* (power) regulated the kingdom, hence the structural integration of the state. The Taoists used this *shih* in describing the "pervading power" of *Tao*, and it is mainly in this sense, linked to technical skill, that it is used in the Manual.

stalks may be entwined and twisted, from top to base their *ch'i* (essence) flows uninterrupted through the whole form. As to the *shih* of the flowers, although they may be numerous and mixed, facing in various directions and scattered, each is naturally expressive of the joy of flowers. Their essence and the law of their being *(li)* is constant. As to the *shih* of the leaves, although they may be scattered, or dense, intertwined, and seemingly in disorder, they are never too few or too numerous, or actually in disorder, for all have their *li*.

Further details may be added, such as bees, wasps, butterflies and other insects hovering around to gather the fragrance of the flowers. They climb along stems and alight on leaves. Whether the insects are half-hidden or exposed to view, each should be drawn according to its nature. They should never be superfluous ornaments.

Among the leaves, distinction should be made between the dark and light tones; and they should seem to screen the flowers from the glare. The flowers should be placed in various positions and should be joined naturally to their stems. The (lesser) stems are straight or inclined, and, to be natural, should be properly joined to the main stem.

If, in the composition of a picture, the conception *(i)* is not reached through thought *(ssu)*, the whole effect will be blocked, like an old Buddhist priest trying to patch a garment with a hand trembling with age. How can one possibly express the divine and the wonderful in this way? That is why the *shih* is a prized element in a painting. It pertains to the spirit *(ch'i)* that should pervade the whole picture. Examination of details should yield further evidence of the divine principle. In this way an expert hand reveals itself. There are, however, many ways to obtain the *shih* in a painting, and all are elusive. One must seek them among the methods of the ancients; and if they can not be found there, they must be sought in the natural *(chen,* true) forms of the plants. In seeking the true forms of plants, one should observe them under various circumstances, in wind, in dew, in rain, and in the sun. The variety of aspects will become clear according to the degree of attentive observation.

METHOD OF PAINTING STEMS

Generally, in the painting of flowering plants, whether the style is in fine, delicate brushstrokes or the free-sketch *(hsieh i)* manner, the moment at which the brush is poised to begin is like that in a game of chess, when a whole plan of action *(shih)* should be in one's mind before the first move. The life movement engendered by the spirit *(ch'i)* should animate the whole picture. Only in this way will it avoid being stiff and lifeless. In establishing the structure *(shih)* of plants, it is necessary first to distinguish between the wood-stemmed plants and the grasses. The former are like old men, while the latter are delicate and graceful. In painting grasses, their *shih* should be established through the three basic positions of pointing upward, hanging down, and leaning horizontally; in each of these three positions there are additional forms of branches forked, crossing, shooting out, bent, and broken off. Among the stems branching off are some high and some low, some in front and some in back; any form like the character *i*[6] should be avoided. In the crossing of stems it should be clearly indicated which are in front and which in back, which are thick and which delicate; any form resembling (a cross, as in) the character *shih* should be avoided. When stems incline to one side, it should be clearly indicated which point up and which point down, which extend horizontally and which vertically; one will then avoid coiled forms like the character *chih.* There are three more things to avoid: when stems point upward, there should be a reason, and care should be taken not to make them appear stiff in their straightness; when stems bend, they should have life movement *(sheng tung)* and not appear to be exhausted; when stems are extended horizontally, they should cross each other but not seem to prop each other up. Flower and stems resemble a man with four limbs and a head: even though the countenance is beautiful, if the four limbs are weak or incomplete, how can the man be whole.[7]

[6] See Appendix, Sec. IX, for Chinese characters cited for forms.

[7] The integration of the composition of the plant is reinforced by analogy to that of man physically and psychologically, and by implication, to the Wholeness and unifying power of the One (Heaven, Spirit, *Tao*) on Earth and among all things (Four).

METHOD OF PAINTING FLOWERS

Whatever the species, large or small, it is necessary to indicate whether flowers are in full bloom, half open, placed high or low, facing front or back. Even when massed together, flowers are not identical. They should not be upright without that graceful air lent by their suppleness. They should not bend without the pleasing effect that perfect balance gives. They should not be side by side without the charm in their variety that arises from their being together. They should not be joined without the design that is the result of their being placed strategically in the composition. They should be facing upward or inclined naturally; and, as they turn toward each other, some intimation of feeling should be conveyed in their gaze. While there is variation in their positions and poses, there is clearly also a harmony.

Besides color, light and dark tones should be apparent, not only in a group of flowers but in one flower and even in one petal. Color and tones should be deep at the heart and light at the edges. Thus it should be when the flower is rendered according to its mode of being.[8] In a flower not yet open, the petals at the center are of deeper tones of color; when the flower is fully opened, they are light. When some of the flowers on a stem are past full bloom, their color is faded, while the color of others in full bloom on the same plant is fresh, and those not yet opened are of a dark tint. Flowers should not all be in the same tones of one color; there should be variation presented by a judicious use of light tones; accentuation of dark tones by lighter ones will give results beautiful to the eye.

METHOD OF PAINTING LEAVES

When one has learned to establish the structural integration (shih) of the main stem and stalks of a plant and the drawing of

---

[8] Fa, as "mode of being," in its use in the sense of dharma.

the flowers on the stems, one should then proceed to add the leaves. How can one be indifferent or careless about the *shih* of leaves? The naturalness of the flower on its stem depends on its *shih,* and the whole movement and pattern of that *shih* depends on the *shih* of the leaves. It is by the manner in which leaves are drawn and painted that flowers can be shown in various conditions and moods.

If ink is the medium, the face of leaves should be dark, their backs light. If color is used, the face should be a dark green and the backs a light green. For the back of the leaf of the lotus or water lily, a green mixed with white should be used. Only the leaf of the begonia is red on its back. What has been said about the *shih* of leaves may be applied generally to all herbaceous plants whose flowers blossom in the spring and fade in the autumn.

METHOD OF PAINTING THE PEDUNCLE

The stems of both ligneous and herbaceous plants have peduncles that support the buds, the buds being wrapped by the calyx. The peduncles may not be identical, but each supports and envelops a bud containing all the petals.

In plants with large flowers, such as the peony and the hibiscus, the peduncle holds the bud within it. The hibiscus bud is green, the receptacle part a gray-green. The peony bud is green inside and red outside. In general, when flowers are seen full face, their centers are visible and the peduncle is hidden. When the back is seen, the flowers will show the peduncle and not the center. With the side view, they show half the peduncle and half the center. The receptacle of the begonia is joined directly to the stem without a peduncle. In the magnolia and the day lily the petals are joined at the base in the peduncle.

When there are many petals, there also are many sepals; when there are five petals, there are five sepals. Some flowers have a receptacle and no peduncle, and others have a peduncle but no receptacle. And there are flowers that have both.

METHOD OF PAINTING THE HEART

In the peony and the hibiscus the heart is deep at the base of the petals. In the lotus the heart is pale, with yellow stamens. The magnolia, the red lily, the day lily and the tuberose have six petals and also six stamens tipped with anthers; from the base of the flower rises the pistil, which has no anther. Among the many kinds of chrysanthemum are some with centers visible, others with centers hidden; their shapes, color, tones, and the number of blossoms on a stem vary a great deal. The begonia has a large and rounded center. The receptacle of the orchid is light red; that of the marsh orchid is pale green. The heart of the marsh orchid is white sprinkled with red. It is important to place and paint correctly the heart of a flower among its delicate petals. The hearts and countenances of flowers are unlike those of human beings.

METHOD OF PAINTING INSECTS AMONG HERBACEOUS PLANTS

When painting insects that live among herbaceous plants, attention should be given to rendering their appearance when flying, fluttering, chirping, or hopping. Flying, the wings of insects are unfurled; returning to rest, folded again. Those that chirp vibrate parts of their forewings against their haunches, making the sharp sounds that are their song. Those that hop straighten their bodies, poised, as it were, on tiptoe, giving an impression of lively skipping. Bees, wasps, and butterflies have a pair of large wings and a pair of small. Insects that live among grasses have six pairs of long and short legs.

Butterflies are of many sizes and colors, the most common being the black, white and yellow ones. Their forms and colors are actually so varied that it would be impossible to enumerate them all. The ones marked with black have large wings and trailing tails like queues. Butterflies painted among spring flowers have pliant wings; the lower part of the body is enlarged because they are about to lay their eggs. Those painted among autumn flowers have strong wings and lean bodies, lengthened at the tail because they are growing old. They have eyes, mouths and antennae. When they fly, (a tube-like part of) their mouths is coiled; when they alight, this part of the mouth extends to penetrate the flower and draw its nectar.[9]

Insects around herbaceous plants are of various sizes, large and small, long and short; their colors change with the seasons. When the plants are in full leaf, their color is completely green, and when they begin to shed their leaves, their green gradually turns to yellow. While insects are ornamental touches to paintings of plants, they should nevertheless be added according to seasons and under the proper conditions.

RULES OF PAINTING BUTTERFLIES PHRASED FOR MEMORIZING

In painting most things, the head is the first part drawn. But in painting butterflies the wings are done first, for they are the most important part of the butterfly. It is there the divine quality *(shen)* is to be found.

When the butterfly is flying, only half the body is visible. At rest, the whole body may be seen.

On the head of the butterfly are two antennae; in between them is the mouth. When it is drawing nectar, (the tube-like part of) the mouth is extended; when it is flying, its head is drawn in. Flying in the morning, its wings are straight up, opposite each other; resting at night, its wings are folded. It flutters among the flowers, and where there are flowers there also should be butterflies adding their decorativeness to the colors of the flowers, like a beautiful lady accompanied by her maids.

RULES OF PAINTING PRAYING MANTIS PHRASED FOR MEMORIZING

Although the praying mantis is a small creature, it should nevertheless be drawn and painted with its own kind of majesty.

[9.] "The mouth parts of moths and butterfies are especially adapted for sucking nectar from flowers. If the head of a butterfly be examined, there will be found a long sucking tube, which when not in use is coiled on the lower side of the head between two forward-projecting appendages." (Comstock, *A Manual of the Study of Insects,* p. 192).

Painted at the moment it is about to seize its prey, it should have its own aspect, which is similar to that of a tiger. The look of its two eyes shows it will devour the object. Its nature is greedy and gluttonous. Such a ferocious insect may be included in paintings, much as war songs may be played on instruments of peace, like the lute and zither.

RULES OF PAINTING FISH PHRASED FOR MEMORIZING

Fish must be painted swimming and darting with vitality. They should appear startled by a shadow, or they should be floating idly, opening and closing their mouths. As they float on the surface, dive, or glide through the water grass, the clear waters envelop them or ripple off them. Deep in one's heart, one envies them their pleasure. As with human beings, they should have *i* (idea, meaning). If one fails to render this aspect of their divine quality and merely copies their appearance, even painted in a stream or mountain torrent, the fish will look as dead as on a platter.

FLOWERS OF HERBACEOUS PLANTS WITH FOUR AND FIVE PETALS

Poppy *(Yu mei jen hua,* beautiful people of Yu flower; *Papaver rhoeas).* Garden balsam *(chin feng hua,* golden phoenix flower; *Impatiens balsamina).* Begonia *(ch'iu hai t'ung,* autumn *hai t'ang; Begonia evansiana).*

Narcissus *(shui hsien,* immortals of the water).

FLOWERS WITH LONG PEDUNCLES AND FIVE AND SIX PETALS

Day lily *(hsuan hua,* flower of maternity; *Hemerocallis graminea).*
Pink *(chien lo,* snipped gauze; *Dianthus barbetus).*[1]

[1.] The literal translation of the Chinese name quite fortuitously offers a description of the tailor's term "pinking," cutting the edge of a piece of cloth in an indented pattern.

LARGE FLOWERS WITH MANY AND DENTATE PETALS

Peony *(shao yao,* herbal spoon flower; *Paeonia albiflora).*
Hollyhock *(Shu k'uei,* mallow of Shu; *Althaea rosea).*

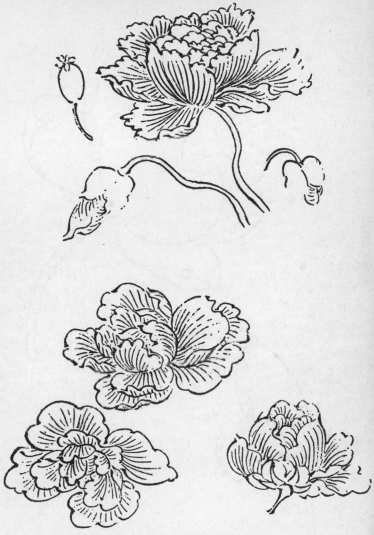

Poppy *(ying su,* seed for the oriole; *Oriolus chinensis).*
Hibiscus *(fu yung,* fairyland flower; *Hibiscus mutabilis).*

Lotus or water lily with large round petals and pointed tips.

Wisteria *(tzu t'eng hua,* purple climber), of the ligneous class. (Mid-right,) monkshood *(seng hsieh chu,* Buddhist slipper aster; *Aconitum fischeri).* (Mid-left,) marigold *(chin chan hua,* golden cup flower). (Lower right,) bleeding heart *(yu erh mou tan,* fish's son variety of the *mou tan; Dicentia spectabilis).* (Lower left,) red azalea *(tu chuan hua,* little cuckoo flower; *Rhododendron indi-cum).*

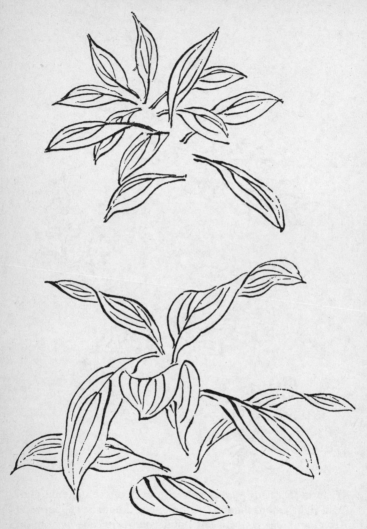

EXAMPLES OF TAPERING LEAVES OF HERBACEOUS PLANTS

(At top,) red lily; (below,) white lily.

EXAMPLES OF ROUND LEAVES IN GROUPS

(Beginning at the top,) begonia; hollyhock; and tuberose.

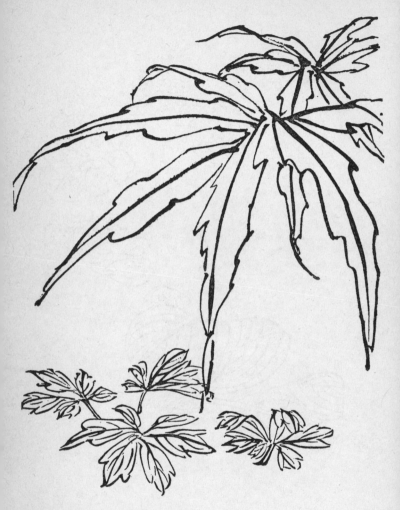

EXAMPLES OF PRONGED LEAVES

(At the top,) mallow; (below,) monkshood.

EXAMPLES OF DENTATE LEAVES

(At the top,) the *ying su* poppy; (below,) the *yu mei jen* poppy.

EXAMPLE OF CIRCULAR LEAVES

The forms of lotus leaves should be varied: turned over, facing up, half-covered, and curled. They should never be round and flat as a board.

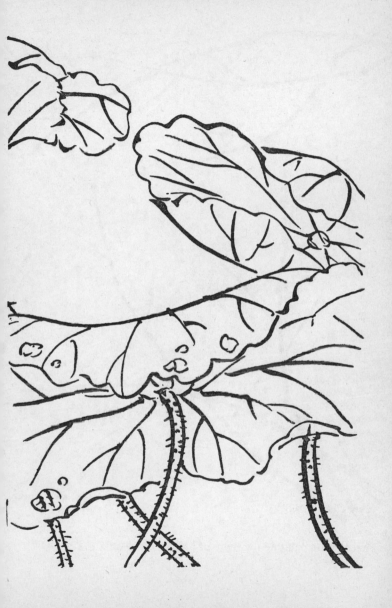

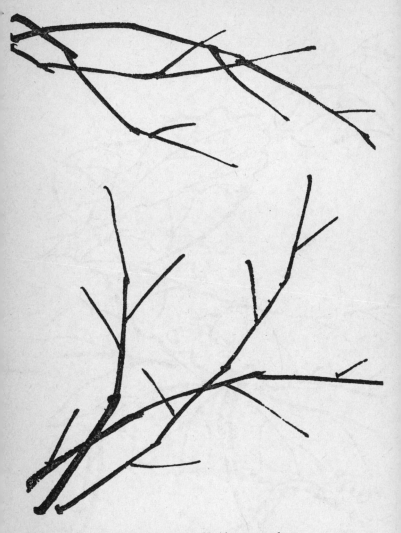

First steps in painting the stems of herbaceous plants.

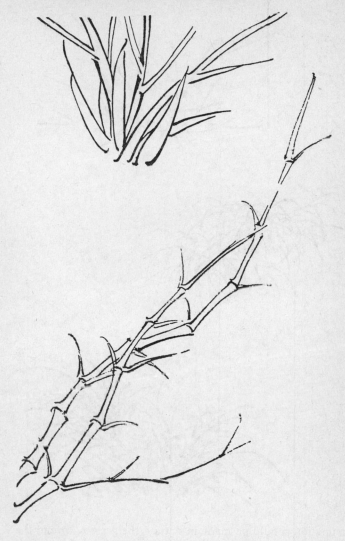

Base of stems of the peony; and the jointed stems of the poly-gonum.

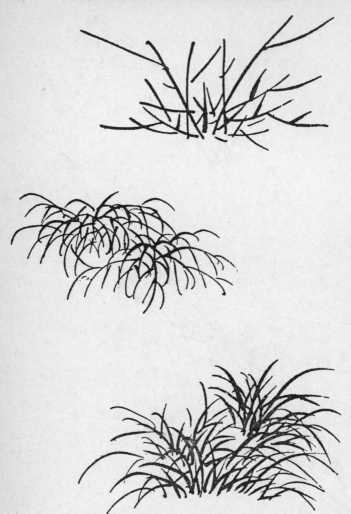

Distinction should be made in dotting the grasses around the base of plants in spring, when they are delicate, or in summer, when they flourish, or in autumn, when they are a little drawn,

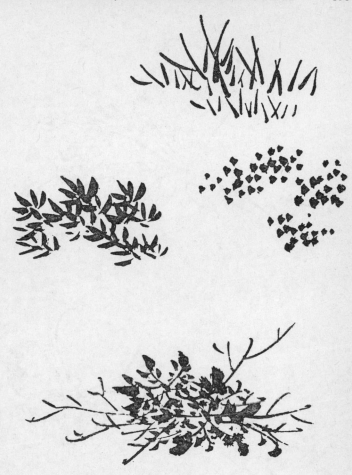

or in winter, when they are withered. When they are represented in the same stages of development as the flowers of the four seasons, they will be lovely.

EXAMPLES OF INSECTS FOR PAINTINGS OF GRASSES AND PLANTS
Butterflies.

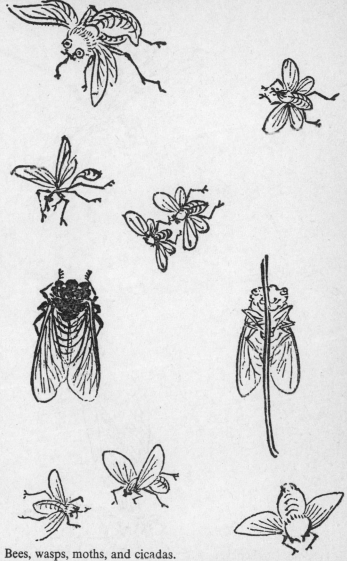

Bees, wasps, moths, and cicadas.

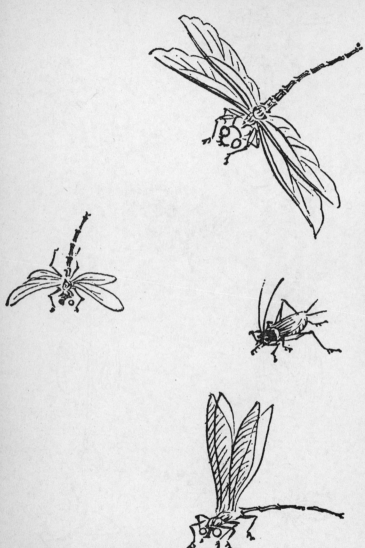

Dragonflies and cricket.

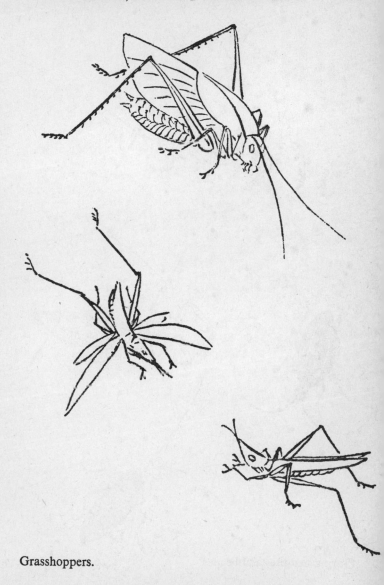

Grasshoppers.

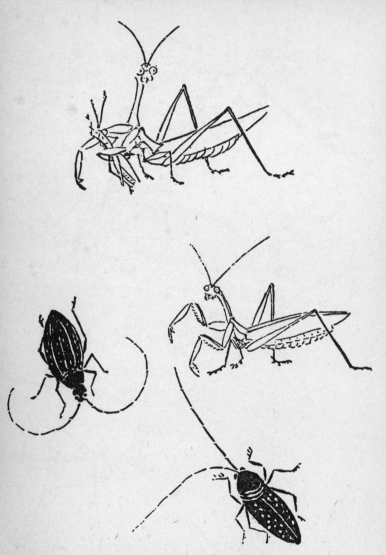

Praying mantises and beetles.

Book of Feathers-and-Fur
and Flowering Plants

DISCUSSION OF THE
FUNDAMENTALS OF PAINTING
FLOWERING PLANTS AND
FEATHERS-AND-FUR¹

THE introduction to the *Hsuan Ho Palace Catalogue of Paint-ings,* of the XII century, described plants as possessing in essence the Five Elements and the Breaths *(Ch'i)* of Heaven and Earth (nature); in the alternating action of the *Yin* and *Yang* (the Two *Ch'i),* the process of exhalation brings plants to full flower and that of inhalation causes them to fade.² Among all the numerous varieties of grasses and plants, it is impossible to distinguish and name all of those with wood stems. Neverthe-less, their forms and colors adorn all of civilization, though that may not have been nature's prime intent. Are they not evidence of the harmonizing power of the *Ch'i?* Poets frequently men-tioned them, and they are the subjects also of painting.

In the period of the Five Dynasties, Huang Ch'uan excelled in combining the methods of various masters of the past. His sons Chu-pao and Chu-ts'ai carried on the family style and for this were celebrated in their period. From Sung times, the meth-

¹· As in the preceding book, the title-page and the text heading are slightly dif-ferent; the classification, however, is usually called *Birds and Flowers. Ling mao* (feathers and fur) refers literally to birds and animals, though it is often used only for birds, as here, presumably in the sense of "feathers and down." "Flowering plants," in this book, refers to ligneous or wood-stemmed plants, including trees, shrubs and bushes.

²· The complementary action of the *Yang* (exhalation of the *Ch'i)* and the *Yin* (inhalation) was described as accounting for the cycle of the seasons. Also, spring-summer was *yang,* autumn-winter, *yin.*

ods and style of the Huang family set a standard. In the Sung period, Hsu Hsi appeared and, single-handed, changed the old methods. He has therefore been described as unique, without rival before or after. Some have classed him with Huang Ch'uan and Chao Ch'ang, but he alone achieved the divine *(shen)* and the wonderful *(miao)*. He bequeathed these gifts to his grandsons Ch'ung-ssu and Ch'ung-chu, who faithfully carried on his methods; truly, they followed in the steps of their grandfather.

Those who are learning to paint and are looking for models among the masters should choose to follow Huang Ch'uan and Hsu Hsi. Let them study their works to be influenced by their gifts, and then seek among the other masters points that will help in rendering a breath of the divine *(shen)*. In this way, they will be free of the commonplace and the undisciplined, and they may progress according to the *Tao*.

METHOD OF PAINTING BRANCHES AND STEMS

The branches and main stems of ligneous plants are different from those of herbaceous plants. Grasses are supple and lovely, whereas wood-stemmed plants are old and rugged. There are differences, too, wrought by the changes of the four seasons.

Among spring plants, plum, apricot, peach, and pear all differ in structure; moreover, the branches and stems of each vary. The old trunk of the plum tree should be gnarled, with lean branches and twigs. Thus the *shih* (structural integration) of the plum tree exhibits both strength and tortuousness. The branches of the peach tree should be straight, upward pointing and sturdy. The branches of the apricot tree should be rounded, sleek and curving. The characteristics of these three trees present a basic pattern from which one may learn the structure of others. The roots and joints of the pine and cypress should be twisted and gnarled. The trunk, main stems, and stalks of the dryandra and of bamboos should give an effect of height and purity. If one draws a branch bent, curved, or jagged, one should place it pointing upward, downward, or horizontally, where there is space or where the foliage is rather sparse. Each position should be studied for the *shih* of the particular branch. In drawing or painting a branch, the brush should be held obliquely, and the stroke should start with the tip; it should not be held vertically. In painting fruit, their *shih* requires that they hang from the branch, that being their nature.

METHOD OF PAINTING FLOWERS

The flowers of most trees and ligneous plants have five petals: for instance, plum, apricot, peach, pear, and camellia. But the flowers of plum, apricot, peach, and pear are different in color and in the shape of their petals. The flowers of the tree peony, that perfect blossom, are naturally different from all the others; the petals of the many kinds of peony have a great variety of forms. The red peony has long petals and a center like a rounded knot or button. The lavender peony has short and rounded petals, and its center is flat. The pomegranate, camellia, plum, and peach trees have blossoms with numerous petals. The flowers of the magnolia open like the lotus. The flower of the hydrangea is similar to a cluster of plum blossoms. Among the ramblers are the cinnamon rose *(chiang wei)* and the pink and the red rose *(mei kuei)*. When in bud, the white rose *(fen t'uan)*, the pale yellow moon rose *(yueh chi)*, the white or yellow climber *(t'u mi)*, and the banksia rose *(mu hsiang)* all resemble each other; when their flowers open, they are different in color. The petals of the *yen p'u* vine are like those of the white jasmine, though of a different size. The red cassia resembles the flower of the mountain alum *(shan fan)* tree of Honan, but one blooms in the spring and the other in the autumn. In the flowers of the quince *(hsi fu)* and tamarisk *(ch'iu ssu)*, of the wild plum family, the calyx must be clearly defined from the base of the flower. Among the various kinds of plum blossoms, one should indicate the difference in petal forms and centers—for instance, between those of the green-calyx plum *(lu ngo)* and the wax or winter plum *(la mei)*.

These various blossoms open in the course of the seasons. Everyone can see them and, with a little attention, get to know the various forms and colors. Various regional species, herbs, and sprouts may occasionally be included in paintings, but space does not permit discussion of the details of their forms and appearance.

METHOD OF PAINTING LEAVES

Leaves of herbaceous plants are young and supple, those of ligneous plants are old and thick. This is a fixed principle. There are, however, some trees, such as peach, pear, wild plum, and apricot, whose leaves sprout in the spring at the same time as their blossoms; and, although these are ligneous, their leaves are young and supple. Leaves that grow in autumn and winter should be painted in deep, dark tones. Because grasses and the leaves of herbaceous plants are young and supple, a few should be drawn turned over. The leaves of the cassia, orange, and camellia can endure frost and snow without wilting and wind and dew without being shaken. Their leaves, though dark and rich in color, should still be rendered with variations of tone; the distinction should be clearly made between the characteristic light and dark tones of their faces and backs. The folded or turned-over leaf should be dark green on its face, light green on its back. After painting the leaves, one adds their veins, of thickness or thinness depending on the form of the leaf and of tones in accordance with those of the rest of the leaf.

Having discussed the tones of green for leaves, we should now proceed to the use of red for leaves, keeping in mind the difference between those that are young and fresh and those that are fading. Leaves sprouting in spring often have tips of red. In autumn, when leaves begin to fall they first turn red. For young leaves not yet in full foliage, rouge red should be used. For leaves that are about to drop, umber should be used. I have observed, in examining old paintings of flowers and fruit, that the ancients had a way of painting a few withered leaves that insects had fed on among the dark green leaves. By such touches they adorned their works. One should know how to do this.

METHOD OF PAINTING THE CALYX

The blossoms of plum, apricot, peach, pear, and wild plum are five-petaled. The calyxes are of the same number, with sepals shaped like the petals. Blossoms with pointed or tapering petals usually have calyxes so formed; and similarly those with rounded petals.

The calyx of the blossom of the sturdy thorn tree *(keng, Hemiptelea davidi)* is connected with the thorns. From the calyx of the tamarisk blossom hang fine red threads. The calyx of the camellia is composed of several layers like fish scales. The calyx of the pomegranate is long with many sepals.

The color of the plum-blossom calyx changes, as the flower does, from green to red. The calyx of the peach blossom is both red and green, that of the apricot both red and black. The calyx of the wild plum is a dark red. Each blossom is turned at a particular angle, some showing their stamens, some their calyxes. The calyxes of the *yu lan* and *mu pi* magnolias in bud are green and reddish brown. The cinnamon rose has a long green calyx, red at the tip. Here, then, are various calyxes that one should be able to identify.

METHOD OF PAINTING THE HEART AND STAMENS

The calyxes of the blossoms of trees and ligneous plants are rooted in the hearts of the flowers; when, for instance, the blossoms of plum and apricot are seen full face, the calyx is not visible but the heart is the source both of the flower inside and of the calyx outside. It is the real *(shih,* substantial, living) core of the flower. At the center point are also the five small dots where the stamens issue; their ends are tipped with yellow anthers. The stamens of plum, apricot, and wild plum blossoms are not all alike: those of the plum are thin, while those of the apricot and the peach, flowering in different seasons, are luxuriant. Moreover, the stamens of the white plum are few and thin, while the red plum stamens are numerous and luxuriant, though not like the apricot's. Blossoms vary, and they may be identified by their hearts.

METHOD OF PAINTING THE BARK OF TRUNKS AND STEMS

Like their blossoms, the stems or trunks of ligneous plants are different from those of herbaceous plants. In painting the bark of the peach and *t'ung* trees, the brushstrokes for modeling *(ts'un)* should be drawn horizontally. For the pine and juniper the *ts'un* should be drawn like the scales of a fish. The bark of the cypress should be knotty, that of the plum tree should look old. The bark of the apricot should be a reddish purple. The stems of the cinnamon rose should be smooth and shining, those of the pomegranate lean and dry, and those of the camellia green and sleek. The bark of the wax or winter plum, like the ordinary plum, should have an old look. If, in painting the roots and trunks, the proper *ts'un* are used in drawing the bark, the forms of trees and ligneous plants will then be perfect.[3]

GENERAL BACKGROUND OF BIRD PAINTING

In the Six Styles of Poetry, poets frequently alluded to birds, animals, grasses and trees. In the exposition of the four seasons in the *Yueh Ling* (Monthly Regulations, Book IV, *Li Chi* or Book of Rites), it is recorded when birds sing or are silent and when plants flourish or fade. When flowers and plants are associated with birds and animals in the *Shih* (Book of Poetry) and the *Li Chi,* naturally they should also be associated in painting.

The flowers and birds in the great works of the T'ang and Sung periods were superb. As to birds, there were many kinds. The cranes of Hsueh Chi and the sparrow hawks of the Kuo (brothers, Ch'ien-yu and Ch'ien-hui) were renowned in ancient times. Were there others after them? Certainly! After Hsueh Chi there were many who excelled in painting cranes. After the Kuo brothers, many who excelled in painting eagles and hawks. Pien Luan excelled in painting peacocks; Wang Ning, parrots; Li Tuan and Niu Chien, pigeons; and Ch'en Heng, magpies. Ai Hsuan, Fu Wen-yung, and Feng Chun-tao excelled in painting quail; Fan Cheng-fu and Chao Hsiao-ying, pied wagtails; Hsia I, waterfowl; Huang Ch'uan, chickens and mandarin ducks; Huang Chu-ts'ai, pigeons and partridges; Wu Yuan-yu, swallows and yellow orioles; the Buddhist monk Hui-ch'ung, seagulls and egrets; Ch'ueh Sheng, crows and rooks; Yu Hsi and Shih Ch'ing, ringed pheasants. Many, including the Buddhist monk Mu Ch'i, excelled in painting wild geese. Many excelled in painting fighting cocks, chickens, geese, ducks sleeping and wild geese swimming. Some

[3.] Four paragraphs following this section are omitted. They summarize in rules the instructions given earlier for painting the various parts of plants and flowers.

excelled in painting certain kinds of birds among flowers; some, still better, were able to paint all kinds.[4]

Mountain birds and water birds vary according to their habitat, and their feathers change in texture and color in the course of the seasons. The form of their beaks, wings, tails and claws vary according to whether they are flying, singing, resting, eating or drinking. These positions are illustrated later in pictures, and should be learned also by observing the birds.

STEPS IN PAINTING BIRDS

In painting birds, begin with the long stroke for the upper part of the beak and then complete that part of the beak. Next comes the long stroke for the lower part of the beak, and then complete that part. To dot in the eye, place it near the point at which the beak opens. The head is drawn next, and then the back, from the neck down along the wings. Proceed with the breast, then the curve of the stomach, and then the tail. Finally, add the strokes for the legs and claws. The shape of most birds resembles an egg; we will go on with this.

COMPLETE RULES OF BIRD PAINTING PHRASED FOR MEMORIZING: THE FORM AND STRUCTURE OF HEAD, TAIL, WINGS, FEET; THE DOTTING OF EYE; THE POSITIONS OF FLYING, SINGING, DRINKING, PECKING

One should know well the whole form of the bird. Birds are born from eggs. And their forms resemble eggs, with head, tail, wings, and feet added. Flying, their power *(shih)* is in their wings. When the wings are spread, they are raised and light. When the head is lifted, the beak is open, as when a bird sings on a branch. When a bird is perched on a branch, the position of the feet is firm and secure, in no way uncertain. On the point of flying, the tail quivers. And with the quivering of the tail, the bird takes off. One should

---

[4] In this paragraph, which gives an idea of the varieties of birds as specialized subjects, some names are retained, though not all of them are identifiable today; where a string of names appears, no longer significant, they are omitted and are covered by a phrase such as "there were many who . . ."

catch the quality *(shih)* of flight in the outspread wings; one should catch the hopping from branch to branch, the bird never for one moment still. All this describes the forms of birds in various positions.

There is much in the manner in which the eyes are drawn that may help to give an effect of aliveness *(shen)*. When drinking, the bird is as though it were descending in its flight; eating, it seems about to begin a dispute; angry, it seems about to fight; joyful, it seems about to break into song. When two birds are perched together or flying around each other, they should seem to be turning their heads to look at each other. As in a portrait, the whole work depends on how the eyes are drawn. There should be method in placing and drawing the eyes. Then the whole form will be true *(chen)*. Each detail has its reason *(li)*. And that is the only way to produce lasting results.

RULES OF PAINTING SLEEPING BIRDS PHRASED FOR MEMORIZING

In general, one knows how birds look flying, singing, drinking, and pecking. But one may not know how they look asleep. A bird asleep on a branch has the eyes closed, the eyelids firmly folded. Unlike any animal, birds tuck their beaks under their wings and their feet into the down on their stomachs. Observing birds asleep brings to mind the saying, "When chickens sleep they perch high, when ducks sleep they lower their beaks and tuck them under their wings. Birds that perch to sleep bend and draw in their legs." Although only the habits of chickens and ducks are mentioned, the remark applies to all kinds of birds. One should know about this in painting; for good results it is essential.

RULES OF PAINTING THE BEAKS AND TAILS OF TWO KINDS OF BIRDS
PHRASED FOR MEMORIZING

In painting birds, one should note two general classes, mountain birds and water birds. Mountain birds necessarily have long tails; in flight their wings are very light. Water birds have short tails; swimming, they bob their heads into the water. One should know these characteristics in order to render their forms.

Birds with long tails should be drawn with short beaks; they sing beautifully and fly high. Those with short tails should be drawn with long beaks; thus they are able to catch fish and shrimps under water. Cranes and egrets have long legs. Seagulls and wild ducks have short legs. Although they belong in the category of water birds, their legs are characteristic and should be clearly defined.

Mountain birds live among trees and in the woods. Their plumage is of the Five Colors. The *luan* phoenix, the *feng* phoenix, and the cock pheasant are resplendent in reds and greens. Water birds are constantly bathing in clear water, and therefore their bodies are always clean and glistening. Wild ducks and wild geese have blue and green plumage, seagulls and egrets have white. The color of the mandarin duck differs according to its sex: the female has feathers of the Five Colors, the coloring of the male resembles that of the wild duck. The kingfisher is brilliant as though ornamented, its feathers green and blue with touches of violet. Its beak and claws are of a shade of cinnabar. It is the most beautiful of the water birds.

EXAMPLES OF FLOWERS OF LIGNEOUS PLANTS WITH FIVE PETALS

(At the top,) pear blossoms; (below, back and front views of the)
Golden Thread peach *(chin ssu; Hypericum ascyrion).*

FLOWERS WITH EIGHT AND NINE PETALS

(At the top,) white jasmine; (below,) gardenia.

Peony (an example of a flower with numerous petals).

(At the top,) cinnamon rose; (below,) pale yellow moon rose.

EXAMPLES OF LEAVES OF LIGNEOUS PLANTS

(At the top,) leaves of the peach tree; (center,) leaves of the apricot tree; (and bottom,) leaves of the plum tree.

When the plum tree flowers, it is bare of leaves; when the apricot flowers, its leaves are still at the stage of just sprouting. This point is added for the sake of authenticity (*shih*, realness).

(At the top,) gardenia; (below,) camellia.

EXAMPLES OF PAINTING BRANCHES OF LIGNEOUS PLANTS

Extended, these branches may be used for the peach and orange trees. (At the bottom,) branches with thorns, suitable for the cinnamon rose and the pale yellow moon rose.

A hanging and bent branch, suitable for the old branches of the peach, pear, wild plum, and camellia.

EXAMPLES OF FIRST STEPS IN PAINTING BIRDS

(Downward, starting at right:) In painting birds begin with the beak. The eye is placed above the upper part of the beak. Before completing the eye, draw in the head. Draw in the feathers around lower part of face and top of shoulders.

(Top left:) Use large and small half-circle brushstrokes; then long and short tapering strokes. Draw in carefully the tips of the wings.

Step by step, draw in the tail. And the feathers and down along the spine and under the tail. Breast and stomach should be placed ahead of the legs. Lastly, add the legs. The feet either grasp a branch or are spread out. Claw spread out. Claw grasped like a fist.

EXAMPLES OF BIRDS ON BRANCHES

Bird perched, turning its head. A side view, facing downward.
And a side view, facing upward.

EXAMPLES OF BIRDS FLYING OR PERCHED

(At the top,) drawing in its wings, about to come to rest. (Next,) flying upward. (At the bottom, left,) with wings raised investigating its feathers; and (right,) head down, looking at its feet.

EXAMPLES OF BIRDS UPSIDE DOWN AND FIGHTING WHILE FLYING

A bird painted perched on a branch is different from one painted
in a cage. It should have life-movement *(sheng tung),* its *shih* being
an impression of being about to fly, turning to one side, bending over, or looking up; for its form is never rigidly set. Often,
however, it may stop a moment and may perch, and may be seen
front view. The example shows a bird hanging upside down, about
to fly down, giving an impression of change and further lively
movement.

Painting two birds fighting in the air is difficult. The effect *(shih)* should be of birds aroused, with wings spread, heedless of what happens to their bodies. Their manner of fighting while flying is to dart swiftly at each other, pecking at throats. Such an effect may be achieved only through the spirit *(shen,* divine quality); it is not to be found just in the form *(hsing)* or the principle *(li).*

EXAMPLES OF WATER BIRDS

Mountain birds have long tails, water birds short ones.

APPENDIX:

KEY TERMS

TRADITIONAL CHRONOLOGY

LIST OF REFERENCES

KEY TERMS

THE pictographs and ideograms of Chinese writing often illustrate their meaning more vividly than an explanation. Particularly, the terms of Chinese painting become more significant on examining the old forms of the words. The old forms are among the earliest known Chinese writing; simpler than the characters used today, they show more clearly the components of a word.

A number of key terms are briefly analyzed here. A few characters associated with the concept of *Tao,* apart from other senses in which they are used, are included after the *tao* character. The modern form of each character, written with a brush, is given first, at the left, followed by one or more of its old forms. When the components of a word are of special interest, as in the *tao* character, the parts are separately presented, after the character itself, either with the modern form of the part first or in only an old form or forms, when they are easily recognizable. Following the key terms, a group of characters mentioned in the text are shown: first, a few that illustrate points in the discussion in Part One but are not among the key terms of painting; second, those that are cited in the Manual for their forms, regardless of the meaning of the words, in connection with drawing and brushwork.

The characters are arranged in the following groups:

I   The character *tao*
II   Synonyms and terms descriptive of *Tao*
III Basic terms of painting borrowed from Chinese thought
IV The First Canon: *Ch'i yun sheng tung*
V   The Second Canon: *ku fa*
VI Other basic terms borrowed from Chinese thought
VII Other terms of painting
VIII Characters, not among the key terms of painting, which are discussed in Part One, Chapters I–IV
IX Characters cited for their forms, regardless of their meaning, in Part Two, Selections from the Manual

I The character *tao*

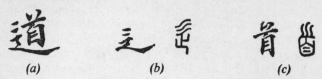

(a)   (b)   (c)

(a) *tao:* road, path, way; method, standard, doctrine; the Way

(b) *ch'o:* a foot taking a step; step by step

(c) *shou:* head

II Synonyms and terms descriptive of *Tao*

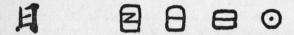

jih: sun, day; symbolically, the Sun, *Yang,* Heaven, *Tao*

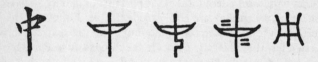

chung: center, middle; "center of the four quarters"; the Mean, the Center, *Tao*

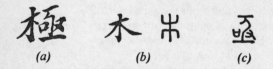

(a)   (b)   (c)

(a) *chi:* ridgepole, the extreme, utmost; the *T'ai Chi,* Great Ridgepole or Axis of the Universe and of the Wheel of Life, the Absolute, *Tao*

(b) *mu* (modern and old forms): wood, tree; roots and branches of the whole tree

(c) chi: haste, urgency; the old form here depicts man standing between two lines representing Heaven and Earth, shown with a mouth-form (left) and hand (right), calling out and signaling, as it were; also can be interpreted as striving through words (mouth) and deeds (hand) to live according to the concepts associated with the *T'ai Chi*

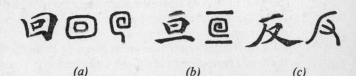

     (a)   *(b)*   *(c)*

Words applied by Taoists to *Tao* (modern and old forms)
(a) hui: to return to or from; a turn or revolution
(b) hsuan: to revolve; a complete and continuous revolving between lines representing Heaven and Earth
(c) fan: to turn over; a drawing of the motion of the right hand turning something over

III   Basic terms of painting borrowed from Chinese thought

理   玉   里

    (a)   *(b)*   *(c)*

(a) li: principle; reason, essence, inner law; Neo-Confucianist "fitness of things"
(b) yu: jade, a symbol of purity and the vitality of life
(c) li: lane, thoroughfare; markings, grain, as of wood, and veins, as in a piece of jade, thus the very essence of its purity and substance

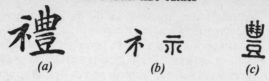

(a)   *(b)*   *(c)*

(a) li: rituals, ceremony, and conduct befitting an occasion; the sense of fitness

(b) shih (modern and old forms): signs or omens in the heavens; the will of Heaven discernible in the movement of the sun, moon, and stars hung in the heavens (the two lines at top)

(c) li: sacrificial vessel (the green sprigs or branches in the vessel symbolized plenty and other benefits)

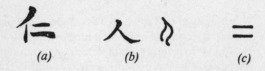

(a)   *(b)*   *(c)*

(a) jen: Goodness; "the virtue that must unite men" (Wieger, p. 73)

(b) jen (modern and old forms): man, mankind

(c) erh: two (representing relationship)

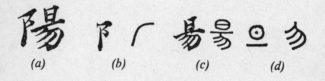

(a)   *(b)*   *(c)*   *(d)*

(a) yang: clear, light, hot; dryness, fire, red, day; upper, outer, front, open; South; south of a mountain and north of a river; male or positive element, force, and principle, Sun, spring-summer, Heaven, Spirit

(b) fu: mound; hill, mountain

(c) yang: sun, light; the sun radiating heat and light—composed of *(d) tan:* dawn; sun above the horizon; and *wu,* a phonetic, used as a negative, also to indicate motion of jerking, waving, or, as here, radiating

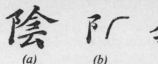

(a)   (b)   (c)   (d)

(a) yin: shady, dark, cold; moistness, water, black, night; lower, inner, back, closed; North; south of a river and north of a mountain; female or negative element, force, and principle, Moon, autumn-winter, Earth, Matter

(b) fu: mound; hill, mountain

(c) yin: cloudy, shaded, dark; a coiled cloud; the moment when clouds cast shadows, as indicated by its components *(d) chin:* now, the moment; *yun:* cloud

The Eight Trigrams around the *Yin-Yang (T'ai Chi)* emblem: from the Heaven trigram, at top, of three unbroken lines, clockwise, the trigrams of Fire, Thunder, Mountain, Earth (directly below Heaven), Water, Wind, and River

IV The First Canon: *Ch'i yun sheng tung*

(a)   (b)   (c)

(a) ch'i: vapor, breath; air, manner, influence, weather; *Ch'i*—Breath of Heaven, Spirit, Vital Force, the vivifying principle; the concept is symbolized in the two parts of the character, shown in *(b)* and *(c)*, each in two versions and old forms

(b) ch'i: vapor, breath

(c) mi: rice, grain; interpretations of grain and the four cardinal points, thus sustenance in every sense throughout the universe

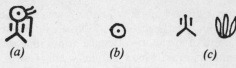

(a)   (b)   (c)

(a) an ancient form of *ch'i;* the two parts *(b)* and *(c),* depicting "sun" and "fire," form a double symbol of power and life; the bird form might have been intentional, to suggest the association of a bird with the sky-air element and the spirit

(b) jih: sun

(c) huo: fire

(a)   (b)   (c)   (d)

(a) yun: to turn, revolve; a circuit; composed of *(b)* and *(c)*

(b) ch'o (old form): step by step

(c) chun: a legion, army with chariots; composed of two parts *(d),* from which the meaning of revolving is borrowed

(d) pao: figure bending to enfold an object; by extension, to wrap, to enclose; bundle, group; and *che:* chariot, carriage (represented by axle, two wheels, and body of chariot); by extension, to roll, to revolve

(a)   (b)   (c)

(a) yun: rhythm, harmony; the meaning from its parts, shown here in old forms

(b) yin: utterance (of sound or word)

(c) yuan: official; border; roundness (as of a cowrie shell) and, by extension, rhythm

(a)   (b)   (c)   (d)

(a) sheng tung: life-movement or producing movement of life

(b) sheng (old form): to grow, to bear, to produce; to live; life (picture of a plant sprouting out of the earth)

(c) tung (old form): to move, stir, arouse; to set into action or motion by strength of one kind or another, the meaning aptly described by its two parts *(d)*

(d) chung (two versions): heavy, weighty; important; and *li* (modern and old forms): sinew, strength

V The Second Canon: *ku fa*

(a)   (b)   (c)   (d)

(a) ku fa: basic structure

(b) ku: bone; framework, structure

(c) and *(d)* the second word *fa,* meaning rule, model, means, method, law, *dharma,* shown in its two parts: *(c) shui* (modern abbreviated and full forms, and an old form): water, active and still; also a symbol of the source, spirit, rebirth, reflecting *Tao; (d) ch'u* (modern and old forms): past, gone, emptied; to remove, to get rid of; an empty vessel and cover, thus, by extension, to clarify, to purify

VI   Other basic terms borrowed from Chinese thought

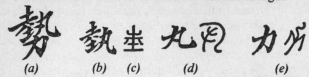

(a)   (b)   (c)   (d)   (e)

(a) shih: to maintain strength; power, authority; structural integration, style, effect

(b) i (upper half of *shih*)*:* to cultivate the earth, composed of *(c)* and *(d)*

(c) lu (old form): earth, represented as a plant growing and multiplying out of the earth

(d) chi (modern and old forms): to do, hold, grasp; by extension, to cultivate

(e) li (lower half of modern and old *shih*)*:* sinew, strength

shih: solid, substantial; actual, authentic, real, true, living quality; represented by the idea of a string of cowrie shells, an ancient form of money, under one's roof, thus of material wealth and of richness in other ways; the old forms of the three parts of the word are—*mien:* hut, roof; *kuan:* to string or tie together; and *pei:* cowrie

hsin: heart, heart-mind

(a)   (b)   (c)   (d)

(a) ssu: thought, to think (that which rises from the heart-mind up through the brain and head, represented

by a drawing of a skull, as in the upper half of the old form of the character *(b)*

(c) i: idea, meaning, conception; the intention from the heart-mind formed or uttered in words; the upper half of the old form *(d)* shows a face with a short line in the mouth representing sounds or words issuing and, as with *ssu* (thought), arising from the heart-mind

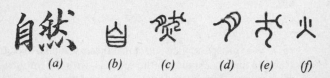

(a)   *(b)*   *(c)*   *(d)*   *(e)*   *(f)*

(a) tzu jan: certainly; of course; naturalness, spontaneity; self-existent

(b) tzu (old form): nose, beginning; self; personally, characteristically, certainly

(c) jan (old form): yes; certainly; the early origin of this character may be seen in its parts *(d, e, f)* representing the sacrifice of the flesh of a dog in ancient times, an offering of filial piety and thus a gesture of utmost affirmation

(d) ju: pieces of meat *(e) ch'uan:* dog *(f) huo:* fire

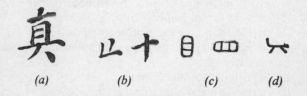

(a)   *(b)*   *(c)*   *(d)*

(a) chen: genuine, true, real; hence, spiritual, divine, and according to nature (the composition of the character denotes that what ten or many eyes have gauged and found straight and true was set up as a standard; or what had been perceived as complete and perfect (ten) was established as true—what the Taoists called "perfectly true")

(b) *shih* (abbreviated and full, modern forms): ten
(c) *mu* (old forms): eyes
(d) *wu* (old form): base, pedestal, platform

VII   Other terms of painting

(a)   (b)   (c)

(a) *ching*: prospect, view, circumstances, seasonal aspect
(the sun and its aspects in the seasons, with the implication that circumstances are right and natural when
guided by the sun)
(b) *jih* (old form): sun
(c) *ching* (old form): lofty, high; central in importance,
and pivotal

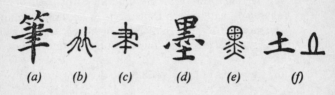

(a)   (b)   (c)   (d)   (e)   (f)

(a) *pi:* brush, writing brush with a bamboo holder
(b) *chu* (old form): bamboo
(c) *yu* (old form): a hand writing with brush
(d) *mo:* ink, composed of two words indicating ingredients in early times
(e) *heh* (old form): black, soot
(f) *t'u* (modern and old forms): earth

(a)   (b)   (c)   (d)

(a) hua: to draw, to paint (see *pi*, "brush," above, for the upper part of the character depicting a hand tracing with a brush, to which is added here a picture of a subject in a given, framed space)

(b) hsieh: to write; also to draw, to paint; the origin of the character is lost but from its two parts *(c* and *d)* the meaning, by extension, is suggested of setting thoughts and ideas in order in writing and painting

(c) mien (modern and old forms): hut, house, roof

(d) yeh (old form): magpie (it has been suggested that neatness and trimness were associated with the magpie, thus *hsieh* might originally have contained the idea of setting things in order under one's roof and in one's head)

VIII　Characters, not among the key terms of painting, which are discussed in Part One, Chapters I–IV

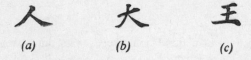

(a)　　　　　*(b)*　　　　　*(c)*

(a) jen: man (indicated by a pair of legs, in contrast to *ta,* greatness and completeness)

(b) ta: great; greatness, wholeness; by extension, true maturity

(c) wang: king, emperor; the ideal ruler, exemplifying "sageliness within, kingliness outwardly," and functioning as intermediary between Heaven and Earth, and by extension, all the various unifying and harmonizing analogies of *Yin-Yang;* the old form, similar to the above modern form, was interpreted in the early dictionaries as representing the lines of Heaven, Earth and Man, linked by the central stroke, but more recent theories suggest that the character originally indicated a figure, upright, with arms outstretched and a head (line at top), standing on the line representing "earth"

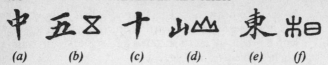

(a)   (b)   (c)   (d)   (e)   (f)

Characters pertaining to aspects of the concept of the Center

(a) chung: center; Center, Mean, *Tao* (see *chung* under *tao* character)

(b) wu (modern and old forms): five (representing the Five Points, Four and One)

(c) shih: ten

(d) shan (modern and old forms): mountain

(e) tung: east; a drawing of the sun rising and seen through tree in the east, composed of the two parts *(f)*

(f) mu and *jih* (old forms): wood or tree, and sun

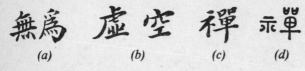

(a)   (b)   (c)   (d)

(a) wu wei: "no action," non-assertiveness, outer passivity with inner activity

(b) hsu and *k'ung:* empty; Taoist "emptiness"

(c) ch'an: meditation; *dhyana;* Zen; composed of two parts, shown in their old forms *(d)*

(d) shih: sun, moon and stars, the universe; *tan:* one, singleness

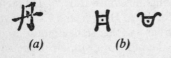

(a)   (b)

(a) and *(b) tan* (modern and two old forms show a substance brewing in a caldron, as in the preparation of cinnabar, a favorite ingredient of the elixir of alchemy and also the source of various reds for painting): pill, drug, elixir; red; used also in expressions such as *lien tan* (alchemy) and *tan ch'ing* (to paint)

遠 近　開 合　起 伏　龍脈
(a)　　*(b)*　　*(c)*　　*(d)*

Terms, used technically, that express aspects of the complementary and unifying action of *Yin-Yang*
(a) yuan chin: "far-near"; perspective
(b) k'ai ho: "open-together," and *(c) ch'i fu:* "rise-fall," pertaining to arrangement, balance, sequence and rhythm in elements of a picture
(d) lung mo: "dragon-veins"; connective brushstrokes and sections of a composition

形　　象
(a)　　*(b)*

(a) hsing: form, shape *(b) hsiang:* likeness, symbol

IX Characters cited for their forms, regardless of meaning, in Part Two, Selections from the Manual

介　个　求　心　人　乂　井　分
(a)　*(b)*　*(c)*　*(d)*　*(e)*　*(f)*　*(g)*　*(h)*

(a) chieh　　*(e) jen*
(b) ko　　　*(f) i*
(c) ch'iu　　*(g) hsing*
(d) hsin　　*(h) fen*

乙　八　品　丁　十　女　之
(a)　*(b)*　*(c)*　*(d)*　*(e)*　*(f)*　*(g)*

(a) i　　　*(e) shih*
(b) pa　　*(f) nu*
(c) p'in　*(g) chih*
(d) ting

TRADITIONAL CHRONOLOGY

B.C.

c. 3000–2205	Era of the legendary Five Emperors and Three Kings (and the Yang Shao culture in Honan; the P'an Shan and Ma Chia Yao cultures in Kansu; the black pottery culture in Shantung, Honan, and Anhui)
2205–1766	Hsia Dynasty
1766–1122	Shang-Yin Dynasty
1122–255	Chou Dynasty
255–207	Ch'in Dynasty
207–A.D. 220	Han Dynasty

A.D.

220–264	Three Kingdoms (Wei, Wu, Shu Han)
265–420	Chin (Tsin) Dynasty
265–589	Six Dynasties (Wu, Easter Chin, Sung, Southern Ch'i, Liang, Ch'en)
589–618	Sui Dynasty
618–906	T'ang Dynasty
907–959	Five Dynasties (Later Liang, T'ang, Chin, Han, Chou)
960–1280	Sung Dynasty Northern Sung 960–1126 Southern Sung 1127–1280
1260–1368	Yuan Dynasty
1368–1644	Ming Dynasty
1644–1911	Ch'ing Dynasty K'ang Hsi 1662–1722 Ch'ien Lung 1736–1795
1912–	Republic

LIST OF REFERENCES

THE following list gives full references for works cited in the text and footnotes. The records of Chinese painting are contained in the two major Chinese compilations, the *Wang Shih Hua Yuan* and the *Li Tai Ming Hua Chih;* the essays and other writings referred to are therefore not separately listed; available translations of works or excerpts from them are given in the footnote references. A fuller bibliography on aspects of Chinese painting and related material is offered in *The Tao of Painting,* Volume 1.

ACKER, WILLIAM REYNOLDS BEAL. *Some T'ang and Pre-T'ang Texts on Chinese Painting.* Leiden, 1954.

ANDERSSON, J. GUNNAR. *Children of the Yellow Earth.* London and New York, 1934.

———. "On Symbolism in the Prehistoric Painted Ceramics of China," *BMFEA,* 1 (1929).

———. *Preliminary Report on Archaeological Research in Kansu.* (Bulletin of the Geological Survey of China, Ser. A, no. 5.) Peking, 1925.

———. "Researches into the Prehistory of the Chinese," *BMFEA,* 15 (1943).

BAILEY, L. H. *The Standard Cyclopedia of Horticulture.* New York, 1925. 3 vols.

BMFEA. Museum of Far Eastern Antiquities, Stockholm. *Bulletins* 1–24 (1929–52).

BRUCE, J. P. *Chu Hsi and His Masters.* London, 1923.

BUDGE, E. A. WALLIS. *The Gods of the Egyptians.* London, 1904. 2 vols.

442   LIST OF REFERENCES

BULLING, A. *The Meaning of China's Most Ancient Art: An Interpretation of Pottery Patterns from Kansu (Ma Ch'ang and Pan-shan) and Their Development in the Shang, Chou and Han Periods.* Leiden, 1952.

BURNET, JOHN. *Early Greek Philosophy.* 4th edn., London, 1948.

CH'U TA-KAO (tr.). *Tao Te Ching.* London, 1939.

CLARK, CYRIL DRUMMOND LE GROS. *The Prose-Poetry of Su Tung-p'o.* Shanghai, 1935.

COMSTOCK, J. H. and A. B. *A Manual of the Study of Insects.* Ithaca, N.Y., 1926.

COOMARASWAMY, ANANDA K. *The Transformation of Nature in Art.* 2nd edn., Cambridge, Mass., 1935.

CREEL, HERRLEE GLESSNER. *The Birth of China.* London, 1936; New York, 1937.

DALCQ, A. M. "Form and Modern Embryology," in *Aspects of Form,* edited by Lancelot Law Whyte. London, 1951.

EITEL, ERNEST J. *Notes and Queries on China and Japan.* Hong Kong, (1874?).

ELIOT, T. S. *Four Quartets.* London and New York, 1943.

FORKE, ALFRED. *The World-Conception of the Chinese.* London, 1925.

FREEMAN, KATHLEEN. *Ancilla to the Pre-Socratic Philosophers.* Cambridge, Mass., and Oxford, 1948.

———. *The Pre-Socratic Philosophers. A Companion to Diels, Fragmente der Vorsakratiker.* Cambridge, Mass., and Oxford, 1947; 2nd edn., 1949.

FUNG YU-LAN. *A History of Chinese Philosophy.* Translated by Derk Bodde. Princeton, 1952–53. 2 vols.

———. *A Short History of Chinese Philosophy.* Edited and translated by Derk Bodde. New York, 1948.

———. *The Spirit of Chinese Philosophy.* Translated by E. R. Hughes. London, 1947.

GILES, HERBERT A. *A Chinese Biographical Dictionary.* London and Shanghai, 1898.

———. *A Chinese-English Dictionary.* 2nd edn., revised and enlarged, Shanghai and London, 1912. 2 vols.

————— (tr.). *Chuang Tzu, Mystic, Moralist and Social Reformer.* 2nd edn., revised, Shanghai, 1926.

GRAY, RONALD D. *Goethe the Alchemist: A Study of Alchemical Symbolism in Goethe's Literary and Scientific Works.* Cambridge (England), 1952.

HUME, ROBERT ERNEST (tr.). *The Thirteen Principal Upanishads.* 2nd edn., revised, London, 1934.

JOHNSON, OBED S. *A Study of Chinese Alchemy.* Shanghai, 1928.

JUNG, C. G. European Commentary, in *The Secret of the Golden Flower: A Chinese Book of Life.* Translated from Chinese into German by Richard Wilhelm. Translated into English by Cary F. Baynes. London and New York, 1931.

KARLGREN, BERNHARD. *The Chinese Language.* New York, 1949.

—————. "Grammata Serica," *BMFEA,* 12 (1940).

—————. "Legends and Cults in Ancient China," *BMFEA,* 18 (1946).

KOSUGI, HOAN and KODA, RENTARO. *Zenyaku Kaishien Gaden.* Tokyo, 1935–36. (Complete Japanese translation of the *Chieh Tzu Yuan,* including the Chinese text of the K'ang Hsi and Ch'ien Lung editions.)

LAUFER, BERTHOLD. *Jade, A Study in Chinese Archaeology and Religion.* 2nd edn., South Pasadena, Calif., 1946

LEGGE, JAMES (tr.). *Confucian Analects, The Great Learning, The Doctrine of the Mean.* Chinese text, translation, and notes. (The Chinese Classics, I.) 2nd edn., revised, Oxford, 1893.

—————. *The Li Ki* (The Book of Record of Rites). Translation and notes. (Sacred Books of the East, XXVII, XXVIII.) Oxford, 1885. 2 vols.

—————. *The She King; or, The Book of Poetry.* Chinese text, translation, and notes. (The Chinese Classics, IV, 1 and 2.) Hong Kong and London, 1871. 2 vols.

—————. *The Shoo King; or, The Book of Historical Documents.* Chinese text, translation, and notes. (The Chinese Classics, III, 1 and 2.) Hong Kong and London, 1865. 2 vols.

LEGGE, JAMES (tr.). *The Works of Mencius.* Chinese text, translation, and notes. (The Chinese Classics, II.) Hong Kong and London, 1861.

————. *The Yi King* (The Book of Changes). Translation and notes. (Sacred Books of the East XVI.) 2nd edn., Oxford, 1899.

LI CH'IAO-P'ING. *The Chemical Arts of Old China.* Easton, Pa., 1948.

Li Tai Ming Hua Chih (Notes on Famous Painters of All the Dynasties), *c.*847. Reprinted in 1922 facsimile edn. of the *Wang Shih Hua Yuan.*

LIAO, W. K. (tr.). *Han Fei Tzu.* London, 1939.

MAERZ, A. and PAUL, M. REA. *A Dictionary of Color.* 2nd edn., New York, 1950.

MALRAUX, ANDRÉ. *The Twilight of the Absolute. (The Psychology of Art,* III. Bollingen Series XXIV.) New York, 1950.

MAR, P. G. "The Use of Precious Stones in Ancient Medicine," *The China Journal of Science and Arts* (Shanghai), XXXIV: 5 (May, 1941).

MARCH, BENJAMIN. *Some Technical Terms of Chinese Painting.* (American Council of Learned Societies, Studies in Chinese and Related Civilizations, 2.) Baltimore, 1935.

MARTIN, W. A. P. *The Lore of Cathay.* New York, 1901.

MAYERS, WILLIAM FREDERICK. *The Chinese Reader's Manual.* Shanghai and London, 1874.

MISCH, GEORG. *The Dawn of Philosophy.* Edited in English by R. F. C. Hull. London and Cambridge, Mass., 1950.

PETRUCCI, RAPHAEL (tr.). *Kiai-Tseu-Yuan Houa Tchouan, Les Enseignements de la Peinture du Jardin Grand comme un grain de Moutard: Encyclopédie de la Peinture Chinoise.* Paris, 1918.

PICASSO, PABLO. "Statement by Picasso, 1923," in *Picasso: Forty Years of His Art.* Edited by Alfred H. Barr, Jr. (Museum of Modern Art.) New York, 1939.

RADHAKRISHNAN, S. (tr.). *The Bhagavadgita.* London, 1948.

RUFUS, W. CARL and TIEN HSING-CHIH. *The Soochow Astronomical Chart.* Ann Arbor, 1945.

SAKANISHI, SHIO (tr.). *The Spirit of the Brush: Being the Outlook of Chinese Painters on Nature from Eastern Chin to Five Dynasties.* (Wisdom of the East Series.) London, 1939.

SIRÉN, OSVALD. *A History of Early Chinese Painting.* London, 1933, 2 vols.

———. "Shih T'ao, Painter, Poet and Theoretician," *BMFEA,* 21 (1949).

——— (tr.). *The Chinese on the Art of Painting.* Peking, 1936.

SOPER, ALEXANDER COBURN (tr.). *Kuo Jo-hsu's Experiences in Painting (T'u-Hua Chien-wen Chih).* (American Council of Learned Societies, Studies in Chinese and Related Civilizations, 6.) Washington, 1951.

SOWERBY, A de C. "Animals in Chinese Art," *Journal of the North China Branch of the Royal Asiatic Society* (Shanghai), LXVIII (1937).

SUZUKI, DAISETZ TEITARO. *Essays in Zen Buddhism.* 1st Series, 2nd edn., New York, 1949. 2nd series, 2nd edn., New York, 1950. 3rd series, London, 1934.

———. *An Introduction to Zen Buddhism.* 2nd edn., London, 1948.

———. *Studies in the Lankavatara Sutra.* London, 1930.

——— (tr.). *The Lankavatara Sutra.* London, 1932.

TAKI, SEI-ICHI. *Three Essays on Oriental Painting.* London, 1910.

TAYLOR, A. E. *Socrates.* London, 1932.

THOMPSON, D'ARCY WENTWORTH. *On Growth and Form.* 2nd edn., Cambridge (England), 1952. 2 vols.

TOMITA, KOJIRO. "Brushstrokes in Far Eastern Painting," *Eastern Art,* III (1931), Philadelphia.

TSCHICHOLD, JAN (ed.). *Chinese Color-Prints from the Painting Manual of the Mustard Seed Garden.* London and Basel, 1952.

UYEMURA, ROKURO. "Studies on the Ancient Pigments in Japan," *Eastern Art,* III (1931), Philadelphia.

WALEY, ARTHUR. *An Introduction to the Study of Chinese Painting.* London, 1923.

———. *Three Ways of Thought in Ancient China.* 2nd edn., London, 1946.

WALEY, ARTHUR (tr.). *The Analects of Confucius.* London and New York, 1939.

——— (tr.). *The Way and Its Power.* London, 1934.

Wang Shih Hua Yuan. Collected writings on painting compiled by Wang Shih-chen, with supplement by Chan Ching-feng. Preface dated 1590, but published some years later by Wang Ch'ien-ch'ang. 1922 facsimile reproduction of the original Ming edition.

WIEGER, LÉON. *Chinese Characters. Their Origin, Etymology, History, Classification and Signification.* Translated by L. Davrout. Peking, 1940 (lithographic reissue of 2nd edn., 1927).

——— (tr.). *Les Pères du Système Taoiste.* Chinese text and translation of the *Lao Tzu, Lieh Tzu,* and *Chuang Tzu.* (Cathasia serie culturelle des hautes études de Tien-tsin.) Paris, 1950.

YAN TSZ CHIU. "Chemical Industry in Kwang Tung Province," *Journal of the North China Branch of the Royal Asiatic Society* (Shanghai), L (1919).

YETTS, W. PERCEVAL. *Symbolism in Chinese Art.* (China Society Lecture, 1912.) London, 1912 (pamphlet).

INDEX

VINTAGE CRITICISM: LITERATURE, MUSIC, AND ART